FROM PROUST TO CAMUS

From Proust to Camus

PROFILES OF MODERN FRENCH WRITERS

by

ANDRÉ MAUROIS

Translated by
CARL MORSE and RENAUD BRUCE

DOUBLEDAY & COMPANY, INC.

GARDEN CITY, NEW YORK

1966

Library of Congress Catalog Card Number 66–20938
Copyright © 1966 by André Maurois
All Rights Reserved
Printed in the United States of America
First Edition

Grateful acknowledgment is made for receiving permission to translate and quote material from works by the following authors:

ALAIN: From *Les Dieux, Propos*, translated by permission of Editions Gallimard.

SIMONE DE BEAUVOIR: From *The Second Sex*, reprinted by permission of Alfred A. Knopf, Inc., and Jonathan Cape, Ltd.

ALBERT CAMUS: From *The Rebel, The Myth of Sisyphus, The Stranger* (British title—*The Outsider*), translated by permission of Alfred A. Knopf, Inc., and Hamish Hamilton, Ltd.

PAUL CLAUDEL: From *L'Echange, Tête d'Or*, translated by permission of Mercure de France. From *The Satin Slipper*, originally translated by John O'Connor, retranslated by permission of Sheed & Ward, Inc., and Sheed & Ward Ltd. From *L'Annonce Faite à Marie* (*Tidings Brought to Mary*), originally translated by Wallace Fowlie, copyright © 1960. Retranslated by permission of Henry Regnery Company, Inc.

GEORGES DUHAMEL: From *Le Combat*, translated by permission of Literary Publications, Inc. (*Poet Lore*).

ANDRÉ GIDE: From *Journals 1889–1951*, translated by permission of Alfred A. Knopf, Inc., and Martin Secker & Warburg, Ltd.

REYNALDO HAHN: From *Hommage à Proust*, translated by permission of Editions Gallimard.

JACQUES DE LACRETELLE: From *La Bonifas, Hauts-Ponts Sabine*, translated by permission of Editions Gallimard.

ANDRÉ MALRAUX: From *L'Espoir* (*Man's Hope*), *Les Conquérants*, translated and used by permission of Random House, Inc., and Editions Gallimard. From *La Condition Humaine*, translated by permission of Editions Gallimard.

FRANÇOIS MAURIAC: From *Souffrances du Pécheur, Bonheur du Chrétien, Les Mains Jointes*, translated by permission of Editions Bernard Grasset. From *La Pharisienne*, translated by permission of Eyre & Spottiswoode and Editions Bernard Grasset. From *Désert de l'Amour*, retranslated by Renaud Bruce by permission of Farrar, Straus & Giroux, Eyre & Spottiswoode and Editions Bernard Grasset. From *Nœud de Vipères* (*Vipers' Tangle*), translated by permission of Sheed & Ward, Inc., and Sheed & Ward Ltd.

MARCEL PROUST: From *Remembrance of Things Past*, translated and used by permission of Random House, Inc., Chatto & Windus Ltd., and Editions Gallimard.

JULES ROMAINS: From *Les Hommes de Bonne Volonté* (*Men of Good Will*), translated by permission of Alfred A. Knopf, Inc., and

Librarie Ernest Flammarion. From *Les Humbles,* translated by permission of Alfred A. Knopf, Inc. From *La Vie Unanime,* translated by permission of Librarie Ernest Flammarion.

ANTOINE SAINT-EXUPÉRY: From *Citadelle (Wisdom of the Sands),* originally translated by Stuart Gilbert, retranslated by permission of Harcourt, Brace & World, Inc., and The Bodley Head Ltd. From *Pilote de Guerre (Flight to Arras), Terre des Hommes (Wind, Sand and Stars), Vol de Nuit (Night Flight),* translated by permission of Harcourt, Brace & World, Inc., and William Heinemann Ltd.

JEAN-PAUL SARTRE: From *Les Mots,* translated by Bernard Frechtman. © English translation by George Braziller, Inc. Originally published in French under the title, *Les Mots,* © 1964 by Librarie Gallimard. All rights reserved. Reprinted by permission of George Braziller, Inc., Librarie Gallimard and Hamish Hamilton, Ltd.

MARCEL THIÉBAUT: From *Entre les Lignes,* translated by permission of Librarie Hachette, Editeur.

PAUL VALÉRY: From *Collected Works of Paul Valéry, Discours de Réception à L'Academie Française, Speech at Jansons-de-Sailly (1932).* Translated by permission of Bollingen Foundation and Librarie Gallimard.

PREFATORY NOTE

MOST OF the chapters in this book were prepared for a course for American students. The essays on Alain, Gide, Malraux, Sartre, Simone de Beauvoir, and Camus were not part of this group but written later. I have revised the Claudel, Saint-Exupéry, and Mauriac chapters in order to account for a number of new and significant publications. If this series were to be a comprehensive survey of French literature during the first half of the twentieth century it would, of course, be necessary to add many names—Romain Rolland, Péguy, Colette, Martin du Gard, Giraudoux, for example—plus a number of living writers. Such a new volume will require extensive readings. Will the gods give me enough time? I hope so.

A. M.

PUBLISHER'S NOTE

CARL MORSE is responsible for the translation of the chapters on Proust, Bergson, Valéry, Gide, Alain, Simone de Beauvoir, Sartre, and Camus. RENAUD BRUCE has translated the chapters on Claudel, Mauriac, Duhamel, Saint-Exupéry, De Lacretelle, Romains, and Malraux.

The original French edition was published under the title *De Proust à Camus,* and did not include the articles on Gide, Sartre, and Simone de Beauvoir, which appear in this volume. These articles were published in French in a subsequent volume entitled *De Gide à Sartre.*

CONTENTS

FROM PROUST TO CAMUS

MARCEL PROUST

THE WRITERS of 1900 would have been greatly surprised, I think, if anyone had told them that one of the greatest of their number—he who would give new life to the art of the novel and introduce contemporary philosophical ideas and scientific discoveries into the realm of art—was a young man who was sickly, unknown to the public (and to most men of letters), and considered by those who had met him socially as possibly intelligent but not capable of creating a great work. This error persisted for a long time, surviving even the publication of the first volume of *A la Recherche du Temps Perdu*. It was the same kind of error that Sainte-Beuve made about Balzac, and one that shows how very cautious and modest critics should be.

I. THE MAN

For knowing Proust we have at our disposal Léon-Pierre Quint's fine biography, the letters, and the eyewitness accounts of his friends. The best critical analysis of Proust's life, character, and work is Edmund Wilson's in *Axel's Castle*.

Born in Paris in 1871, Marcel Proust was the son of Professor Adrien Proust, a prominent doctor who later became inspector of the French Service of Hygiene; his mother, Jeanne Weil, was Jewish; she seems to have been loving, sensitive, and cultured, and remained to her son throughout his life the image of perfection. It was from her that he acquired a "horror of falsehood, moral sensitivity, and especially, a sense of infinite goodness." André Berge has discovered in an old album one of those lists of questions with which young girls used to torment young men, and to which Proust had responded when he was fourteen.

"What is your idea of unhappiness?"

"Being separated from my mother."

"What is your bête noire?"

"People who are insensitive to what is good," he replied— "who don't appreciate the pleasures of affection."

He was throughout his life to have a horror of people who did not value "the pleasures of affection." Fear of causing anyone pain remained a dominant instinct with him. Reynaldo Hahn, who was perhaps his best friend, has told how, in leaving a café, he would give tips to everyone in sight; one to the waiter who had served him, then, catching sight in a corner of another waiter who had done nothing, he would rush over and give that waiter a ridiculously high tip, saying:

"It must be so painful to him to be left out!"

Finally, just as he was about to enter his carriage, he would suddenly head back to the café:

"I believe," he would say, "that I forgot to say goodby to the waiter; and that isn't nice!"

Gentil . . . Nice . . . This word played an important role in his speech and in his behavior. One must be nice, not hurt anyone, please people—and to that end he multiplied the number of wildly generous gifts—gifts embarrassing even to those who received them—overly flattering letters, solicitudes. What lay behind this *gentillesse?* Partly a fear of displeasing, a desire to win and to retain the affection and attention a weak, sickly person needs, but partly too a sensitive and vivid imagination which enabled him to picture the sufferings and desires of others with painful precision.

Illness doubtless aggravated this naturally acute sensitivity

—for Proust had been, from the age of nine, an invalid. Asthma attacks obliged him to be very careful of his health, and only the wonderful gentleness of his mother could sooth his high-strung nerves.

We know what the life of a Parisian child of well-to-do middle-class family was like around 1880: walks on the Champs-Elysées with an old governess; meetings with little girls with whom he played and who would later become *"les jeunes filles en fleurs";* a turn sometimes about the Allée des Acacias where he might catch a glimpse of Mme. Swann, voluptuous and triumphant, in her handsome victoria.

Proust spent his holidays in Illiers, not far from Chartres, his father's native region. The landscapes of la Beauce and le Perche became, in his book, those of Combray. The pilgrim may go there today and seek out Swann's "way" and the Guermantes "way."

In Paris Proust attended the Lycée Condorcet (a breeding ground for writers), where he found himself in a brilliant class. Even at that early age this marvelously gifted child, endowed and trained in the love of the classics by his mother, felt the need to record certain of the things he saw in words.

Suddenly a roof, a glint of sun on a plain, the smell of a road, made me stop because of a special pleasure they gave me, and also because they seemed to be hiding, beyond what I saw, something which they were inviting me to come and grasp and which, in spite of my efforts, I could not manage to discover. Since I felt that that something was to be found in them, I remained motionless in that spot to look, to breath, to try to make my mind go beyond the image and the smell; and if I had to catch up with my grandfather in order to continue my walk, I tried to find him again with my eyes closed. I concentrated on remembering the exact line of the roof, the hue of the stone which, without my understanding why, had seemed to me pregnant, ready to open, to deliver up that of which it was but the covering.

The child, to be sure, was far from knowing the import of this strange urge; but one day, having tried to capture one of these sights on paper—that of three steeples turning on the plain, separating, coming back together, overlapping, as the observer shifted position—he experienced, on finishing the page, that very special satisfaction he was later to know so often, the joy that comes to the writer when he has freed himself of a feeling or sensation by giving it, through the magic of art, an intelligible form. "And I felt myself," he writes, "so entirely freed of those steeples and of what they concealed that I began, like a chicken who has just laid an egg, to sing at the top of my lungs."

Meanwhile he had reached his final year at the Lycée Condorcet, the year devoted to philosophy. This is an important event in the life of any educated young Frenchman. Proust had an excellent teacher, Darlu, during that crucial year, and he retained a taste for philosophical systems throughout his life. Later he was to transpose the essential themes of the most illustrious philosophy of his time—that of Bergson—into the novelistic mode.

What would he do with his life? He founded, together with his friends, Daniel Halévy, Robert de Flers, Fernand Gregh, and a few other Condorcet schoolmates, a little literary magazine: Le Banquet. His father would have liked to see him go into the Cours des Comptes but he was little inclined to do so; he liked to write; he also liked to mingle in society. How people criticized him for his taste for drawing rooms! In literary circles he was immediately set down for a snob and worldling. Yet which of those who treated him so scornfully was his equal? The fact is that the particular social groups a writer portrays are much less important than the way he sees and describes them.

"Every social station," says Proust, "has its interest, and it can be as intriguing for the artist to depict the manners of a queen as the behavior of a dressmaker." High society has always been one of the milieus most favorable to the making of a novelist who wants to observe the passions. Feelings assume greater intensity in circumstances of leisure. It is at court in the seventeenth century, in the drawing rooms in the eighteenth, and in "society" in the nineteenth that the French novelist was afforded the opportunity of finding actual comedies or tragedies, comedies and tragedies which attained full development, first, because the principals had the time for them, and second, because a sufficiently rich vocabulary made it possible for them to express themselves.

As for saying that Proust was a dupe of society—that he was snobbish to the point of not seeing that all classes can be interesting, dressmaker and queen alike—is to reveal that one has read and understood him poorly. For Proust was at no time a dupe of society; he undoubtedly exercised in society not only his *gentillesse* and his extraordinary good manners, but also his affection—for there are in society, as in every human context, people worthy of being loved. Moreover, there was often a good deal of irony beneath these obliging externals. The depravity of a Charlus or the selfishness of the duchess of Guermantes is consistently offset by the faultless goodness of a bourgeoise like his mother (who, in the book, became his grandmother), the common sense of a woman of the people like Françoise, or the nobility of those he calls "the French of Saint-André-des-Champs," meaning the people of France as they are depicted by a simple sculptor on a cathedral portal. But society was his field of observation, and he needed it.

To see him as the friends of his youth saw him, we must imagine him as Léon-Pierre Quint has described him to us:

"Large black, shining eyes, a gaze of great gentleness, an even gentler, somewhat breathless voice, extremely elegant dress, broad silk shirt-fronts, a rose or orchid in the buttonhole of his frock-coat, one of those flat-brimmed top-hats which in that day and age one deposited next to one's chair when visiting. Then, gradually, as his illness advanced and, too, as intimacy gave him the courage to dress as he wished, he began to appear in drawing-rooms, even in the evening, in his pelisse, which he wore summer and winter for he was always cold."

In 1896, at twenty-five, he published his first book, *Les Plaisirs et les Jours* (*Pleasures and Days*), with complete lack of success. The presentation of the book was calculated to put off fastidious readers. Proust had arranged for a cover drawn by Madeleine Lemaire, for a preface by Anatole France, and for music by Reynaldo Hahn to be interspersed throughout the text. This overly sumptuous edition, the odd assortment of patrons, did not convey an impression of seriousness. Yet for the really good critic who might have managed to find the few grams of gold buried among all these stones, there was plenty of matter there for a fine display of prognostic powers!

Reading *Les Plaisirs et les Jours* carefully one already detects some of the themes of the Proust of *A la Recherche du Temps Perdu*. It contains one unreal and bizarre short story in which Baldassare Silvande, near death, asks the young princess he loves to stay with him a few hours; she refuses, for her selfishness will not allow her to give up her pleasure, even for a dying man. This theme will recur when Swann is dying and expresses his anguish to the duchess of Guermantes, who does not let that stop her from going off to a dinner party.

There is another story in *Les Plaisirs et les Jours*—*La Confession d'une Jeune Fille* (*A Young Girl's Confession*)—in which the heroine kills her mother by letting a boy kiss her while her mother (who has a heart condition) watches the scene in a mirror. This theme will recur on the one hand when Mlle. Vinteuil makes her father so unhappy, and on the other when the narrator (or Proust himself) causes his grandmother grief because of his weakness and inability to work.

Such unresolved "chords" are found in every artist, complexes which begin to vibrate whenever a subject of matching resonance awakens them, and which alone are capable of generating that special music for which we love a particular writer. This is also the reason why certain writers always rewrite the same book; why Flaubert excoriates, in each of his novels, his unrepentant romanticism; why Stendhal three times recreates the young Beyle as Julien Sorel, as Fabrice del Dongo and as Lucien Leuwen; why Proust, at twenty-five, sketches, in the clumsy melodies of *Les Plaisirs et les Jours,* the great symphony that will be *A la Recherche du Temps Perdu,* and later, in *Jean Santeuil,* an unfinished novel not to be published in his lifetime, all of the themes of his future work.

But at that point he was too much engaged in life to depict it with proper detachment. He himself points out that to become a great artist one must rise above one's own existence. What is important is not that that existence be especially interesting nor that one have a powerful intellectual mechanism at one's command, but that that mechanism be able, as pilots say, to "lift off." Before Proust could "lift off," certain events had to remove him from real life.

Circumstances, and doubtless, too, the inner prompting of his genius, produced the desired effect. First his asthma got worse; he would soon no longer be able to tolerate the country. Not only trees, flowers, but even the faintest plant-smell brought in from outside by a friend would give him terrible choking spells. He continued for a long time to spend his summers by the sea, at Trouville or Cabourg; later, however, he had to forgo even this annual jaunt.

Meanwhile he had made a discovery that was to play a very large part in his life and art; he had discovered Ruskin. He himself translated two of Ruskin's books: *The Bible of Amiens* and *Sesame and Lilies,* larding his translations with notes and prefaces. The two men had points in common:

both had led sheltered childhoods with over-protective parents; both had lived the lives of well-to-do amateurs of art, lives that have their dangers—the danger especially of cutting a man off from contact with hard realities—but also their advantages: that of preserving the sensitive skin that allows the aesthete thus protected to perceive the subtlest of nuances. It was through Ruskin that Proust learned to understand—much better than Ruskin himself—works of art. It was because of Ruskin that he made pilgrimages to the cathedrals of Amiens and Rouen. It was Ruskin's mind that brought the dead stones to life for him. Proust, who by this time no longer traveled, found the strength to go to Venice in order to observe—embodied in palaces that were "sinking but still pink and standing"—Ruskin's architectural ideas.

The only way we ever know reality is through great artists. Ruskin was for Proust one of those mediating writers we require to put us in touch with things. Ruskin taught him to examine at close range a flower-filled thicket, clouds, waves, and to depict them with an attention to detail that recalls some of the drawings of Holbein or those of the Japanese. Ruskin saw things with almost microscopic vision. Proust adopted this way of looking at things, but he pursued it much further than his teacher and applied to feelings that attention to detail for which Ruskin had set the example. Without his great love of Ruskin, it is likely that Proust would never have found himself. Thus Proust's innumerable descendants in France are equally descendants of Ruskin, even if they have not themselves read him. For a single copy of a book, transplanted by chance and fallen upon a mind that was receptive ground for that particular way of feeling, is enough to introduce to a patch of ground a plant that did not previously exist and that suddenly thrives and overruns it.

In 1903 his father died; in 1905, his mother. Was it feelings of remorse in relation to this woman who had so much believed in him yet never lived to see the fruits of his work, or was it illness alone that drove him at this point to withdraw completely from the world? Or were both illness and remorse but pretexts for the subconscious need to put to paper a work that was almost finished in his mind? It would be hard to say. In any event, it was at about this time that the life his friends recall and have reported to us, the life of the legendary Proust, began.

This is the time of the room lined with cork to keep out noises, of the windows sealed to shut out the imperceptible yet baneful scent of the chestnut trees on the boulevard, of fumigation measures that produce a suffocating stench, of woolens Proust dons only after toasting them in front of a fire, by consequence of which they are as tattered as old flags riddled with grapeshot. This is also the period when Proust, in bed most of the time, fills the twenty notebooks that comprise his book. He goes out only at night, and then only to seek out some detail he needs for his work. He often sets up headquarters at the Ritz, questioning the waiters and the maître d', Olivier, about the conversations of the diners. If he feels it necessary—in order to describe them better—to see the hawthorn bushes of his childhood again, he braves the country in a closed car.

In this manner, from 1910 to 1922, he writes *A la Recherche du Temps Perdu*. He knows his book is a beautiful book. It would be impossible for him not to know it. The man who wrote pastiches of Flaubert, Balzac, and Saint-Simon, pastiches that show so perfect an understanding of these great writers, was too discerning a literary critic not to appreciate the fact that he too was constructing one of the major monuments of French literature. But how was this work to be launched? He had no "literary position" and, furthermore, as was mentioned earlier, if he had a "rating," it was negative. Because he was rich and considered a snob, serious writers were inclined to mistrust whatever this dabbler might produce.

He submitted his manuscript to *La Nouvelle Revue Française*. They turned it down. He finally managed, in 1913, to get an initial volume published (*Du Côté de chez Swann: Swann's Way*) by Bernard Grasset and at his own expense. It met with little success. Almost immediately, moreover, the war interrupted publication, and as a result the second volume did not come out until 1919, this time with *La Nouvelle Revue Française*. The honor of "launching" Proust goes to Léon Daudet. Thanks to him, Proust received, in 1919, the Prix Goncourt, the prize which has brought recognition to so many writers of talent. With the publication of this second volume he became famous, and his work quickly found the public it deserved, not only in France, but in England, America, and Germany. There had always been an affinity between Proust and Anglo-Saxon literature.

"It's strange," he says in a letter of 1910, "that in all the various genres—from George Eliot to Hardy, from Stevenson to Emerson—there is no literature that has an effect on me comparable to that of English and American literature. Germany, Italy, often even France, leave me indifferent. But two pages of *The Mill on the Floss* make me weep. I know Ruskin loathed that novel, but I reconcile all these enemy gods in the Pantheon of my admiration. . . ."

From the appearance of the first volumes, the whole world knew that they were in the presence not only of a great writer but of one of those rare "inventors" who bring something entirely new into the history of letters.

Fame came in 1919; he was dead in 1922. At the time he achieved widespread recognition he had only a few years left to live, and he knew it; he spoke constantly of his illness and imminent death. No one believed him; his friends smiled; they considered him a *malade imaginaire*. Meanwhile he kept to his bed, working, correcting, finishing his work, adding passages, pasting in new bits, so that his proof sheets came to resemble, like his woolens, tattered flags. Moreover, dying or not, he made himself sick by his dreadful living habits, by overindulgence of soporifics, and by a work schedule that was all the more feverish because of his doubts as to whether he would be able to finish his book in time. During this period he told Paul Morand: "I'm writing you a long letter, which is stupid because it brings me closer to death."

He might have lived a few more years if he had taken care of himself; but he contracted pneumonia, refused to see doctors, and died. A few days before this illness, he had written on the last page of the last notebook the word: *Fin*.

The account of his death is an oft-told and moving story. He endeavored to dictate notes correcting and completing the account he had given in his book of the death of Bergotte, the great writer he had invented. He had said: "I shall finish this passage on the instant of my death." He attempted to do just that and one of the last words he uttered was the name of his hero. Bergotte's death, as Proust relates it, ends with the following passage:

He was dead; dead forever? . . . Who can say so? . . . Certainly no spiritualist experience, any more than any religious dogma, gives proof that the soul continues to live. What can be said is that everything occurs in life as if we came into it with the burden of obligations contracted in some anterior life. There is no reason on earth why we should feel obliged to do good, to be thoughtful, even polite, nor any either why the trained artist should feel obliged to start a piece again twenty times over when the admiration it will excite will have little effect on his body's being eaten by worms, like the patch of yellow wall one artist, whose life will never be known, painted with such great craft and subtlety. All of these obligations, which are not ratified by present life, seem to belong to a different world, one founded on goodness, moral sensitivity, sacrifice, a world entirely different from this one and which we come out of in order to be born on this earth. . . .

Wherefore the idea that Bergotte was not dead forever is not improbable.

They buried him, but, throughout the night of the wake, in the lighted windows, his books opened in threes, mingled together like angels with extended wings, seemed the symbol of resurrection for the one who was no longer. . . .

What a wonderful page. Let us try to be faithful to its spirit and, in order to bring the work to life, light the lamps of our attention at the sides of that great structure, *A la Recherche du Temps Perdu.* Let us speak no longer of Proust but of his book. Of the life let us retain only that part which helps us understand the work: his sensitivity, which, though excessive even from childhood, was to permit him to grasp those nuances of feeling hardest to perceive; that respect for goodness first stirred by love of his mother; the regret, sometimes deepened to remorse, of having caused some person pain; his illness, that marvelous weapon the artist uses to protect himself from the world; and finally, the need, from childhood, to capture, through style, complex and fleeting sensations. Never was the calling of writer clearer; never was a life more totally dedicated to one work.

II. INVOLUNTARY MEMORY

What is the subject of this work? It would be a great mistake to think one had explained *A la Recherche du Temps Perdu* by having said: "It's the story of a high-strung child, of his growing-up in life and in society, of his friends and relatives, of his love for several young girls—Gilberte, Albertine—of Gilberte Swann's marriage to Saint-Loup, and of the unusual love relationships of Monsieur de Charlus." The more such statements one collects, the farther one is from identifying what makes Proust original. As the Spanish critic Ortega y Gasset so well put it, it's exactly as if someone asked you to explain Monet's painting and you replied:

"Monet is a man who painted cathedrals, views of the Seine, and waterlilies." You would thereby be stating a fact, but not *a fact about the nature of Monet's art*. Sisley also painted views of the Seine; Corot too painted cathedrals. What makes Monet what he is is not his subjects, which were provided to him quite by chance, but a special way of seeing nature. Ortega y Gasset uses a symbolic anecdote to illustrate this idea. There was, he relates, a little hunchback who came to the library every morning and asked for a dictionary. When the librarian asked him, "Which one?" he would say, "I don't care. I need it to sit on."

Similarly with Monet, or Proust. If you had asked them: "What subject do you want to take up? . . . What person do you want to portray?" they would have answered, "I don't care. Subjects and people exist only to enable me to be myself."

And if Monet is a special way of seeing nature, Proust is above all *a special way of evoking the past*.

Are there then several ways of evoking the past? There are indeed. One may, first of all, evoke the past intellectually, by trying to reconstruct back from the present those circumstances that led to the present. For instance, I am presently engaged in writing a study on Proust. If I ask myself why, I recall that the original suggestion that I do a group of studies on a number of outstanding contemporary Frenchmen was made to me by the President of Princeton University during a lunch that took place in the Bois de Boulogne. I might perhaps, with a little effort, summon up the Bois of that moment, recall the people present at the lunch and, little by little, succeed, through a series of operations of the mind, in reconstructing a more or less accurate picture of that segment of the past.

Sometimes, too, we try to reconstruct the past by means of documents. If, for example, I wish to picture Paris in Proust's time, I will read Proust, I'll question people who knew him then, I'll read other books written during the same period and, slowly, I'll succeed in putting together some sort of picture which will (or will not) resemble the Paris of 1900. Proust finds this mode of evocation totally inappropriate to the creation of a work of art. We can never succeed in giving a true impression of time, nor can we revive the past through intellectual reconstitution. What is needed is *evocation through involuntary memory*.

How does this involuntary evocation occur? *Through the coincidence of present sensation and memory*. Proust relates that he had for a long time forgotten everything about Combray when, one winter day, his mother, noticing he was chilled, suggested he have a cup of tea. She sent for one of those cakes called *madeleines*. Proust mechanically lifted to his lips a spoonful of tea in which he had allowed a bit of madeleine to soak, and the instant the sip of tea mixed with cake crumbs touched his palate he shuddered, permeated by a delicious pleasure he couldn't comprehend. This pleasure made life's pains seem unimportant, its briefness illusory.

What caused this great joy? He felt the joy to be related to the taste of the tea and cake but surpassing it infinitely. Where did it come from? What did it mean? He took a second sip and slowly succeeded in discovering that the taste that was giving him such powerful sensations was that of the tiny piece of madeleine his great-aunt Léonie, on Sunday mornings in Combray when he came to say good morning, would offer him, having first dipped it in her tea. And this sensation, an actual sensation from his past, goes on to evoke for him—with a clarity much more precise than that of intellectual memory—everything that was going on at Combray at that time.

Why is this particular mode of evocation so powerful? *Because the representations of memory, which are generally fleeting because they have no strong sensations to reinforce them, now find support in a present sensation.*

If you want to know exactly what transpires here in the realm of Time, consider the relationship of a stereopticon to

Space. A stereopticon shows you two images; these two images are not exactly alike because each is directed at only one of the two eyes; and it is precisely because they are not identical that they give an impression of depth. An object that has actual depth, on the other hand, provides both eyes with two different images. It is as if the viewer were saying: "Every time I have received from the self-same object two images that do not exactly coincide, I have perceived that the cause was a three-dimensional object seen from two different points; since I am now having trouble making the two images presented to me coincide, I know I am dealing with a three-dimensional object." Whence the illusion of spatial depth created by the stereopticon. Proust discovered that the combination Present Sensation-Absent Memory is to Time what the stereopticon is to Space. It creates the illusion of temporal depth; it allows one to recover, to "feel" time.

To sum up: *At the source of Proust's work lies an evocation of the past through involuntary memory.*

III. TIME RECOVERED

The past being thus conjured up, what does Marcel, the book's hero, see? At the center, he sees a country house, in Combray, and living in it his grandmother, his mother, his aunt Léonie (a character of homely and powerful comic quality), and a number of servants. He sees a country garden. Often in the evenings, one of the neighbors, M. Swann, comes to pay his acquaintances a visit; he comes alone, without Mme. Swann. As he arrives he opens the little garden gate, which sets a little bell ringing. For the child, the lands surrounding the house are divided into two "ways": Swann's Way, where M. Swann's house is, and Guermantes Way, where the castle of the Guermantes family is located. To Marcel the Guermantes are mysterious, inaccessible beings; he has been told that they are descendants of Geneviève de

Brabant; they partake of a fairy-tale existence. *Thus life begins with the age of names.* The Guermantes are nothing but a name; Swann himself, and especially Mme. Swann, and Swann's daughter, Gilberte, are names.

One by one these names give way to actual people. Once the Guermantes are known, they lose much of their magic. To Marcel the child the duchess of Guermantes was something like a saint in a stained-glass window: the grown Marcel lives in her house in Paris. He sees her go out every day, he is present when she quarrels with her husband, and he learns to appreciate not only her wit but her selfishness and heartlessness as well. In short he learns that these men's and women's names, which had seemed so beautful to him as a child, masked a rather commonplace reality. Romance does not reside in the real but in the distance between the real world and that of the imagination.

For love, too, Proust describes an *age of words,* an age during which man believes he can identify himself completely with another person and pursues an unattainable communion. But the person we imagine has no relation to the actual person to whom we will be joined for life. Swann marries an Odette born of his imagination and finds himself faced with a Mme. Swann he doesn't love, "who isn't his type." Marcel, the narrator, ends up loving Albertine whom he found at first meeting common, almost ugly, and he too learns that in love one gets a hold on nothing, one can never possess another. He tries to confine Albertine, to hold her prisoner. He thinks he can hold her, absorb her through this kind of coercion; but it's a chimera. Like the world, love is only illusion.

These two sides of Marcel's childhood—Swann's Way and Guermantes' Way—had both seemed to him vast and mysterious worlds; but when he had explored both, he found nothing in either worthy of deep attachment. The two sides had seemed to him separated by an unbridgeable gulf. And then—forming in a way a kind of great arch above the novel—they are joined; for Swann's daughter, Gilberte, marries Saint-Loup, a Guermantes. So the opposition of the two *ways* was also nothing but a lie. Reality is totally known, and *it is entirely illusory.*

Toward the end of the book, however, Marcel receives a second sign, which resembles that of the *petite madeleine* and which is to artistic conversion what the call to grace is to religious conversion. He is on the point of entering the home of the Guermantes, when he puts his foot down on two uneven steps and, as he regains his balance, steps on a paving-stone that is "poorly dressed, not quite as high as the one next to it," and at that very moment all the gloomy thoughts in his mind vanish before a happiness exactly like the one the taste of the madeleine had once brought him.

"Just as when I was tasting the madeleine, all worry about the future, all intellectual doubt was wiped out. A profound love intoxicated my eyes, impressions of freshness, dazzling light revolved close by me each time I retraced that step, one foot on the higher stone, the other foot on the lower stone. . . . I succeeded, forgetting the Guermantes, in recapturing what I had felt; the dazzling and indistinct vision was brushing by me as if it had told me: 'Catch me on the fly if you have the power to do so and try to solve the riddle of happiness I set you . . .' And almost immediately, I recognized it, it was Venice—which I had never been able to describe to my satisfaction, and which the sensation I had once felt on two uneven flagstones in St. Marks had just restored to me with all of the other sensations of that day."

Thanks once again to the coupling of Present Sensation and Past Memory, he experiences the joy of the artist. A bit later, when he asks to wash his hands and is given a rough napkin, the unpleasant feel of this cloth brings the sea to his mind. Why? Because a very long time ago, thirty or forty years, the napkins in a seaside hotel had the same feel. These shocks are identical to that of the madeleine. Again the writer succeeds in grasping, seizing, "recovering" a tiny segment of time. He enters the age of realities, or rather of the one reality, which is that of art. He feels now that he has but one duty, that of going in quest of such sensations, *in quest of lost time*. Life as we live it is of no importance, is nothing but lost time. "Nothing can be truly transfixed and known except under the aspect of eternity, which is that of art." Recreating lost impressions through memory, mining that vast deposit, the memory of the grown man, and transforming its remembrances into a work of art—such is the task he sets for himself.

At that very moment, in the town-house of the Guermantes, that sound of a step, of my steps in showing M. Swann out, that surging, ferruginous, interminable, high-pitched, and clear jingling of the bell that told me that M. Swann had finally left and that Maman was going to come upstairs—I still heard them, I heard those very steps, steps situated nonetheless so far back in the past. . . . The point in time at which I heard the noise of the bell of the garden of Combray, so far in the past and yet so much within me, was a point of reference within that vast dimension that I had not known I had. I became dizzy from seeing down below me—and at the same time in myself, as if I were miles tall—so many years. . . .

If at least there remained to me enough time to finish my work, I would not fail to stamp it with the seal of this time of which the idea impressed itself on me with such force today, and I would describe in it men, though it should make them look like monstrous beings, as occupying within time a place different in range from that very restricted one which is allotted to them in space, a place, on the contrary, extended limitlessly because they touch simultaneously like giants, immersed in the years, on periods lived by them, so distant—between which so many days have intervened—in time. . . .

Thus the novel ends, as it began, on the idea of time.

When one has just finished rereading Proust's entire novel, it is dumbfounding to think that some critics have accused him of having no plan. On the contrary, this whole vast novel is structured like a symphony. Wagner's art undoubtedly had a great influence on all the artists of this period. Even more perhaps than a symphony, *A la Recherche du Temps Perdu* is constructed like a Wagnerian opera. The opening pages are a prelude in which the major themes are stated: time, M. Swann's ringing of the bell, the literary calling, the *petite madeleine*. Then a great arch is thrown up from Swann to Guermantes; and, at the end, all the themes recur—the madeleine being recalled in connection with the steps and the rough napkin; Swann's bell ringing as it did in the opening pages; and the work ending with the word *time*, which has been its central theme.

What deludes the superficial reader is that within this very brilliant and very rigorous plan the evocation of memories does not occur in logical and chronological sequence, but rather, as in dreams, through free association and involuntary memory.

IV. THE RELATIVITY OF FEELINGS

What sets this work apart? First of all, Proust's art is rich in aesthetic, scientific, and philosophic learning. Proust views his characters with the intense and dispassionate curiosity of a naturalist observing insects. Seen from the height to which Proust's flawless intellect rises, man once again takes his place in nature, which is that of a lustful animal among other animals. Even his vegetable side is vividly revealed. The "budding girls" are—more than just on the level of imagery —a necessary season in the brief life of the human plant. Even as he admires their freshness, he is already taking note of the imperceptible little signs that foretell their ripening, maturity, and subsequent seeding and dessication: "As on a plant on which the flowers bloom at different times, I had seen them, in old ladies, on that beach in Balbec, these hard seeds, these tubercular lungs that my friends would one day be."

Particularly striking in this regard is the passage in which Françoise, a hardy and parasitic plant, is described as living in symbiosis with her employers; the description of Charlus as a fat bumblebee and Jupien as an orchid at the beginning of *Sodome et Gomorrhe;* and the scene at the Opéra in which land words are slowly submerged by aquatic words, and one seems to see the characters, who have become transformed into sea monsters, through a glaucous film. The "cosmic side" of the human drama is not better expressed in even the best of the Greek myths.

Love, jealousy, vanity, are illnesses—literally—for Proust. *Un Amour de Swann (Swann in Love)* is the clinical description of a case from its beginning to its end. In the painful precision of this pathology of the feelings one senses that the observer has experienced the sufferings he is describing but that, like certain courageous doctors who are able completely to separate their suffering self from their thinking self and make notes on the daily progress of a cancer or advancing paralysis, he analyzes his own symptoms with a heroic technicalism.

The scientific side of Proust's style is remarkable. Many of his finest images are taken from physiology, physics, or chemistry. Reading at random, we find in the space of a few pages:

> For three years my mother took no more notice of the paint one of her nieces was putting on her lips than if it had been invisibly and totally dissolved in some liquid; until the day when a touch extra, or perhaps some other factor brought on the phenomenon known as supersaturation; all of the paint hitherto unperceived crystallized, and my mother, confronted with this riot of color, let it

be known that it was a disgrace and cut off all relations with her niece. . . .

People who are not in love maintain that a man of intelligence should only be made unhappy by a woman who is worth being unhappy for; this is rather like being amazed that someone should deign to suffer from cholera by reason of a creature as tiny as the comma bacillus. . . .

Neurasthenics are unable to believe people who assure them that they will be gradually calmed by staying in bed and receiving no mail and reading no newspapers. Similarly are lovers—viewing the matter from the midst of an opposite state, and not having begun yet to try it out—unable to believe in the salutary power of breaking it off.

These beautiful, precise analyses comprise what one might call a *breakdown of classical categories of feelings.* For a long time moralists contented themselves with general terms of ill-defined content and agreed that the interplay—properly choreographed—of such abstractions as Love, Jealousy, Hate, and Indifference formed the substance of our emotional lives. Stendhal attempted to clarify these murky terms by distinguishing between *amour-goût, amour-passion,* and *amour-vanité,* and by explaining the phenomenon he called "crystallization." In this he took up the work of the generation of late eighteenth-century chemists who, having ceased to believe in the four elements, had isolated a certain number of simple substances. But Proust went on to show that these "indivisible" atoms are in reality complex universes composed of an infinity of feelings again divisible infinitely.

What happens in real life, he tells us, is that at certain times in our existence (particularly in adolescence and at the "roving stage" that comes in late middle age), we are in a receptive state, just as at certain times of weakness or fatigue we are at the mercy of the first germ that happens to attack our organism. We are in love not with such and such a particular person but with the person who happened

to be present at the moment we felt that mysterious need for
an encounter. Our love casts about for a person on whom it
can settle. In each of us is a play all set to begin, lacking
only the actress who will play the lead. She will inevitably
appear; moreover, she can vary. Just as in the theater a
certain role can be played by a leading actor and then by
understudies, so in a man's or woman's life the role of loved
one can be played successively by performers of unequal
quality.

The woman whose face is before us more constantly than
light itself—since, even with our eyes closed, we do not
for an instant cease to cherish her beautiful eyes, her fine
nose, to figure out all the possible ways of getting to see
them once more—this unique woman, we are well aware
that it would have been another who would have been
the unique woman for us if we had been in a town other
than the one in which we met her, if we had walked in
other quartiers, if we had frequented a different drawing
room. Though we think her unique, she is innumerable.
And yet she is solid, indestructible in the eyes of him who
loves her, for a long period irreplaceable by any other.
The fact of the matter is that this woman has done nothing
except arouse, by various magical summonses, a thousand
components of tenderness, existing in us in a scattered
state, which she has brought together, united, eliminating
all spaces between them; it is ourselves who, by giving
her her features, have provided all the substance of the
loved person.

If we were honest with ourselves we would admit that a
pre-existing feeling lay behind our choice of object; we
would ask ourselves frankly: "Who am I going to love?"
We would acknowledge that it is only by chance that the
happiness or sorrow we feel is linked to a particular person,
and that in actuality our heroines, like Proust's, play only a
few performances of the lead in the play that lasts the length
of our emotional lives.

Why do we choose certain heroines and not others? For their beauty? No, says Proust. What really motivates the civilized man is the curiosity aroused by mystery and obstacle. Valéry's beautiful lines are appropriate here:

Allez! . . . Que tout fût clair, tout vous semblerait vain.
Votre ennui peuplerait un univers sans ombre
D'une impassible vie aux âmes sans levain.
Mais quelque inquiétude est un présent divin.
L'espoir qui dans vos yeux brille sur un seuil sombre
Ne se repose pas sur un monde trop sur:
De toutes vos grandeurs, le principe est obscur.
Les plus profonds humains, incompris de soi-même,
D'une certaine nuit tirent les biens suprêmes
Et les très purs objets de leurs nobles amours.
Un trésor ténébreux fait l'éclat de vos jours;
Un silence est la source étrange des poèmes.[1]

A mystery is the strange source of our loves . . . Happiness, Proust teaches, is not in reality but in our imaginations. Strip our pleasures of our dreams and nothing is left. According to him, love—that love existing in us even before it has an object—this roving and fluid love "stops at the sight of one particular woman simply because that woman will be almost impossible to attain. From that moment on, one thinks less about the woman, who becomes hard to picture in one's mind, than about the ways of getting to know her. A whole anxiety process is set in motion and serves to fix our love on her who is the object of our love though barely known to us. The love becomes boundless; it no longer

[1] Come now! . . . Were everything clear, all would seem to you vain./Your boredom would populate a shadowless universe/With an impassive life made up of unleavened souls./But a measure of disquiet is a divine gift./The hope which, in your eyes, shines on a dark threshold/Does not have its basis in an overly certain world;/The principle of all your grandeurs is obscure./The deepest human beings, not understood by themselves,/Draw from a certain night the greatest riches/And the very pure objects of their noble loves./A shadowy treasure is responsible for the light of your days;/A silence is the strange source of poems.

occurs to us to think how little place the real woman has in it. . . . What do I know of Albertine? One or two profile views against the sea. . . ."

We may not even know the least thing about the loved one. When Marcel is on his way to Balbec, his train stops in a village station, and during the short time it is stopped he sees a lovely girl selling milk to the passengers. The train starts up again almost immediately, and Marcel carries away with him nothing but this rare and fleeting vision. But it is precisely because that vision is devoid of any content that the most intense of feelings can come to be attached to it.

Proust finds it so true that imagination is everything to love that in describing love's physical realities—which men naïvely believe to be the principal object of their desire— he always depicts them in a somewhat ridiculous or even manifestly unpleasant light. Reread the ghastly scene between Jupien and Charlus, or the scene in which the narrator, after wanting to for so long, is finally able to kiss Albertine:

> I should very much have liked, before kissing her, to be able to invest her once again with the mystery that she had for me on the beach, before I knew her, recover in her the land where she had once lived; in her place at least, if she were yet unknown to me, I could introduce all the memories of our life in Balbec, the sound of the wave breaking beneath my window, the cries of the children. But, in letting my gaze pass over the lovely pink globe of her cheeks, whose softly incurved surfaces disappeared gradually at the feet of the first plaits of her beautiful black hair, which ran in undulating mountain-chains, raised their sheer foothills, and modeled the waves of their valleys, I could not help saying to myself:
>
> "—Finally, not having succeeded in doing so in Balbec, I am going to know the taste of the unknown rose that is Albertine's cheeks. . . ."
>
> I told myself this because I believed that there is a knowledge to be gained through the lips; I told myself that I was going to know the taste of that carnal rose

because it had not occurred to me that man, a creature obviously less rudimentary than the sea-urchin or even the whale, still lacks a certain number of essential organs, and, in particular, possesses none for kissing. He compensates for that absent organ with the lips, and thereby achieves a result perhaps somewhat more satisfying than if he were reduced to caressing his beloved with a horny tusk. But the lips, fashioned to carry to the palate the savor of that which tempts them, must content themselves, without being aware of their delusion and without acknowledging their disappointment, with wandering on the surface and with running up against the barrier of the impenetrable and desired cheek. Moreover, at that very moment of actual contact with the flesh, the lips, even allowing for the possibility that they might get better at it with practice, would doubtless not be able to taste any better the savor that nature in fact prevents them from possessing, for in that desolate zone where they can find no nourishment, they are alone, sight, then the sense of smell, having deserted them some time since. First, to the degree that my mouth began to approach the cheeks which my eyes had proposed to it for kissing, those eyes, shifting position, saw new cheeks; the neck seen from closer up and as through a magnifying glass, revealed, in its coarse graininess, a robustness that altered the character of the face. . . . Just as, in Balbec, Albertine had often appeared to me differently, now, in the short journey of my lips toward her cheek, I saw ten Albertines; this single girl being like a several-headed goddess, the one that I had last seen, if I tried to come close to her, gave way to another. At least as long as I had not touched that head, I saw it, a light perfume came from it to me. But, alas! —because for kissing, our nostrils and our eyes are as ill-positioned as our lips are ill-fashioned—suddenly, my eyes stopped seeing; in turn, my nose flattening itself no longer perceived any odor and, without knowing any better for all that the taste of the desired rose, I became aware, from these odious indications, that I was finally in the process of kissing Albertine's cheeks.

Compare this description of "odious" sensations to Rousseau's ecstasy in describing Julie's and Saint-Preux's kiss, and you will get an idea of the vast distance separating an objective philosophy of love, i.e., a philosophy that believes in the reality of love and of the loved object, and a subjective philosophy like Proust's, which teaches that love exists only within ourselves and that anything that brings it to the level of the real, anything that satisfies it, kills it.

Just as an air-observer, because of the height at which he glides, sees enemy and home lines simultaneously and thereby attains a kind of painful, yet inescapable, objectivity, so Proust in love sees simultaneously the mind of the lover and the mind of the woman loved, as well as the image the one has of the other—or even, soaring above time, contrasts with calm cruelty his present, aching soul and his future, healed one. Nothing more deeply interests him than such marvelous panoramic vistas: the Faubourg Saint-Germain set sitting in judgment on the Verdurin set, and simultaneously, the Verdurin set sitting in judgment on the Saint-Germain set; the art of the present seen from the future and impressionism seen from the present; the pro-Dreyfus and the nationalist factions caught in the same photograph by one flawless and impartial lens.

But why does this detachment, this scientific calm result in a maximum of aesthetic emotion? It would seem to be because the essential goal of art is to divert the emotions from actual life and gear them onto the reserve motor of fiction. A *moral fiction,* one that claims to set forth *rules of action,* by its very nature stirs up precisely all that it should lay to rest. The moment moral judgment intervenes, aesthetic emotion ends, for the same reason a statue is a work of art and a nude woman isn't.

Stendhal was well aware of this, and his Napoleonic Code style aims at striking a tone of lofty distance. But Proust knew even better how to give a work that implacably ob-

jective quality that is one of the necessary conditions of
beauty.

"If the phenomena of the world," Flaubert says, "present themselves to you as transposed to the service of an
illusion to be described, so much so that all things, including
your own existence, seems to you to have no other useful-
ness . . . dive in." Swann, at Mme. de Sainte-Euvert's
soirée, detached through his love from the world and finding
in that world the charm "of that which, being no longer a
goal to our will, presents itself to us *in itself,*" seems a fine
symbol of that archetypal artist, of that flawless mirror
Proust so often approached to the point of merging with it.

V

Proust and Flaubert agree in believing the only real universe to be that of art and the only genuine paradises to be
those one has lost. Is this a philosophy the average man can
accept? Clearly not. "The wind rises; we must try to live!"
And it's hard to live without believing in the reality of feelings. In fact, a form of love exists that is quite different from
the love-malady Proust describes—a happy, mystical, absolute, loyal love, the total acceptance of another person, the
love of which Mme. de Renal and Mme. de Mortsauf are
the fictional—and thousands of women the living—heroines.
Proust described this kind of love only in the guise of maternal love. But we know, from the portrait he created of his
grandmother, that feelings of loyalty and self-denial were not
at all foreign to him.

As for himself, he reserved all his powers of loyalty for his
art; but when art attains such awareness, places such demands on the artist, it bears a remarkable resemblance to
religion. When Bergotte dies, Proust recalls what the pious
devotion of a painter like Vermeer must have been in trying
to reproduce with an absolute perfection a tiny patch of

yellow wall; even thus do we imagine Proust's patient courage in hunting down exactly the right words in order to render a particular fountain, a particular clump of hawthorn, or the miracle of the *petite madeleine*. Reynaldo Hahn has described one such moment of devotion, and it is with this picture of Proust at prayer that I wish to leave the reader:

The day of my arrival we went walking together in the garden. We were going by a border of Bengal rose-bushes when he suddenly stopped talking and stopped. I stopped too, but he then started walking again, and I followed suit. Soon he stopped once again and said to me with the childlike and rather sorrowful sweetness that characterized his manner and voice all his life: "Would you mind terribly if I stayed behind for a bit? I would like to see those little rosebushes again. . . ." I left him. At the turning of the path, I looked behind me. Marcel had retraced his steps back to the rosebushes. Having taken a complete turn about the château, I found him still in the same spot, staring fixedly at the roses. His head bent forward, his face intent, he was narrowing his eyes, his brows slightly knit as from an effort of intense concentration, and with his left hand he was obstinately pushing between his lips the end of his little black mustache, which he was nibbling. I sensed that he had heard me approach, that he saw me, but that he did not wish to speak or move. So I went on without uttering a word. A minute went by, then I heard Marcel calling me. I turned around; he was hurrying toward me. He rejoined me and asked "if I were angry." I laughingly reassured him that I was not, and we resumed our conversation where we had left off. I didn't question him about the interlude of the rosebushes; I made no comment, no joking allusion: somewhere I understood that it would not be right to. . . .

How many times thereafter I witnessed similar scenes! On how many occasions I observed Marcel in these mysterious moments when he was communing totally with nature, with art, with life, in these profound minutes when his entire being, concentrated in a transcendent effort, alternately, of penetration and aspiration, went into, so to speak, a state of trance, when his superhuman intelligence and sensitivity, at times through a series of piercing lightning-flashes, at times through a slow and resistless process of infiltration, reached the root of things and perceived what no one can see—what no one, now, will ever see.

At such moments of grace, the artist's mysticism is very close to that of the believer.

HENRI BERGSON

As we have seen, *A la Recherche du Temps Perdu* begins and ends on the theme of Time; it has been shown that the nature of memory was one of the problems that most interested Proust. Bergson's philosophy, which is the philosophy of *la durée* (duration) and the philosophy in which Time and Memory are the principal players in the drama of life, follows a course parallel to that of Proust's thought. The whole period was dominated by this philosophy. In the history of ideas in France it has played a role comparable (and complementary) to that of Cartesian philosophy. It has led fine minds into religious thought. It has inspired artists, Proust and Péguy among them, and has obliged scientists to revise their conclusions. One must attempt, then, to describe at least its principal features.

Alain, the philosopher who taught me philosophy, was not a Bergsonian. He accepted Bergson but not the school. He often said, however, that nothing was more unprofitable in studying a great man's work than splitting hairs, arguing, and disproving. He believed one should do one's utmost to immerse oneself in a system, to make as good a case for it as possible, and embrace it as one's own, at least during the period one was studying it. Criticism did not seem to him justifiable unless based on thorough understanding, and no understanding is possible without some attempt at sympathy. I shall try then to set forth the elements of Bergsonism sympathetically. This account will be neither complete nor

scholarly—far from it. Both my time and my learning are
limited. Those who desire further enlightenment are advised
to turn to Bergson himself, who is not a difficult author.
I shall attempt here only to indicate the general line of the
Bergsonian inquiry and the nature of its originality.

I. LANGUAGE AND REALITY

Most men do not see reality. They spend their whole lives
dealing with symbols—words—not people and things. To
say that "Turkey is still (or is no longer) loyal to the British
alliance" is not to reproduce a segment of reality; it is to
place certain ill-defined words in a certain order. What is
Turkey? If by this word one means the Turkish government,
one should, before speaking, be acquainted with that government's workings, be familiar with the individuals that make
it up, weigh the intensity of their feelings. If instead one
means the country Turkey, one should have traveled in
Turkey, have studied its various provinces and classes, have
been friends with a cross-section of Turks. But such study
would be too time-consuming. For life and action require
rapid decisions. So we content ourselves with the label on
the file-drawer and say "Turkey," hoping that others—ministers of state, ambassadors—will perhaps know what's inside
the files themselves.

The human mind is above all an instrument of action
and should accept the tools of language. They are imperfect
but indispensable. However the mind must from time to time
re-establish contact with the real. If it does not, abstract
words and the concepts they represent end up at odds with
one another in unreal and dangerous conflicts. An "intellectual" of the left forms a conception of a vague aggregate of
relationships he calls *capitalism* and battles furiously against
this monster; an intellectual of the right forms a conception

of a vague aggregate of relationships he calls *socialism* and starts warring against this specter. For these two fanatics a walk-out is only a duel of abstract words. Contrarily, for the manufacturer who has grown with his plant, who knows its every cog, who has worked with his employees—and for the intelligent and well-informed worker—the factory is a living thing whose needs and failings they intuit. Both these latter arrive at proper solutions to industrial problems through an instinct based on their profound knowledge of men and machines and not through abstract reasoning.

In speaking of a woman they do not know well, men will say she's complicated, unpredictable, deceptive. They analyze her words and ponder her behavior but fail to understand. But to the man who has long loved this woman and who sees her thoughts from the inside, this whimsical personality is the most consistent and understandable one in the world. He doesn't reason; he intuits. Similarly, it is in vain that a foreigner talking about the misfortunes of France analyzes all the elements of the decisions made at the time of the 1918 Armistice. He sees nothing but confusion. He finds it impossible to explain certain reversals in policy, certain periods of inaction. But a Frenchman who loves and knows his country in depth—even if he disapproves— understands and excuses. He places himself inside French society, thinks with it, senses in his own mind the reactions of the various groups, and feels an aggregate impression taking shape within him which corresponds to the actual behavior of France—for France is made up of the same elements as he is. He does not reason; he knows.

"We know truth," says Pascal, "not by reason alone but through the heart as well; it is through the latter that we have knowledge of first principles. And it is upon these perceptions of the heart and of instinct that reason should rely and base its discourse." For example, the heart—or instinct—tells us that man is free, that the mind is distinct from the body, and that some actions are good and some bad. But it sometimes occurs that the discursive intelligence, meaning that intelligence which expresses itself in language and words, runs counter to these instinctual truths and that, by means of skillful verbal jugglings, it professes to prove that the world is all matter and that our actions are completely determined. According to Bergson, the philosopher's job is to rediscover the things concealed behind opaque and ill-defined symbols. He maintains that philosophy should be essentially a return to the real and a return to simplicity. To *discursive* knowledge, which is its principal tool, philosophy should add (and sometimes oppose) *intuitive* knowledge, which, piercing the web of symbols—lilies floating on the pond of reality—plunges into life itself. But does a form of knowledge other than discursive knowledge exist? Can we think without words? Is it possible to place oneself at the heart of things? Indeed it is. Great poets know nature through intuition, not reason. "Beneath the thousand nascent actions that give outward expression to a feeling, behind the banal, social word that expresses an individual state of soul, it is the feeling, the state of soul pure and simple they seek after. And to encourage us to exercise the same effort on ourselves, they contrive to make us see something of what they have seen: through rhythmic arrangements of words, which come to form organic groups and live a life of their own, they tell us, or rather suggest to us, things language wasn't made to express." This recalls the Valéry of *Charmes*. And like the creative poet, the painter, the man of action, the scientist is capable, too, of going beyond concepts and of merging for an instant with things themselves.

"Careful now," say opponents of Bergsonism. "If you deny the primacy of intellect, you take humanity back to the age of superstition and magic. You destroy the achievement of the eighteenth century; you endanger the accomplishments of reason, which are already so much threatened today." But Bergson never denied the role or the value of the intellect.

He only said that beyond intellect, intellect itself can open the way to something superior to intellect. If the great statesman can on occasion have a sudden and brilliant intuition of what his people want, it is not because he denies the intellect; it is because, by dint of using his intellect to grasp all the details of the problem, he comes to be at one with the object of his thought.

Bergson is much too intelligent to make war on intellect, much too reasonable to make war on reason. He does make war, however, on that particular kind of intellectualism which accepts "the chaff of words for the kernel of things," on that particular kind of discourse in which reasoning has done away with reason. Descartes himself, father of rationalists, had many an intuitive prompting, and the reasonable Voltaire, in *Candide,* makes fun with good reason of the abuses of reason. The scientist and mystic, Pascal, understood that there is room for the *esprit de finesse* as well as the *esprit de géométrie.* As for the danger of tyranny from the rule of discursive reason, one observes it when the French Revolution veered away from its original goals and fell, during the Reign of Terror, into a bloody verbalism. Bonaparte, a man of swift intuition, was able, subsequently, to see beyond the verbiage of the orators to the *facts* whose aggregate constituted the givens of the problem France. Is there anyone willing to argue that Bonaparte was not intelligent? But "he used intelligence to go beyond intelligence." "There is," says Péguy, "a great mob of men who think in ready-made ideas. There are ideas that are ready-made even while they're being conceived, just as ready-made overcoats are already ready-made while they're in the process of being made up." Bergson wants to dress reality to measure. He uses the same symbols, the same words as other philosophers, but he quickens his discourse, just as poets do, with images—often telling and beautiful ones; and he regains contact, behind the curtain of words, with living quivering nature.

II. THE BODY AND THE SOUL

And so we find ourselves in quest of a kind of knowledge lying beyond words and which we shall call intuitive—as opposed to discursive—knowledge. *Intueri* means to look within. Intuition is the mode of thought that consists of taking oneself, by means of the mind, to the center of the object being studied and of grasping its truth from within. "That's a handsome definition," says the anti-Bergsonian, "but to what reality does it correspond? How could one bring oneself by means of the mind to the center of anything? Whether a person, a country, or an object, one's only chance of grasping it lies in analysis, the description of each of its parts, as one sees them from outside, then the synthesis of all those elements. But that synthesis itself takes place in the mind. You can't get outside of yourself and enter into an exterior reality. To what, concretely, can one apply your intuitive method?" To what? replies Bergson. Why first of all to that very thought you claim we can't get outside of. When you yourself are the subject, there's no question about your being on the interior of the subject. If you should describe your interior life to another person, you would doubtless do so by using words; you would describe your visions, your dreams, your feelings, in the form of discourse. This is necessary in order to be understood. But if you carry on a conversation with yourself, if you really try to find in yourself the *"données immédiates* of consciousness," you can and should do so through pure intuition.

"Granted," says the anti-Bergsonian, "but that's a pretty sterile kind of contemplation. I concentrate on myself, I do not allow myself to use words, I listen, but I don't hear anything. If this intuition business goes on for very long, I'll fall into a kind of slumber in which I watch the transparent stream of my thought go by like a drowsy shepherd watching

water flow." All of Bergson's early work is devoted to showing
that we can, on the contrary, recover, by way of this simple
and silent interior contemplation, infinitely precious elements
of thought hitherto hidden from us by a vocabulary entirely
derived from that system of knowledge which describes the
exterior world.

The system of knowledge that describes the exterior world
is entirely based on the notion of quantity. It requires fixed
and measurable relationships, numbers, diagrams, a space
that answers to mathematical laws. Interior life has nothing
to do with quantity; it is the realm of quality. One grief isn't
twice or ten times as intense as another. You can't square
love. Feelings and sensations increase and decrease in a different way entirely, a way one can attempt to express in images
but never measure. The same thing is true of perception of
the *durée*. The flow of time is one of the givens, or *données,*
consciousness provides to everyone. We have a clear awareness that each moment is different from the preceding one,
even if none of the spatial relationships has changed in the
interval. We know that this interior time is subjective and
not measurable. But we are such slaves to geometrical ways
of thought that the time we speak of is almost always objective time, measured by the movements in space of sand,
say, or a pendulum.

"And what disadvantage do you see in not experiencing
the sensation of pure *durée* and in transposing temporal
data into spatial data?"

"The very serious drawback that since Time is not of the
same nature as Space, we would thereby render certain problems unintelligible. Recall, for example, the problems Zeno
posed to the Greek philosophers of antiquity, problems no
one could solve. . . . 'Let us assume,' says Zeno, 'that the
fastest of human beings, Achilles, tries to overtake the slow-
est of animals, the tortoise. I maintain that if the tortoise has
the slightest head-start, Achilles will never catch up with it.
For while Achilles is covering the distance separating him

from the tortoise, the latter will move ahead a little. Achilles will then have to cover this new distance. But while he is doing that, the tortoise will advance again, very little, but a little nonetheless. This will go on endlessly. And thus Achilles will never catch up with the tortoise.'"

Such is the absurd conclusion Zeno's discursive, geometric thought leads us to. Intuitive understanding, which in this instance is the equivalent of common sense, knows on the contrary and beyond the shadow of a doubt that Achilles will catch up with the tortoise. Then what is wrong with Zeno's argument? The trouble is that his whole argument is falsified by the transposition of a continuous movement in time into a segment of space that can be cut up at will. Discursive thought in this instance confuses movement with the spatial trajectory that describes it. Intuition easily provides the correct answer or, to be more specific, demonstrates that the only problem is that of a misuse of words. It reinstates the factor of *durée* and the unbroken flow of time.

When Einstein's theory first came out, a thousand absurd conclusions were immediately drawn from it. A man traveling in a capsule at almost the speed of light could, it was said, come back after an interval of time that would be only two years to him but two centuries to those who stayed on the ground. He would have aged only two years and would have become a contemporary of his descendants. A man traveling at exactly the speed of light would never age, since the same light rays would always accompany him and present him with the identical view. Again, common sense balks. Bergson shows that these fabricators of hypotheses are confusing spatial time, that of signs and simultaneities, with interior, living time, the time in which one grows old. The traveler in the first capsule would, in fact, be dead long before the projectile came to earth two centuries later.

Another *donnée immédiate* of consciousness is the idea of freedom. We know we are free and responsible. A mechanistic philosopher like Taine, however, tells us that all of our thoughts and motions are as much determined as physical and chemical phenomena. "Vice and virtue are products like sugar and vitriol." And indeed, if we look for motives and explanations for our actions, we find them easily enough, and action does seem to be determined. But if we put ourselves back into the *durée* at the moment of the act, we are obliged to admit that the decision, taken as it was in an instant and without reflection, had in most cases nothing behind it except our nature. "We all more or less resemble the poor suitor who was always late, sometimes because he had overslept, sometimes because he had missed his train, sometimes because he'd forgotten his watch—and who in the last analysis was always late because being late was part of his nature and mental make-up." Acting according to one's mental make-up, pursuing action that has no explanation other than our own nature, is precisely what Bergson and common sense call acting freely. The problem of freedom, like so many others, seems difficult only because it is badly formulated.

The implications of Bergson's method are clear. Because his thought is simple and does not allow ready-made ideas to mask actuality, he recovers that freshness of intuition and common sense shared by all great philosophers. When subjected to this intense light, many problems fade away, for they were false problems in the first place, spawned by a defective vocabulary.

In his second work, *Matière et Mémoire (Matter and Memory)* Bergson tackles the body-mind problem. A number of his predecessors—Taine, for example—had denied the existence of the mind. To them the brain was a kind of factory in which all our thoughts are manufactured. The idealists, on the other hand, upheld the paradox of pure thought and denied the reality of the exterior world. Bergson seizes on the intuition of the real and shows that common sense is right. Common sense does not believe that a couple of pounds of gray matter can contain all the configurations of our life.

Common sense believes that mind is distinct from matter but also that matter exists. All of the experiments on localization in the brain support common sense. A part of the brain can be eliminated without loss of any mental image. A lesion of the brain can cause aphasia, that is, destroy certain motor mechanisms controlling the tongue and lips, but it does not destroy memory of the images corresponding to the forgotten or lost words. The brain, says Bergson, is simply an organ of transmission between mind and the motor organs. He conceives the relationships between mind and body as follows:

All the images that at every moment bombard the senses are stored in the mind. The *entire* past is always present in the mind. The brain, however, is a sorting agent that admits only those images useful to action. These images are summoned up by a particular state of the body. In sleep, action being no longer pertinent, this evocation is free, and it may be the most distant memories and the most bizarre combinations of images that then correspond to a given state of the body. Proust speaks somewhere of the woman born of a cramped position of his thigh. Such is the realm of dream. The man who allows the realm of dream to invade the realm of action is mad. What happens to the mind if the body disappears? This is the problem of the immortality of the soul. Bergson's answer tends to the affirmative. Lacking the body to transmit and articulate thoughts in space, the mind no longer has any means of communicating with matter; however, "the life of the mind cannot be considered an effect of the life of the body. . . . On the contrary everything occurs as if the body were merely used by the mind, and therefore we have no reason to suppose that the mind should disappear with the body. . . ." If we hang up the telephone, the mind of the person we were speaking to does not thereby cease to exist. And the brain is just like a telephone system. The view that the soul survives after death—which is that of most religions —seems to Bergson more likely to be true than not.

III. LIFE AND CREATION

Our intellect, born of the battle of mind and matter, a weapon forged for this battle, a collection of formulae for imposing on matter the forms the mind desires, is a tool ill-equipped for understanding life. It has, moreover—in order to explain the variety and evolution of the forms of life—come up with a number of rather feeble theories. These can be divided into two groups: mechanistic and finalistic.

Mechanistic explanations maintain that the entire universe —that equally of living things and of inert matter—functions in accordance with the blind working of immutable laws. The mechanist sees life as merely one of the fortuitous properties of matter. He explains the formation of organs and the evolution of species as the accumulation of tiny, measurable changes. But this account is inadequate. First of all, experience does not show that acquired characteristics can be passed on to future generations. Furthermore, evolutionism does not explain how absolutely distinct sequences come to the same result—how, for instance, the arthropod eye has the same essential features as that of mollusks. Above all, it doesn't explain life itself, or the action of living things on their surroundings. Matter left to itself is inert; it tends toward immobility. Life, on the other hand, tends to create. Any attempt to explain life by death is doomed to failure.

Finalistic theories are no more acceptable. These would maintain that life has as its object the realization of some plan, of some particular future state of matter, a state which is already known at the present time, for otherwise it would not be possible to talk about it. But none of the facts justifies this view. If life were working according to some pre-established plan, it would in the course of history show an ever-increasing degree of harmony. "Just as a house, as the stones go up, increasingly expresses the architect's idea." But we observe nothing of the kind. Disharmony among species is increasing rather than decreasing. "There are some species which are at a standstill, others which are retrogressing." The world of living things does not correspond to any plan in process of being worked out, but rather to a creation which proceeds unceasingly by virtue of an initial motion. This motion is alone responsible for the unity of the world, "a unity of infinite variety, superior to any the intellect might invent, for the intellect is but one of its aspects, one of its products."

This then is roughly how Bergson conceives of the life process. Its basis is a simple source, a creative force which he calls the *élan vital* and which transmits itself from seed to seed. This primal force is common to all life, animal and vegetable. "Just as the wind sweeping into a crossroads breaks up into divergent currents of air which are all but one and the same gust," so the *élan vital* impels to the conquest of matter species which are but emanations of one and the same force. Harmony in nature does not lie ahead in the future as the finalists would have it; it lies behind in the past, in the original afflatus.

Then what are animal forms? They are the shape of the resistance matter sets up against the vital force. If the wind blows on the sand at a beach, that sand will take symmetrical and distinct forms; it will assume regular wavy patterns. Each of these wrinkles of sand is actually of infinite complexity; it could be broken down into millions of grains of sand, and each of those grains could again be broken down into atoms, protons, and electrons. But the simple explanation of this entire phenomenon is the wind. Similarly, the simple explanation of evolution is the creative will. Everything happens as if some superior being had sought to realize itself and could do so only by relinquishing in the process—as does the wind in blowing over water and sand—a part of its force. Our body is the negative mold of our lack of force, the boundary separating our free will from matter.

Creation then is like a burst of force from a single center spreading out in diverse series, each of which is sooner or later arrested by the resistance of matter, just as fireworks blossom and fade. But the force of creation is continuous. Bergson calls this center of force *God*. "God so defined has nothing ready-made about him; he is life unceasing, action, freedom. Creation so conceived is not a mystery; we experience it in ourselves when we act freely."

And what is the end of this continuous creation? Asking such a question means falling back into the errors of finalism and attributing a plan to God. But Bergson's God is a poet, not a geometrician. That creation is an end in itself, and perhaps the only end, is indicated to us by nature in the joy attendant on any act of creation. "He who is certain, absolutely certain that he has produced a viable and durable work, has no further use for praise and feels beyond mere fame—because he is a creator, because he knows it, and because the joy he feels in it is a divine joy."

IV. MORALITY AND RELIGION

Among the *données* of consciousness, one finds, in nearly all men, a sense of moral obligation. We know without reflection and without coercion that certain actions in certain circumstances are wrong. We are often prepared to sacrifice personal interest in order to preserve the peace of mind and heart that only "a good conscience" can give. Where does this sense come from? Bergson's originality as an ethical thinker lies in his reply that this sense arises from two different sources, and that there are two moralities.

The first is the morality of societies. Man, like the wolf and dog, is a social animal. He can live only in groups. The size of the group varies over the course of history. Sometimes it's a family, sometimes a tribe, sometimes a religious order, sometimes a sect, sometimes a nation. But since man is not able to live without the group, he always needs its approval. Indeed, the judgment of the group, which is known instinctively, is never absent from the consciousness of any member of the group. This herd instinct can be stronger even than the instinct for self-preservation. It explains why the wolf, or the soldier, prefers death to flight. Even Robinson Crusoe, alone on his island, remains a moral man—for the isolated man believes that this abnormal situation will not last and prepares himself to face the judgment of the herd on his return.

That this social morality is bound up with the approval or disapproval of a group is clearly demonstrated in time of war or revolution. Certain of the support of the herd, ordinarily moral people are at such times prepared to commit against people opposed to the group, the most heinous and cruel kinds of acts. The fact that all men do not do this—and that some of them maintain, even in time of battle, a spirit of charity—indicates that another form of moral consciousness exists.

This second kind of morality is expressed by such words as: selflessness, giving of oneself, spirit of sacrifice, charity. But if it remained at the level of such concepts it would inspire few acts. Example is much more powerful. In order to be convincing, this higher and broader morality must be incarnated in certain exceptional individuals. Everyone has asked himself, at moments when all ordinary rules of conduct seem inadequate, what such and such a person he admires or reveres would have expected him to do in similar circumstances. "Founders and reformers of religions, mystics and saints, unsung heroes of the moral life, all are there; drawn by their example, we join with them as with an army of conquerors." It is never an intellectual process that leads us to imitate them. "It is not by preaching love of one's neighbor that one achieves it. . . . One must in this case pass through heroism in order to arrive at love." The drastic change that leads a man to charity has all the swiftness of intuition. It is an interior *coup d'état.* "So long as you reason over an obstacle it will remain where it is. . . . But you can dismiss the whole thing in one fell swoop by denying it."

The first kind of morality—social morality—is the morality of repose. It has rules that are permanent, or at least valid for a given period of time. The second kind is a morality of movement. It is a thrust, a progress; it means to be, and *is,* ever more demanding. It inclines strongly to poverty and even martyrdom. Like all free creation, it gives joy. The morality of the Gospels is the best example of dynamic morality. The Sermon on the Mount, in its antitheses, sets forth social and sublime morality at one and the same time: "Ye have heard that it was said . . . But I say unto you . . ." Whence two methods of moral training: first, the adoption and inculcation of the customs of the country, of the group— which is the social morality taught in families; and second, the imitation of some person taken as a spiritual model, and more or less complete identification with him—which is mystical morality and that of the Christian.

Thus we arrive at Bergson's ideas about religion. In these we again encounter the two terms he opposes in all of his thought. Again, he draws a distinction between static religion and dynamic religion, the "ready-made" and the "self-creating," the discursive and the real. Static religion externalizes, in the guise of gods or saints, those forces which should regulate our behavior from within. Mankind invents fables, and this myth-making is a defensive reaction of nature against the dissolvent skepticism of the intelligence. "Religion braces and disciplines. In order to perform this function, continuously repeated exercises are necessary. . . . Which means there can be no religion without rites and ceremonies. . . . These religious acts doubtless spring from belief, but they immediately react upon belief and strengthen it; if gods there be, a form of worship must be devoted to them, but the moment a form of worship exists, the gods exist . . ."

In the case of dynamic religion, the soul allows itself to be penetrated by a being immensely more potent than it is. It becomes "love of that which is naught but love. It also gives itself to society, but to a society which is now humanity as a whole, loved through inclusion in the love of that which is its source"—i.e., loved in God. True mysticism, that total communion of the saint with God, is rare, but there is some echo of it deep down in most men. We feel there is a mysterious and infinite force within us. We are in touch with it only in rare moments of exaltation (which are nearly always moments of sacrifice and humility), but we know it exists and we reserve a place for it in our minds. Thus we arrive at a dual religion—the religion of most men—and the religion in which the antique god, the god of the myth-making function, tends to merge with the god "who illumines and restores by his presence exceptional souls."

And what, in Bergson's view, is the mystic quality of these exceptional souls? "It is contact with and consequently partial union with the creative effort life manifests. This effort is *from* God, even perhaps *is* God." The great Christian mystics knew the ecstasy of this union with their God. Their experiences are significant to the philosopher, inasmuch as they help him in his attempt to understand the nature of God. Bergson thinks, as did Alain, that the superiority of Christianity over the religions preceding it lies in the fact that God, in order to be perceived and felt, must become man. "Creation turns out to be an undertaking by God to create other creators, to adjoin to himself creatures worthy of his love."

At this point the physical scientist will protest and point to the misery of man, to his insignificance as regards the infinite universe, to the naïveté of attributing so much importance to this mite. But isn't the physical scientist looking at the universe through the wrong end of the telescope? Isn't the least human being as infinitely complex as the universe itself, and doesn't that universe exist, moreover, only by virtue of being perceived by some consciousness? Isn't he

who understands and conceives the world a world himself?
Such a notion of man's place in the universe may seem
singularly optimistic. It is confirmed, however, by the intensity of the pure joys to which great souls can rise.

V

One sees how much this philosophy is of a piece. It springs
entirely from one swift and intense intuition. Early in life,
Bergson, who was a fine geometrician, was tempted to believe
in the mechanistic disciplines then in vogue. One day, just
after giving his students at the University of Clermont-Fer-
rand a lecture on Zeno, a lecture in which he presented the
problem of Achilles and the tortoise, he continued during his
stroll to meditate about this intriguing, ancient enigma, and
in a moment of sudden illumination hit upon the intuition
of pure *durée*. Bergsonism was born.

From that moment he had his method. Rather than a
method, moreover, this was "the very line of the movement
that leads thought into the density of things." It consists—no
matter what the problem—of seeking the naked core of
reality beyond the ready-made cloak of doctrines and words.
Bergson's intention is to construct for facts a philosophy to
measure, and to rethink one by one all of the great problems of
philosophy. Does he solve them? Indeed no—as no one ever
will. Like any human theory, his has its gaps and weaknesses;
but "a great philosophy," as Péguy so admirably put it,
"isn't one against which there is nothing to say, but one which
has said something."

PAUL VALÉRY

I. THE MAN

IT IS REMARKABLE how many similarities there are between the astonishing and uncomplicated career of Valéry and that of the great writer he most brings to mind—Descartes. Both came to prose via the twin roads of poetry and science. Like Valéry, Descartes began by being "in love with poetry"; he remained in love with it, and his last work was a verse piece written in Stockholm. Descartes didn't want to become a man of letters and volunteered as a soldier so that he could roam "here and there around the world, trying to be an observer rather than an actor in the comedy that is played there." Valéry, too, for a long time refused to be other than an observer in the world. Descartes withdrew to Holland "into the desert of a bustling populace" in order to collect his thoughts. "It's all up to me whether or not I choose," he said, "to live here unknown to anybody; every day I walk through great crowds of people almost as undisturbed as you are in walking your private paths; the men I encounter give me the same impression as might trees in your woods or bushes in your fields. Even the din of all these merchants is no more distracting to me than the noise of a brook." Aren't we already in the presence of Monsieur Teste?

Like Descartes, Valéry spent twenty years in solitary meditation, and like Descartes too, consented only after twenty years to share with readers any part of his investigations. If one adds that both showed the same kind of intellectual courage in setting about to rebuild—from the foundation up—the entire structure of thought, one sees that the parallel between these two men is not artificial and that we are perhaps justified in outlining here—since Valéry has himself provided us with the materials for doing so—the Valerian Discourse on Method.

II. THE LIFE

But first we must say a few words about the man who had these thoughts. Valéry was born in Sète in 1871. He went first to school in Sète and then to the lycée in Montpellier. Here is his own recollection: "I have teachers who rule by terror. They have a staff sergeant's conception of letters. Stupidity and insensitivity appear to be part and parcel of the curriculum. Mediocrity of soul and total absence of imagination in the best of the class. These appear to be the prerequisites for scholastic success. The result is a disastrous state of mind, opposition, a systematic resistance to learning."

This "resistance to learning" is not perhaps essential to the formation of the exceptional mind, but it gives rise, by virtue of the feelings of dissatisfaction it fosters, to the need to reconstruct. The pupil who is "first in the class" is often the adolescent who willingly accepts a pre-digested diet from his teachers. If he isn't fortunate enough to encounter a Socrates or an Alain among his teachers, a teacher who refuses to teach truth ready-made, he runs a great risk of falling asleep and joining at a very early age the Legions of the Dead. The rebellious student, dissatisfied with official truth, seeks salvation by other paths, and sometimes finds it.

Valéry worked, but not in the way his teachers in Montpellier thought he worked. To all appearances he was studying law; in actuality, he was regretting the fact that he wasn't a sailor (for a long time this regret remained so strong that he had a twinge of sadness every time he saw a naval officer), and he was discovering the new poets—Baudelaire, Verlaine, and, later, Rimbaud and Mallarmé. Art already seemed to him "the only thing that made sense," metaphysics "a bunch of foolishness," science "too limited in range," and practical affairs "an abyss, an ignominy leading to a harried existence." He knew a number of literary men. Pierre Louÿs for one, whom he met at Montpellier. And André Gide, whom Louÿs introduced to him. Gide read Valéry his *Cahiers d'André Walter*, which astounded him. Valéry didn't want to be a writer. He had written a number of poems which were promptly published by little magazines and praised by a number of discerning readers. But becoming a writer "by trade" seemed to him both above and below his powers. He wanted to set himself "a goal impossible to achieve," a wish shared in an almost identical form by Goethe.

He did a year of military service. He admired the style of the Military Code. "It is impossible to be precise without being obscure if one attempts to reduce the number of words and sentences to a minimum."—"On Sundays, I save my soul by writing poetry." At twenty-one he went to Paris. He had no particular goal in mind, no plan of existence. He had just gone through a painful love affair which had intensified his intellectual despair. "I was twenty years old and I believed in the power of thought. I suffered incredibly over being and not being. Sometimes I felt I had infinite powers; they toppled when faced with real problems, and the feebleness of my actual powers filled me with despair. I was gloomy, flippant, looked easy to deal with, was tough in reality, extreme in my scorn, absolute in my admiration, easy to impress, impossible to convince. . . . I had stopped writing poetry, I hardly read any more."

How could one fight this kind of romanticism, which was too intellectual to become lyrical? A reading of Poe gave him the idea of seeking salvation in full *consciousness of self*. The ills he suffered from were ills of the mind. Couldn't they be dispelled by analyzing with extreme precision the mechanism producing them?

In going through, like Gide, the painful crisis of adolescence, Valéry did not seek relief, as did Gide, in sensuality, nor as Byron in poetry, nor as most men in action, but rather, as Descartes, in renunciation and cultivation of the self. He settled in Paris on the rue Gay-Lussac in a room where Auguste Comte had spent his early years. There he filled countless notebooks with entries on time, on dreams, on attention, on truth in the sciences, on the functioning of the human mind generally. He doubtless went to see Mallarmé whom he admired and liked, and to see Huysmans and Marcel Schwob, but he was no longer in that state in which one "makes literature." Even Mallarmé's art interested him primarily in its logical and aesthetic aspects. How are such poems constructed? "I track down the vague and the arbitrary as a warden tracks down gypsies."

Monsieur Teste came into being during the "drunken period of his will." A magazine called *Le Centaure* had asked him for something to print. He started working again on a manuscript that was but barely begun, a manuscript in which he had attempted to write the Memoirs of Dupin (Poe's detective hero). It was this manuscript which began with the sentence: "Stupidity is not my strong point." He added to it using notes taken on himself:

"I suffered from an acute case of the need for precision. I was straining toward the limit of the insensate desire to understand . . . I had no interest in anything that came easy to me, considered it almost inimical. . . . I was suspicious of literature, including even the relatively precise operations of poetry. . . . I spurned not only Letters but also almost all of Philosophy as among the Vague Things and Impure Things I rejected with all my heart. . . . Monsieur Teste was born one day from a recent revival of these feelings. That is, he resembles me as closely as a child—begotten by someone at a moment of profound change of his own being—resembles that father who was not himself."

In short, Teste is a projection of Valéry the youth, the absolutist and extremist adolescent, who, not yet having discovered the value of human conventions or that the arbitrary is the only true form of necessity, rejected all action, including that of the artist. It should be noted that this was not a rejection based on powerlessness, but a rejection based on excess of power.

"What people call a superior being is a being who is illusioned. In order to admire him, one must see him—and in order to be seen, he must reveal himself. And all he shows me is that he is the victim of a silly mania for his own name. Every great man is thus stained by an error. Every seemingly powerful mind rests upon the very fault that makes it known."

Thus, since every great man is a false great man (for if he were truly a great man, he would have taken steps to prevent us from knowing about it), Valéry finds it amusing to entertain the notion that the greatest of men must be unknown: it pleases him to imagine for the solitary genius a life something like the one he was himself then leading—somewhat like Mallarmé without the disciples and without the poetry, somewhat like Descartes or Spinoza before they became famous.

How can one possibly describe Monsieur Teste? His most outstanding characteristic is precisely that of having none. "No one notices him. He speaks without gestures, he doesn't smile, he doesn't say how-do-you-do or good-by, he wipes out his thoughts as soon as they spring to mind, and is not happy about finding them present at all . . . What is hard is incorporating what one finds." Idea is nothing, so long as it has not become body, habit. What did Monsieur Teste find? A number of extraordinary means for achieving a little more precision in thought, a vocabulary from which he banished a great many words because he found them imprecise or ill-defined. Teste himself never says anything imprecise;

the power of his intellect is such that, had he so wished, he might have excelled in all disciplines. In order to be a universally acclaimed genius, he lacked only weakness.

But what of Teste ill, or in love? Doubtless he would feel as other men the pleasurable and painful motions of his body, but his mind would study the rules of these motions and regulate them. The narrator accompanies him to the opera and returns with him to his home; he lives in a tiny furnished apartment. No books, no desk—cheerless "abstract" furnishings. It is "any" lodging, "comparable to the any given point of theorems, and perhaps as useful." Indeed, Teste, who has "killed the puppet," can live only in a "pure and banal" place. There, being old and sick, Teste has a painful attack, and, of course, he *thinks* his suffering:

"Wait . . . There are moments when my body lights up . . . It's very strange. I suddenly see inside . . . I can distinguish the thicknesses of the layers of my flesh, and I am aware of areas of pain, convolutions, poles, aigrettes of pain. Do you see these living figures? This geometry of my suffering? Some of these flashings look exactly like ideas.

"What can a man do? I fight everything, except the suffering of my body, beyond a certain intensity. . . ."

Thus Teste suffers. Then the pain subsides. He falls asleep analyzing sleep and dream. He snores softly. The narrator takes up the candle and tiptoes out.

III. FAME

Valéry was only twenty-four years old when he wrote *Un Soirée avec M. Teste* (*An Evening with Monsieur Teste*). But he was already Valéry. Teste's characteristics are also Valéry's essential characteristics: the need for rigor, the horror of imprecision and of the seeming lucidity with which nearly all men content themselves—and, as a result of this need for rigor, the need to throw all language into question and to require of words a precise content.

This concern for rigor led him to take an interest in another famous man who had been similarly concerned: Leonardo da Vinci. Here again a chance request made Valéry emerge from his silence. At Marcel Schwob's one day he spoke so brilliantly of Leonardo that Léon Daudet, who was present and at that time involved with *La Nouvelle Revue,* asked him, through the intermediary of Madame Adam, to do an article on the subject. This turned out to be *Introduction à la Méthode de Léonard de Vinci.* Actually Valéry uses da Vinci in the article primarily as a pretext for talking about his own special concerns.

In the years after 1895, Valéry pursued—in self-imposed obscurity—investigations whose sole and exclusive aim was the overhauling of his mind and of his language. In order to make a living, he sought out jobs. He worked (with Cecil Rhodes) in the publicity department of the Chartered Company, then in the Ministry of War, where he was long employed in the Artillery Supply Office, and finally, with the Agence Havas. He had, it seemed, forever put aside any idea of becoming known. "A man who renounces the world places himself in a position to understand it."

However, such are the mysterious workings of genius that he was not quite as unknown as he thought. In the lycées and universities there were young men who were imitating those few poems published in little magazines and *An Evening with Monsieur Teste.* Some of them knew his poems by heart, and as with Homer, an oral tradition existed. Other works were known to him alone—the *Manuscrit Trouvé dans une Cervelle,* for instance, which had never been and never will be published.

"Forgetting. Personal work. Notes heaped up in boxes. Marriage. Life. Children. . . ."

So pass twenty years among and far from men, in "the desert of a bustling populace." When he comes to sort out

the notes he has accumulated, he will have enough material
for several full-length books. One will be the *Dialogue sur les
Choses Divines;* another, *Gladiator,* an essay on the nature of
training, on virtuosity. There are notes on love, on eroticism,
pain, the family. All are interesting, some exquisite. If they
were to be brought together in some kind of order, the
French would be stunned to find that they possessed a new
classic. Valéry himself was unaware of his power. Which is
enormous. "Hammered out for years on the smith's anvil, his
mind became a Siegfried's sword,"[1] invincible, at least to
mortals.

Shortly before the war, André Gide who, with several
friends, had recently founded *La Nouvelle Revue Française,*
asked Valéry's permission to print all his old poems in a
volume. Valéry refused, but his friends were insistent. They
had all the old magazine issues where his poems had appeared
searched, and put together a typed copy which they submitted
to the author: "Contact with my monsters," notes Valéry.
"Disgust. I set myself to messing about with them. Retouch-
ings."

So he corrected his monsters, with a concern for music and
resonance, then, taking a liking to this work, decided he
might round off the collection with a short poem of forty or
fifty lines, which would constitute his farewell to poetry.
He began this poem in 1913. He was still working on it
when the war came. He continued working—in the same
state of mind as a sixth-century monk composing Latin hex-
ameters amidst the invasions—with the infinite pains of a man
who believes he is writing the last will and testament of a
civilization and a language. Finally, in 1917, the poem was
finished. It was *La Jeune Parque.*

It was a great success, not in quantity, but in quality. Then
the *Anciens Vers* were published, and the boxes of notes were
opened—and the French, or at least the wiser among them,

[1] Charles du Bos: *Approximations*

knew that they were possessed of both a great poet and a great prose writer. As always happens with those who have chosen to remain obscure, the world cast its most glaring light on Valéry. I shall not recount this portion of Valéry's life. Not that it is less attractive, for no one could have accepted fame with more modesty, simplicity, graciousness, and irony; but Valéry's heroic period is the period of *Monsieur Teste* and *La Jeune Parque*. As he himself said: "the rest is but sound and fury." I have found it necessary, before proceeding as best I can to describe Valéry's method, to lead up to it via the noble phenomenon that was his life; for thus it can be seen that this unrelenting rigor, this desire to wipe the slate clean and reconstruct are not merely an intellectual game, but instead the quest of a determined will. Like Descartes, Valéry lived his method and Monsieur Teste thereby easily carries the day over Monsieur Bergeret.

IV. INTRODUCTION TO THE METHOD OF PAUL VALÉRY

A. *Rigor*

"Not affection, Nathanaël, but love," reads the opening of Gide's *Les Nourritures Terrestres* (*Fruits of the Earth*). In beginning this Introduction to Paul Valéry's Method, I should like to write: "Not clarity, Erixymachus, but rigor." For clarity is not a clear word. What is clear? There are critics and readers who find Valéry unclear. "I am terribly sorry," he says, "to so distress these amateurs of light; it is only clarity that interests me. Alas! I confess I find hardly any. The obscurities attributed to me are but thin and transparent compared to those I find all about me. Happy are those who are sure they perfectly understand themselves! I am possessed, my friend, of that unhappy sort of mind that is never quite sure whether it has understood without realizing it; I have great difficulty distinguishing between what is evidently clear and what is positively unclear."

A shadowy clarity often emanates from works that are considered bright and shining. In speaking of Anatole France in the speech he gave on the occasion of his reception into the French Academy, Valéry spoke of the latter's clarity with more than a touch of irony:

> Immediately pleasing was a language one could savor without giving it much thought, beguiling for its air of great naturalness, and whose limpidity, doubtless, allowed on occasion a hidden though unambiguous thought to show through. . . . His books showed consummate artistry in touching upon the most serious ideas and concerns. Nothing in them gave pause, except perhaps the very marvel of not finding the least resistance.
>
> What could be more precious than the delightful illusion of a clarity that gives us the feeling of being enriched without exertion, of experiencing delight without effort, of understanding without strain, of enjoying the performance without having to pay?
>
> Happy the writers who relieve us of the weight of thought and who lightly contrive a glowing masque of the complexity of things. Alas! Certain gentlemen, whose existence is to be deplored, have taken a quite contrary path! . . . They have set the mind to working upon those voluptuous complexities; they present us with enigmas; they are unfeeling creatures!

I remember Valéry giving a lecture one day at the Vieux-Colombier and saying in almost these exact words:

> Obscure? Me? I'm told so and I try to believe it. But I find myself less obscure than Musset, or Hugo, or Vigny. You're surprised? Look at Musset. I wonder if any one here can explain these lines:
>
> *Les plus désespérés sont les chants les plus beaux*
> *Et j'en sais d'immortels qui sont de purs sanglots.*

[The most desperate are the most beautiful songs
And I know of some immortal ones which are pure sobs.]

I frankly cannot! How can a pure sob be an immortal
song? I find that incomprehensible. A song is a rhythmic
structure; a pure sob is formless. Obscure as I may sometimes be, I have never written anything as obscure as that.

At that moment a young and obviously annoyed man got
up in the audience:

"Really, sir," he said, "you can't be serious. I don't see
anything obscure about those two lines, and I'm prepared to
explain them to you."

"Please go right ahead, sir," said Valéry. "I yield the floor
to you with pleasure."

He got up and lit a cigarette. The annoyed gentleman
stepped up on the stage. In explaining Musset, he did not
succeed in satisfying either Valéry's standard of rigor or even
the audience's less exacting one.

In any case, however, neither clarity nor rigor are necessary in a poem. Valéry doesn't find Vigny's line *"J'aime la
majesté des souffrances humaines"* ("I like the majesty of
human sufferings") "explainable," for there is nothing ma-
jestic about human sufferings. There is nothing grand about
toothaches or anxiety. Still, it is a beautiful line because
"majesty" and "sufferings" strike a beautiful *accord* between
consequential words.

Similarly with Hugo:

Un affreux soleil noir d'où rayonne la nuit . . .

[A ghastly black sun from which night radiates . . .]

Although logically impossible, it makes a marvelous negative.

Valéry the poet grants himself the right to be obscure, or
more precisely to be "musical," just as he grants it to other
poets. But the moment Valéry the prose-writer starts to
put together a string of ideas, he insists on rigor. He tries

never to use a word he hasn't defined and never to assume in those he does use more than they contain in their accepted definitions. In short, he attempts to invest the language of prose with as much mathematical precision as possible.

> I am wary of all words, for the least reflection renders what one has said absurd . . . I have, alas, arrived at the point of comparing those words by means of which one very slowly crosses the space of a thought to thin planks thrown across a chasm, planks that bear crossing but not stopping. The swift-moving man avails himself of them and rushes over and away, but if he lingers the least little bit, that tiny instant snaps them and the whole tumbles into the depths . . .

Nothing detains Valéry, pursuer of exactness. That is why I call his search "heroic." He doesn't accept easy truths; nor does he let universally held opinions—the authority of the experts—stop him. He confronts everything with the same great question: "What is it all about?" Like Descartes, he starts his investigations entirely from the beginning, forcing himself systematically to doubt everything. I am wrong, however, to say "forcing himself," for this doubt is part and parcel of his nature.

B. *The Clean Slate*

What do we know? What have we been taught in school aside from languages and the exact sciences? A metaphysics? Valéry asks this question, having in mind no particular metaphysics but rather whether any metaphysical knowledge is possible. "We can only know what is implicated through our existence . . . Assuming that there were an essence to things, one *word* for the Great Charade—an Ultimate Answer—that word would be only an incidental effect of our behavior."

Before seeking an explanation for the world as a Whole, one must first believe in the possible existence of such an explanation. Valéry doesn't. He includes in his list of "idiotic desires of man": "knowledge of the future, immortal life, belief in the existence of an ultimate answer." If a "supreme thought" existed, "once known, there would be nothing to do but die, for there would be nothing left to come." His fine preface to *Eureka* should be read in this connection: "The question of the totality of things and that of the origin of this All spring from the most simple of wishes: we want to see what came before the light."

All that need be done with regard to this Oneness of the Universe is to admit our obvious ignorance; man, however, translates his feelings into idols. "He puts love on one pedestal, death on another. And on the highest one he puts that which he doesn't know and can't know and which has no meaning." The philosophers' disputations relate not to the nature of things but only to the relationships of certain words which are so broad and abstract as to be devoid of content and impossible to define. Realists, nominalists, idealists, and materialists constitute the different sides in the games of the mind. In these chess matches, each side moves his pawns according to accepted sets of rules. "In the end nothing is proved except perhaps that A is a cleverer player than B."

To which the philosophers will reply that denying philosophy is itself a form of philosophizing. However, I don't think Valéry would let them get away with that dodge. For the philosophers argue in order to make one word triumph over another, whereas Valéry's very different position is to deny that any of these words are subject to precise definition. "With philosophers one need never be afraid of not understanding. Indeed, what one should really be afraid of *is* understanding."

"What one *actually* thinks when one says that the soul is immortal is always capable of being stated in less high-flown terms. . . . All metaphysics of this kind can be considered dishonest, a failure of language, a propensity for making thoughts seem of great import, in short, for getting more

out of the statement one has concocted than one put into it."
—"Time, space, the infinite are clumsy words. Any proposi-
tion that aims to be unambiguous forgoes them." Most of
the so-called "metaphysical" problems are actually problems
of language and very simple-minded. To ask, as do some
philosophers, if the real exists is the equivalent of asking if
the standard meter kept at Meudon is a meter.

What else have we been taught? History. . . . "History is
the most dangerous reaction ever produced by the chemistry
of the intellect. Its properties are well-known. It causes
dreaming, it inebriates entire populaces, encouraging in them
false memories, gives them hyper-sensitive reflexes, keeps their
old wounds open, disturbs their rest, brings on delusions of
grandeur or of persecution, and makes nations bitter, intolerable, and vain."

Given the fact that it dictates behavior to entire populations, is there anything certain about it? Nothing. It cannot
be known. The historians of the French Revolution agree
amongst themselves "exactly as Danton agreed with Robespierre, although with less severe consequences—for the guillotine, fortunately, is not available to them."

The great painter, Degas, once told Valéry how he went
one day with his mother to visit Madame Le Bas, widow of
the famous National Conventionist. On seeing, hanging in the
anteroom, portraits of Robespierre, Couthon, and Saint-Just,
Madame Degas could not help exclaiming in horror:

" 'What? . . . You still have the faces of these monsters in
your house?' "

" 'Shush, Célestine,' " retorted Mme. Le Bas sharply.
" 'Shush. They were saints . . .' "

One readily imagines the same exchange occurring between
Michelet and de Maistre, Taine and Aulard. "Every historian of the *époque tragique* holds out to us the decapitated
head that expresses his preference."

Yet there are some historical facts about whose authenticity all historians are agreed. Charlemagne was crowned

emperor in the year 800, and the battle of Marignan was fought on September 15, 1515. True, but *choosing* among events and documents allows the historian to tell history according to his prejudices and biases. History can be made to justify anything. It teaches absolutely nothing, for it contains everything and provides examples of everything. There is nothing more ridiculous, says Valéry, than talking about "the lessons of history." One can from history deduce all theories of politics, all moral systems, and all philosophical systems.

It is especially dangerous to think that history ever enables us to predict the future. "History," the graybeards say, "is forever a new beginning." To begin with, that is subject to argument. Even admitting that it is true "generally," it is false enough in its particulars to make any prediction absurd. In speaking to a group of lycée students in Janson-de-Sailly, Valéry tried to tell them what he was like at their age, in 1887, and to show them that from the view of the world then available to him it was impossible to deduce what that world would become.

"In 1887, the skies were reserved to the birds. Solids were still solid, opaque bodies still opaque . . . Newton and Galileo reigned in peace; physics was tranquil, its fundamentals absolute. . . . Space was happy in its infinitude, homogeneity. All this has now gone up in smoke. All this has changed even as the map of Europe, the appearance of our streets, has changed. . . . Could the greatest scientist, the most far-seeing politician of 1887 have even dreamed of what we see today, a mere forty-five years later? One cannot even conceive of the processes by which a mind dealing with all of the data of history up to 1887 might have deduced from even the most astute knowledge of the past even a roughly approximate idea of the year 1932."

The so-called exact sciences enable prediction within a closed system and on a certain scale, but in history it is not given to us to isolate the systems and the scale is prescribed.

Thus, all prophesying is a lie. "We enter the future backwards." History is not a science; it is an art; there is a Muse for it. As such, Valéry finds it pleasant enough, but it must be kept in its place. The moment one sets about using this unknown past to plan one's actions with a view to the (unpredictable) future, one is lost. If Napoleon had not been obsessed with the story of Caesar, he would not have had himself proclaimed emperor. "He was an enthusiastic lover of historical accounts and this man, born to create, lost himself in the corridors of history. His decline began the moment he stopped being unpredictable."

Nevertheless, Valéry acknowledges the utility (though a rather negative one) of meditation on the past. "It shows us how frequently projections that are too exact have failed, and, on the other hand, the advantages to be gained from an unceasing over-all preparedness which, without claiming either to shape or defy events—which invariably come as surprises—permits man to move as quickly as possible against the unexpected." Such lessons, however, seem more of a moral than a scientific nature.

The great mistake of the nineteenth century, drunk with the practical achievements of the exact sciences, was to confuse the methods of these sciences with those of false sciences, to which it gave such names as psychology and sociology. "There is the science of simple things and the art of complex things. Science when the variables can be enumerated and their number few, and their combinations clear and distinct." Whereas in the physical sciences, objective control replaced subjective vision of objects, in the historico-political "sciences" an attempt was made to make subjective methods jibe with objective conclusions. History and its daughter, politics, should be humbled and leveled as vigilantly as philosophy. "One cannot pursue politics without taking a stand on questions no sensible man would claim to know anything about. One would have either to be supremely foolish or supremely ignorant to dare to have an opinion on most of the questions politics poses." And he adds elsewhere: "Politics began as the art of preventing people from meddling in affairs which were their concern . . . At a later date was added the art of obliging people to make decisions about things they don't understand."

What's left on our list? Science? It is a collection of recipes and procedures that always work out, and as such is useful and worthy of respect—but "all the rest is literature." Science does not afford, as the men of Zola's generation had naïvely believed, an explanation of the world. It will never do so. Nothing will ever explain the Universe, because the Universe is nothing but a mythological expression. How can one arrive at the concept of something that has no opposite, that excludes nothing, and that resembles nothing else? If it resembled something else, it wouldn't be everything."

Then what is left? Common sense? "Common sense is the ability we once had of denying and brilliantly refuting the existence of opposites . . . Common sense is an entirely local intuition. The sciences daily throw it into confusion, bewilderment, puzzlement. . . . Common sense is no longer invoked except through ignorance. The standard of the average instance has fallen into total disrepute . . . Nearly all the dreams of our fables—flight, perception of objects not actually present, verbal transmission—and other, yet undreamed-of wonders—have in our day emerged from the realm of the impossible and the mind. The fabled has become part of commerce." Common sense is today plainly in disgrace. Something so commonly shared is nothing to pride oneself on.

Thus, truly rigorous thought disproves in turn everything it creates. Isn't the Valerian intelligence, Charles du Bos asked, at bottom a form of nihilism? "In the intellectual realm, there is no more majestically tragic sight than that of the faculty of thought arriving, through its own acuity, at the void and self-negation. This is truly the realm of solitude and of desperate clarity." We shall see, however, that in this solitude, Valéry builds his city, which is the city of civilized men.

C. *The Conventions*

Now that we have the *tabula rasa,* the clean slate, what are we going to construct on the table or write on the board? For there is "some thing." Men think, sometimes reconcile their thoughts and their actions; human societies live and endure. In this disorder and ruin one finds the materials for order. "What are these materials?" we ask Valéry. I believe his reply is: "Conventions, or, if you prefer, fictions."

What is a convention? It is a rule accepted by one or more men. An individual playing solitaire can play only because he has accepted a convention. Two men who are playing écarté together. . . . This agreement is not an expression of some absolute truth. Its only value lies in the fact of its acceptance. For example, it is agreed between us that I will talk for an hour and you will listen. This agreement establishes an order in this room. We might have agreed upon some other convention: that you sing, for instance, and that I listen. This convention would have established a different order. But why are such conventions respected? Because some of the people in this room represent the law. Not through force. They couldn't force you to be quiet. But through an agreed-upon fiction. Now it is in the nature of human societies that they cannot exist except by means of such fictions. "For there is no power capable of establishing order exclusively on the basis of bodily coercion by other bodies."

The instincts are conquered by ideas, by images, and by myths. The movement of a society in the direction of civilization, Valéry thinks, is a movement in the direction of rule by signs and symbols. All society is based on language, which is the primary and most important of the conventions, on

written language, on custom, on observed convention. Society is nothing but a fabric of spells and charms. We do
not perceive the fictive character of our laws because many
of them have become part of us and instinctive. We tip our
hats, we give our word, we clap, we pay for things, we
accept change in return. Each of our actions assumes innumerable ancient fictions. The life of a people whose history is a long one is woven with bonds so numerous that
none of its members any longer knows their origins.

So then what happens? What happens is that, with order,
freedom of mind becomes possible. There is no freedom in
barbarous societies. Take, for instance, a family of apes or
cavemen; the young males obey the father because they are
afraid of him or because some outside danger threatens. Such
is the "state of fact" (as opposed to the state of fiction). In
a contemporary Parisian family, however, danger seems remote or, if it becomes imminent, it is not of the sort that
brings the power of the father into play. Thus, young people
argue: "Why obey one's father? It's only a convention. And
what is more empty than a convention? Why respect it?"
Even thus in eighteenth-century France did people begin to
ask: "Why this King?"

Creators of order, parent to freedom, conventions are
soon threatened by the very order and freedom they have
shaped. Men forget what disorder and pain are like. The
critical attitude sets in. It undermines, then destroys the
conventions. Barbarism is reborn and with it the "state of
fact." "Then it's either Revolution or War. Soon, through
the effects of one or the other, the individual will once again
become unhappy enough to long for the police or death."

Thus, what is most necessary to men is also the most tyrannical of their creations. The strongest underpinning of
civilizations is a fabric of spells and charms. What is useful
about ethics is not the rules it offers (variable, depending on
the time and the place), but the fact that it offers rules.
What is necessary to the life of a country is not that it be a

monarchy, republican, or aristocratic, but that a set of political conventions be accepted by the majority of its citizens. What allows mathematics to create a system of "self-evident" truths is that mathematics is the most arbitrary thing in the world. What makes a poem "wonderfully inevitable" is the arbitrariness of the rules which make its composition possible.

This is a new idea, and one that is peculiarly important and relevant to our day. Almost without exception up until now, men have looked for an absolute truth, the answer to the riddle, the ultimate idea. The modern thinker, like Valéry, no longer believes that he can explain the universe, or even that there is an explanation for it. He makes certain hypotheses about the world that enable him conveniently to group observed phenomena. He doesn't claim that these hypotheses are true. He is certain, indeed, that they will one day be surpassed or replaced. But for a time, they enable one to live. "Modern man has an idea of himself and of the world that is no longer one fixed idea; he cannot help but bring a number of ideas about the world into play; it would be practically impossible for him to live without such a contradictory multiplicity of views."

Thus, Valéry's thought has followed the natural line of all powerful minds. Having as an adolescent made a clean slate of things, he re-establishes in his maturity those conventions he had once rejected. The course of his thought, however, differs in this respect: that he re-establishes those conventions as conventions and not as absolute truths. It is in this respect that Valéry's position is original, different both from Bourget's, which treats convention as some transcendent truth, and from Gide's, which retains toward convention the hostile and defiant stance of the unrepentant adolescent.

D. *The Work of Art*

But the view that the universe is made up solely of human conventions is an indefensible paradox. There is a reality

anterior to fictions and myths. But how can thought deal
with this reality which is, by definition, alien to it? I think
that Valéry, like Proust, would swiftly reply: through the
work of art, and particularly, through poetry, considered
in a very general sense.

Human language inclines to the abstract and is always
straying further and further from the concrete. Poetry enables the mind once again to get in touch with that reality
which is anterior to the mechanistic monsters—our hypotheses and our various "knowledge"—created by that same mind.
Through what means, what *charms* is poetry able to do this?

The function of the poet is to give words their harmonic
value and once again to create—by connecting them, by shifting them about, by catching them unawares in unaccustomed
juxtaposition—that air of mystery surrounding them at birth.
"A poem is not made with ideas nor with feelings; it is
made with words." Valéry is fond of presenting the poet as
a conscious, methodical craftsman, who "fabricates" a poem
just as one constructs a machine, in order to produce a
specific effect. Such "conscious" poets as Poe, Baudelaire,
and Mallarmé are of the line of descent which Valéry so
perfectly continues. "A poem should be a revel of the intellect." It can't be anything else. Here again is the idea of
convention. A poem is a revel, a game so well organized
that it could not be imagined otherwise. "The impression of
Beauty, so desperately sought after, so fruitlessly defined, is
perhaps the feeling of an *impossibility of variation.*" That
is why it satisfies and pleases. It soothes and holds the mind.
It "recaptures" and arrests Time. A rock wears away beneath
the action of the waves, but what possible concatenation of
elements could dislodge one word from one of Baudelaire's
best poems? Here again the arbitrary has created the necessary. This idea of poetry would seem to exclude the in-
spirational. Valéry is fond of making fun of lyricism, which
he considers nothing but "the elaboration of an exclamation."
—"Who would not blush at being Pythia?"—"Inspiration is

that hypothesis that reduces the author to the role of observer." Paradoxical statements that Valéry will at a later date appropriately revise. The fact is that the search for a form by a craftsman is the first concern of all art. Without craft, there is no genius. But the need to make that search would not arise without the presence of feelings of joy or sadness. "Inspiration in poetry and in all the arts is deeply hidden," but it exists. Without Time Lost there can be no Time to recapture.

Valéry is quite aware of this fact, indeed, put it better than anyone: "The Writer makes amends for himself as best he can for some injustice of fate." However much he may try—including in his poems—to be precise, objective, methodical, it is impossible to know him without taking into account his feelings which are never absent. He cannot prevent them from cropping up in his writing. "At the basis of every thought is a sigh." However much the master of the mechanical, Monsieur Teste knew suffering. It won't do to view Valéry as a pure, but inhuman intellect. On the contrary, no man of our time is more sensitive, constant, expansive. But if he knows pain, he does not revel in it as does Pascal. "What do we teach other men in pointing out to them that they are nothing? That life is empty, nature hostile, knowledge illusory? What is the point of beating them over the head with the nothingness they are or telling them once again what they already know?" In concluding, I should like to leave you with this altogether human view of him. Imagine him each morning, at 5 A.M., preparing once again to confront the tasks that were his life's work. He warms up the previous day's coffee, for no one else is up at that hour, then "lets rain upon us his chips of prose, the by-products of a sublime travail. The might of the mind is a beautiful thing. Centuries hence it will be seen that no one had more of an influence on our time than this very simple man."[2]

[2] Alain

V

The nineteenth century, albeit with moments of remorse and some reversions, was the century of positive science and its lively offspring, the machine. We have seen what hopes gave rise to this "triumph of recipes." Intellectual hopes: the hope of finding "the answer to the Universal Riddle." Social hopes: people would readily have agreed to the painting of a mural entitled "Science as the Source of Man's Happiness" on the ceilings of the governmental palaces of the world.

Great hopes are followed by great disappointments. Emboldened by the successes of the scientific method, intoxicated by the strides made in the exact sciences, a number of writers believed that these methods could be applied to the study of man. Many nineteenth-century philosophers were contemptuous of spiritual values—and that without proof and even in the face of contrary evidence—for simple observation shows that the spirit is as important to man as physico-chemical relationships. Man's view of himself changed. He no longer believed in his own power. "The individual of the scientific period loses the faculty of feeling himself to be the center of energy." Whereas the Hindu ascetic and the Catholic saint believed that man possessed a mysterious power over his body and the exterior world, the nineteenth-century scientist affirmed that the entire human process was mechanistic. A disheartening form of humility, for it takes away man's faith in man.

Thought at the turn of the century was characterized by lassitude. France, Lemaître, Barrès were skeptics. I am quite aware that all three, in order to avoid total vertigo, clutched in one direction or another at lifelines that were at best tenuous. This was more the result, however, of the urgent need for finding *some* form of support rather than of any special choice in the matter.

After a century of discoveries which have made us vulnerable to the quite inhuman inroads of "experts," humankind has need of poets, that is, of men capable of re-establishing contact, through an improved use of language, with the basic givens of the human riddle. Europe is dying of ill-made language. It is yet too early to ascertain the distinguishing mark of our time, but doubtless—if we do not come to a disastrous end—it will not be that of having renounced the achievement of the nineteenth century, but rather that of having seen the value, beyond or to the side of science, of a poetic knowledge illuminated by the intelligence.

Thus, it is entirely natural that the best mind of our era should be a poet, and that that poet should be Valéry.

ANDRÉ GIDE

I

As an adolescent I was almost totally unfamiliar with the author most beloved by the adolescents of my generation. Yet he was already very famous by then, and I later learned in letters from Jacques Rivière and Alain-Fournier—both contemporaries of mine—that his work had occupied a special place in their thoughts. But I was a provincial schoolboy in a reactionary province, and the elderly men who were my teachers in Rouen were having me read Homer and Propertius rather than Verlaine and Rimbaud. The most progressive of their number, even if they had got up to France and Barrès, were totally unacquainted with Claudel and Gide.

After the First World War, during which my first book was published, Paul Desjardins, a critic and teacher, asked me to come and spend a few days in an old Burgundian abbey in Pontigny with a group of writers who gathered there every summer. In his letter he told me that one of the attractive features of this session would be the presence of André Gide.

I clearly recall this my first arrival in Pontigny, on a little narrow-gauge railroad train. All the doors opened, and a cluster of literary men emerged from each compartment. Standing on the platform with our host was a clean-shaven man whose features reminded one of certain Japanese masks, a face so striking as to be handsome. This man wore a mountaineer's great-cape, draped with natural elegance about his person, and a broad-brimmed hat with a pointed crown that looked like a sombrero but was made out of some kind of gray velours. This man was André Gide.

We walked back from the station to the abbey, and from this initial conversation I was completely taken with the man. Taken by what? First of all, by an extraordinary impression of youthfulness, a youthfulness that was apparent in his gaze, in the fervor of his voice, and in the probing quality of his thought. Nothing he said was ordinary. Whatever the subject, he would try to elicit from his interlocutor not just the stock-phrases and sentiments that always spring first to the lips, but a deep and genuine response. Most human beings are nothing but phonograph records. Once well acquainted, one knows their repertoire. Gide was alive. And enormously original.

I enjoyed the life at Pontigny. Each day from two to four o'clock there was an open discussion on a set subject. This was the academic side of the session; but the rest of the time one could take walks with Gide, Martin du Gard, or Mauriac, and converse more freely and pleasantly. In the evening, after dinner, everyone got together for "parlor games." Gide was the enthusiastic leader of these, and the almost childlike pleasure he took in playing, for example, at "authors" reinforced that original impression of youthfulness. One side would choose the protagonist of some novel, the other side ask questions and try to guess who it was. On one occasion our side had chosen Goethe's Mephistopheles, and I remember the tone that Gide, our team captain, used in replying to the other team's question "Is he a friend of yours?"

"I certainly like to think so!"

A devilish bit of wit—however, several of our number felt that Mephistopheles and Gide could hardly be fond of one another.

In discussion I was struck by his changeableness. As in any kind of human association, cliques formed quickly at

Pontigny. Gide rarely belonged to any of them for any length of time. When I pointed this out to him, he responded:

"How could I possibly argue if I stuck with one group? In a discussion I'm always on the other person's side!"

In private, he admitted to a fear of solitude and to a capacity for ennui that could reach the intensity of a desire for death. These, in combination with his gaiety at other moments and his youthful inquisitiveness, added up to a mysterious, complex, and engaging person.

During this stay, I told him I was working on a life of Shelley. He said:

"Would you like to show it to me?"

I replied:

"The thing is, it's not finished . . ."

"Precisely," he said. "I only like things that aren't finished. A finished book reminds me of something dead, something one can no longer touch. A book in progress has, for me, all the appeal of a live person."

So I took my manuscript to him at a house he owned in Normandy, not far from the sea, halfway between Le Havre and Fécamp. And that was how I got to know that great white manor house he described in *La Porte Etroite* (*Strait Is the Gate*):

"Like many of the country-houses of the century before last, it has some twenty large windows opening on the garden in the front and as many in the back; the windows are of the small-paned variety. . . . The rectangular garden is enclosed by walls and in front of the house takes the form of a broad and shaded lawn, which is encircled by a sand and gravel walk."

All was lovely, tranquil there—the house set in an autumnal landscape "bordering the sea." And there I came to know the *grand bourgeois* Norman side of Gide's character; the august simplicity of his welcome recalled to me, like a harmonic overtone, the natural dignity and courteousness that had so impressed me in him when we first met. I read him my manuscript. He listened patiently, taking notes, and then tendered criticisms, the aptness and sensitivity of which delighted me. Few men have had such a feeling for language, few men have been as sound in their judgment about what in a book is authentic and what false trappings. The next day he read in turn a few chapters of *Les Faux-Monnayeurs* (*The Counterfeiters*) on which he was then working. I took my leave altogether enchanted—as well as astounded by the difference between the Gide of the legend and the Gide I had just encountered.

I was later to learn that there was, nevertheless, a degree of truth to the legend, and that the description I would have given of Gide after that first meeting wouldn't have been accurate either. The fact of the matter is that there wasn't just one Gide. Indeed, what man *is* just one man?

II

"At that tender age when we would so much like every soul to be all transparency, affection, and purity, I recall in myself nothing but darkness, ugliness, and wiliness." This is an astonishing opening for a confession. On the basis of his autobiography a number of critics have described Gide as a Puritan who, because of an overly strict upbringing, became a rebel out of horror of his family's puritanism. This is an oversimplification.

Gide was descended through his father, Paul Gide, a professor of law, from Midi Protestant stock; and through his mother from a Rouen family, the Rondeaux, wealthy industrialists who had become Protestant through marriage. Both sides of the family were well off. There was a country house at Cuverville, a château at Roque-Baignac in the Calvados region, and a Huguenot family seat in the Southwest (Uzès, Montpellier). Gide was born rich and *grand bourgeois* and rarely concerned himself with the social strug-

gles of his time. His father was affectionate and friendly; his
mother was an austere, devout Protestant. "The one was
charming, gay, tolerant, intellectually cultured; the other
rather oppressively serious, austere, dedicated to the moral
life." As a child Gide was surrounded by clergymen; his
childhood was steeped in the atmosphere of the Bible and
the Gospels. His mother's strictness could only result in some
sort of resistance. He resembled her, feared her, and respected
her. Freudians would say (and have said) that the source of
Gide's inverted sensuality is to be found in his respect for this
overly demanding mother.

His father died when he was twelve. It was an irremediable
loss. There was no longer any one to counter the demands
of his mother, a woman full of detestable virtues whose "anxious solicitude" was to impede the natural development of
the child. He admired that heart "which never allowed anything foul to gain entrance, which beat only for others,"
which devoted itself unremittingly to duty not so much
through piousness as through some innate inclination . . .
But also through fear . . .

Gide's mother was tyrannical: "No peace of any duration
was possible between us. Moreover, I didn't exactly lay the
blame on my mother; she was playing her proper part, it
seemed to me, even when she was plaguing me most. Indeed,
it didn't occur to me that any mother conscientious about
her duty did not seek to subjugate her son, just as I found it
entirely natural that the son should refuse to yield. . . . I
think one could have said of my mother that the qualities
she admired were not those that the persons on which her
affection weighed in fact possessed, but rather those that she
hoped they would feel obliged to acquire. At least that is
how I try to explain to myself that continual labor to which
she devoted herself on behalf of others, on my behalf
especially. . . . She had a way of loving me that sometimes
might have made me hate her and that set my teeth on
edge. Imagine what a relentlessly watchful solicitude, a steady

stream of urgent admonition, relating to your actions, your thoughts, your expenditures, your choice of a fabric, a book, the title of a book, can become. . . ."

Indeed, Gide the adolescent, very much because of his mother, was a very inaccessible person. Ramon Fernandez uses the expression "all buttoned up," which is doubtless, and even literally, accurate. Gide has described to us the clothing he was made to wear as a child:

> I was very sensitive about clothing and suffered a great deal over being so hideously ill-dressed all the time. I wore little tunics that were too small for me, short knickers, striped socks, socks that were too short and bagged out like tulips, hung down unevenly or fell out of sight into my shoes. I have kept the most horrible for the last: the starched shirt. I had to wait until I was practically a grown man before I succeeded in preventing my shirt-fronts being starched. It was the custom, the style, and nothing could be done about it. Try to imagine a miserable child who, every day of his life, during playtime as well as at school, wears where no one can see it, secreted under his jacket, a kind of white cuirass topped by a carcan— for the laundress also starched, doubtless at no extra fee, the collar-band against which the false collar fitted. And since this latter, being either a little too big or too small, did not match on to the shirt properly, painful wrinkles were formed. Just try playing games in a get-up like that!

This starched shirt and over-stiff collar are appropriate symbols for a childhood which allowed no flexibility or freedom.

"Should he live to be a hundred," says Fernandez, "Gide will never stop taking delight in wearing soft shirts and loose attire and letting himself float inside his clothes. And the same thing applies to the rules, conventions, and all the rigid restrictions that buttoned up his soul."

He was all his life to insist on the split caused in him by his double provincial background (Uzès and Rouen) and by the Gide and Rondeaux sides of his family. He used this thesis, which oddly resembles Barrès, to explain his inability to take sides, his abrupt shiftings, his admixture of moral rigor and what most men call vice. It is a fact that from childhood on he suffered from a nervous disorder. The *"Schauder"* of which Goethe speaks, trembling accompanied by tears, an exaggerated sense of guilt that made him turn to "solitary practices"—everything led him to seek refuge in an imaginary world. Artistic creation is a form of compensation. Even as a young boy, Gide wanted to escape from a reality that caused him pain.

At the lycée in Montpellier this bright but abnormal student was "made fun of, beat up, run down." The same thing began all over again at the Ecole Alsacienne in Paris. So he resorted to pretense and began to fake nervous attacks. The doctors were taken in by the act and sent him off for rest cures. He felt himself becoming wicked, a liar. "It was clear that the devil had marked me out, I was totally beset by darkness, and nothing gave me an inkling as to where a ray of light might get through to me. Then it was that the angelic intervention which I shall describe came to wrestle with the demon for my soul." This angelic intervention was his love for his cousin, Madeleine Rondeaux.

It was in the year 1882; he was thirteen, she sixteen. He had always looked to her as a model of goodness, charm, and intelligence. One evening he learned that she was unhappy. Her mother had a lover, and she knew it. He found her in tears, was deeply moved and upset, and fell in love. (This incident would later give rise to a novel, *La Porte Etroite*). The love had a soothing effect on him. "Life no longer meant anything to me without her." They read beautiful books and played music together, but this love had no trace of desire in it. The disquiets of the flesh were allayed by masturbation. All women frightened him. "Even if it had been possible for me to unravel the feminine mystery in one gesture, I should never have made that gesture." In short, he remained until he was twenty-three both chaste and depraved. As Dr. Delay has written, he lived "within a compromise consisting of clandestine gratifications poisoned by a sense of guilt."

And yet, he wanted, even at that early age, to marry Madeleine. It would, he thought, be a mystical union. As for Madeleine, she loved him but was mindful of the opposition of both sides of the family. Her own mother had fled with her lover. Since her father was dead, she was living with an aunt who warned her against the dangers of mistaking adolescent infatuation for love. Madame Gide made it clear that she was very much opposed to any such plan. Madeleine had already suffered a great deal. Should she be allowed to risk such a union? And besides, what did Madeleine herself think of marrying a cousin who told her: "I do not desire you, your body disturbs me, and possessing someone physically horrifies me." He also told this soberminded girl that he was capable, sincerely, of sharing the contradictory ideas and tastes of successive friends. "Your facility for reflecting all colors is a little too . . . chameleon-like," she wrote him. In short, her first move—and the right one—was one of withdrawal.

At twenty, in order to win her over, Gide wrote *Les Cahiers d'André Walter* (*The Notebooks of André Walter*). This work is for him what *Werther* was for Goethe. In both works, a young romantic frees himself of his romanticism by ascribing it to a fictional protagonist. For André Walter is André Gide—and with the inability of nearly all young writers to depict their sufferings in an objective way, the author does not stray far from his own personality.

There are two *Cahiers d'André Walter*. The first is called *Le Cahier Blanc* (*The White Notebook*). Here, the protagonist remains pure; he accepts the pain of the conflict between faith and desire, accepts it almost happily. Gide was throughout his life to derive a certain satisfaction from the conflicts of which he was the site. The habit of moral pain is not without its rewards, and it would not be uncharacteristic of Gide to say that moral pain is the most diabolical of all of pride's disguises.

"Those who seek happiness won't understand this book," says André Walter. "The soul isn't satisfied by happiness, felicities put it to sleep; repose not watchfulness. And one much watch . . . Thus pain is preferable to joy, for it makes the soul more alive. Life lived intensely, that's the great thing; I wouldn't exchange my life for any other; for I've lived several lives, and the actual one has been the least of these."

André Walter (like André Gide) is very much in love with one of his cousins. It's a chaste love, all mixed up with religious notions. The similarity to Byron is striking. Both like to think of their lives as being pulled in two directions: on the one hand, by the devil, the Demon; on the other, by some angelic agent, the soothing influence of a loved person.

André Walter is very much afraid of tainting his soul by surrendering to the flesh. The Demon, however, who takes various forms—even, sometimes, that of a friendly counselor —tells him:

" 'Free the soul by giving the body what it wants.' "

" 'Perhaps so,' " he replies, " 'but the body must ask for things that are possible. If I gave it what it wants, you'd be the first to cry shame.' "

And elsewhere he replies: " 'You tell me, my friend, that one shouldn't worry about the body, but instead let it rule those areas it covets. But the flesh, once corrupted, corrupts the soul.' "

This fear of the flesh makes love for André Walter one unending period of being engaged to marry. Throughout the *Cahier Blanc,* this description of love in which the soul plays a more important role than the flesh, these abstract, high-minded "ineffably Alpine" (Gide's own term) discussions, re-call Rousseau. There is a whole Protestant casuistry of the passions quite apart from that of the Catholic confessional.

The second *Cahier d'André Walter* is called *Le Cahier Noir* (*The Black Notebook*). He is writing a novel—*Alain*—and it is the life history both of Walter and of Gide himself. Gide gives us the notes Walter has made for the composition of his novel. They are of great interest for an understanding of Gide himself:

"Two actors; the Angel and the Beast, adversaries. The spirit and the flesh. . . . Neither materialism nor idealism exists. What does exist is the conflict between them. Realism requires the conflict of these two essences. That's what must be shown. . . . There must be only one character, or rather the brain of one character, in which the drama unfolds, which is the terrain on which the adversaries do battle. These adversaries: the spirit and the flesh—and their conflict, which springs from a single passion, one sole desire: to play the angel."

The conflict that troubles the soul of the adolescent Gide is also the central conflict in Walter's novel. In *Le Cahier Noir,* however, the beast triumphs.

"O Eternal One!" writes Walter, "how long, how long will I go on fighting without feeling you near me? And further, how will these battles end?"

They end in defeat: "The process is always the same; the spirit becomes exalted, it drops its guard, the flesh falls. One prays, one seeks ecstasy once again, and the process starts all over. Once one has gone the round a few times, it loses even the element of surprise; it's heart-breaking." Emmanuèle, who plays the part of the angel in the hero's life, marries another. Walter is left alone. He finishes his novel and has the hero go mad at the end, then dies himself of brain fever.

In this Gide is following the example of Goethe. Goethe got rid of Werther by killing him off; Werther's gunshot freed Goethe. "I call romantic that which is unhealthy, and classic that which is healthy," said Goethe. Werther's gunshot killed the romantic and freed the classic. One might go so far as to say that every man has to kill a romantic in order to be reborn classic. Adolescence, which many people think of as the happiest time of life, is actually the most difficult and painful. Girls and boys alike must negotiate that dreadful time when they suddenly discover—after the magical and sheltered period of childhood—the difficulty of life, the ill-will in men, and the power of the passions. For a certain length of time—one, two, ten years, depending on the individual—one feels as if one were drowning: it is the crisis of Werther. Some never recover; others triumph over it through cynicism; the best succeed in reconciling Angel and Beast. Meredith once said, in effect: "There is no greater error than refusing to recognize man's animal nature." The greatest error? No. Only *one* of the greatest—the other being the refusal to recognize the angelic side of man's nature.

Gide, at twenty-three, killed André Walter; but he did not find the complete life.

The problem was still the same one, and that problem reduced to its simplest terms was as follows: in the name of what ideal do you forbid me to live according to my nature, and that nature, where would it lead me, if I simply followed it? . . . After the publication of my *Cahiers*, although my cousin's refusal had not at all discouraged me, it had nonetheless obliged me to put my hopes off to a more distant day. Moreover, as I have said, my love remained semi-mystical, and if the devil were duping me by making me view as degrading the idea of being able to bring anything carnal into that love, I was still incapable of perceiving that.

Carnal pleasure . . . From this point on it was certain that he wasn't to find it with women. His sexual feeling for the women he loved was inhibited. With him (as with Rousseau and Stendhal) excess of passion dampened physical desire. He nearly succeeded in one attempt he made at normal sexual relations—that attempt with an Ouled Naïl (a young Algerian prostitute) named Mériam. But his mother intervened, weeping when she should have rejoiced. Charles Gide, an uncle to whom he naïvely confided his success, told him with incredible severity that all the perfumes of Arabia would not wash away the stain. This brand of blundering virtue sent him back to the love-objects to which he was naturally inclined—boys. Ah, the accents he found to describe these young Arabs, tanned and drunk with sun and high spirits.

III

This discovery, or rather admission, of his secret sensuality was to unleash a writer quite different from that of the *Cahiers*. These had been succeeded by a number of short, clever, stilted works, one of which was a *Traité du Narcisse* (*Treatise on Narcissus*) (What myth, indeed, could have offered this strange adolescent better sanctuary?) Also in this group were *Le Voyage d'Urien* (*Urien's Travels*) and *Paludes* (*Marshlands*), whose hero, Tityre, is a humorous version of André Walter. All these works showed intelligence and talent, but they bore the stamp of the period, mixing elements of symbolism and art nouveau. It was distinguished, ingenious—empty—work. The 1890 portrait of Gide, which shows him with long hair before a mirror self-satisfiedly verifying the success of his image, reflects this aesthete style.

Africa, Oscar Wilde, and, finally, his mother's death in 1895 completed his liberation. The fact that he had just escaped a brush with tuberculosis made his new-found freedom all the more intoxicating. The burning frenzy of African life, his indulgence in pleasure hitherto shunned, Wilde's impassioned preachings, had finally brought about an internal change. He owed "the courage of his tastes" to Wilde. The odd thing was, however, that even while giving himself

[1] *Marcel Proust*

[2] *Henri Bergson*

[3] *Paul Valéry*

[4] *André Gide*

over to these latter he continued to want to marry Madeleine. His mother died on May 31; on June 17 he became engaged to Madeleine and married her on October 8, having first sought the advice of a doctor who told him: "Get married. Marry without fear. And you will soon see that all else exists only in your imagination."

No medical advice was ever more disastrous. Imagination proved stronger than love, although that love was sincere— and this marriage, which was to have been such a success, ran hard aground, from the wedding trip on, on the reefs of impotence. It didn't sink. Madeleine was doubtless frightened by what she was able to guess of her husband's secret pleasures, but she managed to keep quiet. It caused her great pain, when traveling in Algeria, to see him stroke the bare arms of young Arab boys: "You had the look of a criminal or a madman." But she managed to overcome her disillusionment and to make a fairly happy life for herself from 1895 to 1915. She often had to resign herself, however, to living apart from the husband whose ardors and joys she could not share.

From these ardors—this "resuscitated secret"—issued, in 1897, *Les Nourritures Terrestres* (*Fruits of the Earth*), a book which made Gide one of the dangerous but beloved mentors of the young. Like *Thus Spake Zarathustra, Les Nourritures Terrestres* is a gospel in the root sense of the word—glad tidings. Tidings about the meaning of life addressed to a dearly loved disciple whom Gide calls Nathanaël. The book is composed of Bible verses, hymns, *récits,* songs, rounds, held together on the one hand by the presence of Nathanaël and on the other by the doctrine Gide *seems* to be teaching him. I say *seems* because we shall shortly see that Gide would accept neither the idea of teaching nor that of doctrine.

Besides Nathanaël and the author, there is a third character in *Les Nourritures,* one who reappears in *L'Immoraliste* and who is in Gide's life what Merck was in Goethe's or

Mephistopheles in Faust's. This character, whom Gide calls Ménalque, has sometimes been identified with Oscar Wilde, but Gide told me it wasn't Wilde at all. Ménalque is, indeed, no one unless perhaps one aspect of Gide himself, one of the interlocutors in the dialogue of Gide with Gide that comprises his spiritual life.

The core of the book was a *récit* by Ménalque, one not far different from a *récit* Gide might have given after his African rebirth:

"At eighteen," said Ménalque, "when I had finished my elementary schooling, the mind weary with work, the heart unoccupied, and languishing on that account, the body irritated by confinement, I took to the roads, without destination, working off my wanderlust. . . . I passed through a number of towns and felt no desire to stop anywhere. Happy the man, I thought, who does not attach himself to anything on earth and carries an undying fervor through the constant mobilities of the world. . . .

"I lived," Ménalque continues, "in a perpetual state of expectation of whatever future might come. . . . Each day, hour upon hour, I no longer sought anything except an increasingly direct penetration of nature. I had the precious gift of not being too hampered by myself. The memory of the past had no influence on me except the degree of it necessary to give my life unity. It was like the mysterious thread that bound Theseus to his former love, but didn't prevent him from traversing the freshest of landscapes.

"In the evening, I watched, in unknown villages, the households, separated during the day, come back together. The father came back, weary from work; the children returned from school. The door of the house would open for a moment on a welcome of light, warmth and laughter, then close up for the night. Nothing of all the things that wander could come back in any more. . . . Families, I hate you! snug homes, latched doors, the jealously guarded possessions of happiness. Sometimes, invisible in the darkness, I stood bent toward a window, watching for a long time the daily life of a house. The father was there, near the lamp; the mother was sewing; the chair where a grandparent usually sat remained empty; near the father a child was studying, and my heart swelled with the desire to take him with me out on the roads. . . ."

This *récit* contains the essence of the "tidings" of *Les Nourritures*. First a negative doctrine: flee families, rules, stability. Gide himself suffered so much from "snug homes" that he harped on its dangers all his life.

Then a positive doctrine: one must seek adventure, excess, fervor; one should loathe the lukewarm, security, all tempered feelings. "Not affection, Nathanaël: love . . ." Meaning not a shallow feeling based on nothing perhaps but tastes in common, but a feeling into which one throws oneself wholly and forgets oneself. Love is dangerous, but that is yet another reason for loving, even if it means risking one's happiness, *especially* if it means losing one's happiness. For happiness makes man less. "Descend to the bottom of the pit if you want to see the stars." Gide insists on this idea that there is no salvation in contented satisfaction with oneself, an idea he shares with both a number of great Christians and with Blake: "Unhappiness exalts, happiness slackens." Gide ends a letter to an *amie* with this curious formula: "Adieu, dear friend, may God ration your happiness!"

It would be a mistake to view the doctrine of *Les Nourritures Terrestres* as the product of a sensualist's egoism. On the contrary, it is a doctrine in which the Self (which is essentially continuity, memory of and submission to the past) fades out and disappears in order that the individual may lose himself, dissolve himself into each perfect moment. The Gide of *Les Nourritures Terrestres* does not renounce the search for the God André Walter was seeking, but he seeks him *everywhere*, even in Hell: "May my book teach you to take more interest in yourself than in it, and more in everything else than in yourself!"

IV

There are many objections that might be made to this doctrine. First one might object that this immoralist is at bottom a moralist—that he does teach even though he denies it, that he preaches even though he hates preachers, that he is puritanical in his anti-puritanism, and finally, that the refusal to participate in human society ("snug homes . . . Families, I hate you!") is actually another form of confinement—to the outside.

Gide is too intelligent not to have anticipated this kind of objection. He raises it himself in *Les Faux-Monnayeurs*. In describing Vincent's development, he writes: "For he's a moral creature . . . and the Devil will get the best of him only by providing him with reasons for self-approval. Theory of the totality of the moment, of gratuitous joy . . . On the basis of which the devil wins the day." A subtle analysis of his own case: the beast has found a new way of playing the angel who plays the beast. If the Immoralist weren't a moral being, he would have no need to revolt.

One might further object that this is the doctrine of a convalescent, not a healthy man. . . . But again Gide has taken care to raise this point himself in the very intriguing preface he later added to the book, and to point out further that at the time when he, the artist, wrote *Les Nourritures Terrestres*, he had already, as a man, rejected its message, for he had just got married and, for a time at least, settled down. Moreover, he followed *Les Nourritures* with *Saul*, a play which can only be interpreted as a condemnation of seekers after the moment and sensation. Thus, Gide's wavering course between the angelic pole and the diabolic pole is not at all broken by *Les Nourritures Terrestres*.

How should it be when at the end of the book the master himself advises his disciple to leave him:

"And now, Nathanaël, throw away my book. Free your-self from it. Leave me. Leave me now, you weary me; you hold me back; the love for you in which I have over-indulged myself occupies me too much. I am tired of pre-tending to educate someone. When have I said that I wanted you to be like me? It is because you are unlike me that I love you; I love in you only that which is unlike me. Educate? Who should I be educating but my-self? Shall I say it, Nathanaël? I have never stopped educating myself. I continue to do so. I value myself always and only according to what I could do.

"Nathanaël, throw away my book; take no satisfaction in it. Do not think that your truth can be found by another; more than anything, be ashamed of that. If I secured your food, you would not have the hunger to eat it; if I made up your bed, you would not have the sleepiness to sleep in it.

"Throw away my book. Know that it is but one of a thousand possible stances toward life. Seek your own. What another might have done as well as you, do not do. What another might have said as well as you, do not say; written as well as you, do not write. Attach yourself only to that which you feel exists in you and nowhere else, and make of yourself impatiently or patiently, ah! the most irreplaceable of beings."

But why doesn't Gide require of himself the same rejection he so strongly urges on his disciple? And if he has a horror of any and all doctrine, why isn't he horrified by his own? *He is much too much Gide to be Gidean.* He always protested against people's habit of reducing him to a rulebook when he had attempted, contrarily, to create a rulebook for escape. This is Gide's supreme and perilous leap, the leap that makes him impossible to pin down. What others might find to con-demn in him, this Proteus condemns in himself.

This brings up an extremely interesting question. Why is this subtle, Protean doctrine which constantly denies itself, why after thirty years is this powerful and dangerous book, still such a source of joy and enthusiasm to so many young men and women? Read Jacques Rivière's letters to Alain-Fournier; read in Martin du Gard's *La Belle Saison* the account of the hero's discovery of *Les Nourritures Terrestres;* listen, finally, to some of the young people about you. Many of them intensely admire this book—with an admiration quite beyond the literary. Here is why.

With the discovery of the harshness of life, the magical and sheltered days of childhood are followed, with nearly every adolescent, by a period of rebellion. This is the first adolescent "stage." The second stage is the discovery—*despite* disillusionments and difficulties—of the beauty of life. This discovery ordinarily occurs between eighteen and twenty. It produces most of our young lyric poets.

The special thing about Gide's character, its originality and its force, is that, having been retarded in natural development by reason of the constraints of his upbringing, he went through this second stage when his mind was already relatively mature, the result being that this *retardation enabled him to express the discoveries common to all young people in more perfect form*. In other words, young people are beholden to a retarded and unregenerate adolescent for having so well expressed what they feel. Thus, the necessity, the universality, and the likelihood of endurance of a book like *Les Nourritures Terrestres*. A disciple (as in Wilde's fine story) is someone who seeks himself in the eyes of the master. The young look for and find themselves in Gide.

Readers will find this same lesson in immoralism in *Le Prométhée Mal Enchaîné* (1899). Gide calls this book a *sotie,* a Middle Ages term used to denote an allegorical satire in dialogue form. Prometheus *thinks* he is chained to the peaks of the Caucasus (just as Gide once was by so many shackles, barriers, battlements, and other scruples). Then he discovers that all that's needed is to *want* to be free, and he goes off with his eagle to Paris where in the hall of the New Moons he gives a lecture explaining that each of us is devoured by his

eagle—vice or virtue, duty or passion. One must feed this
eagle on love. "Gentlemen, one must love his eagle, love him
so he'll become beautiful." The writer's eagle is his work, and
he should sacrifice himself to it.

V

This is the end of one important stage in Gide's life and
work. Between *L'Immoraliste,* 1902, a depiction of egoism in
a pure state, and *La Porte Etroite,* 1909, there is no change.
In 1908 he founded—with Gaston Gallimard, Jean Schlum-
berger, and Henri Ghéon—a magazine and a publishing
house: *La Nouvelle Revue Française,* which was to become
one of the great intellectual forums of twentieth-century
France. The founders—joined later by Jacques Rivière and
Roger Martin du Gard—took a lofty view of the independence and disinterestedness of the writer. They worked
neither for recognition nor for the public, but rather "in
order that their eagle might be beautiful." In 1913 Jacques
Copeau founded the Théâtre du Vieux-Colombier, which was
sponsored by the *NRF,* and which had this same ideal.

La Porte Etroite is a book that might be taken as autobiographical since it is the story of the love of two cousins,
Alissa and Jérôme, who have been friends since childhood.
Like Madeleine Rondeaux, Alissa discovers her mother's
misconduct; she considers it an offense against God which
she should redeem through her own purity. She also wants
her love to be a non-physical, mystical love of two minds.
"One fears that Alissa may be found to be less attracted to
heaven than afraid of life on earth." In talking about this
novel, Gide criticized Alissa's attitude and denied that he
had used Madeleine as a model. "She," he said, "was more
human. There was never anything excessive or forced about
her virtue." Alissa is seeking the absolute rather than love.
"O Lord! Keep me from a happiness I could attain too

quickly! Teach me to defer, to put off my happiness until I come to You."

The book is written in an abstract, precise and musical language and made its author—with the support now of the powerful *NRF*—one of the most famous writers of his time. Around 1910 he became a master, first to a relatively small group, then to a growing elite. He had long been a friend of Valéry. He now became a friend of Claudel. Within fifteen years all three would be renowned. His personal life remained very much a secret. We know through Ghéon—who before his conversion accompanied Gide in his travels and on his nocturnal strolls about Paris—that Gide ran considerable risks in following the dictates of his inclinations. Being a divided spirit, however, this did not prevent him from considering conversion to Catholicism from time to time. Many of his friends—Claudel, Charles du Bos, and later Ghéon and Copeau—urged him to it. He spent part of the war working for a Franco-Belgian Refugee Aid Center. A growing number of his acquaintance were converted. He himself reread the Gospels, admiring both their intention and their style, and taking notes from which emerged the brief little book *Numquid et tu?*, a work that gave his Catholic friends high hopes.

In this book he spoke feelingly of the Gospel: "Lord, it isn't because I have been told you are the Son of God that I listen to your word; but your word is beautiful over and above all human suffering, and it is in that that I see you are the Son of God." Actually he adapted the Gospel to his own views. He did not find sin in it; he chose to think that Christ was pure love, and that Saint Paul had rigidified—and falsified—the lesson of the Gospels. Then all of a sudden Gide cut short his exegesis, abandoned these pious endeavors with which his parched and restless heart was no longer pleased and in which his mind saw only dishonest play-acting prompted by the devil. Strange man! He is so afraid of being a hypocrite that he is excessive in his revolts. The fact is that he is emotionally inclined—through his upbringing and through genuine admiration—toward Christianity, but he is contemptuous of those of his friends who have converted and surrendered their freedom of thought.

This whole neo-Catholic movement—and even his own *Numquid et tu?*—is, in Gide's view, a by-product of the war, of the griefs, anguish, and despair experienced during that period. "For there isn't one of these neo-converts whose mind doesn't present some fissure through which the mystic gas can enter. . . . What makes me wary—alarms me—is that the tree can also bear horrible fruits." He retreated back to long-prepared positions. The old Adam triumphed in him. He ceased to have any further intellectual commerce with Claudel, Jammes, and later, Charles du Bos. His, the unbiased mind, could no longer understand theirs. At this time, moreover, his personal life claimed all his attention. During the war a storm had broken out in Cuverville. In reading one of Ghéon's letters, Madeleine Gide had learned about the kind of life her husband was really leading. In love with an attractive and gifted young man, Gide was following him to England. In her pain Madeleine burned all the letters she had ever received from her husband. The writer suffered as much as the man. From that time on, only his *Journal* (kept for so many years) would reveal what he had been.

After turning the tiller toward God in *Numquid et tu?*, this latter disturbance, plus the lesson of the converts, prompted a leap in the opposite direction, towards Evil. "Extremes meet *in me*," he says, and writes a *Conversation avec le Diable*. "First I have him say—Why should you be afraid of me? You know very well I don't exist." But he does exist, not transcendentally but immanently. It is he who dictates Gide's *satanism*, which is a fight, at times a very wily fight, against hypocrisy. As early as 1914, he had sought in *Les Caves du Vatican* (*The Vatican Swindle*) to do battle against morality, against the ninnies, slaves to their systems and positions.

Lafcadio, the hero of this book, is a Gide, or rather, a Super-Gide, dupe to nothing and so free of any attachments that his acts are free. "Free, motivated by nothing. Understand? Neither self-interest nor passion. Nothing." Lafcadio kills without a reason, and Gide is admiring. But he soon stops admiring and perceives the vanity of a search for absolute freedom. For the search itself becomes a motive, and the act ceases to be free.

At this time, however, drunk with sincerity, he wants whatever the cost to unburden himself of his final secret: his inversion. Not only will he confess it; he will glory in it; he will be a martyr. In 1924, he publishes *Corydon*—a theoretical justification—and in 1926, *Si Le Grain Ne Meurt* (*If It Die*)—a full confession. It was indisputably a courageous thing to do. The Gide of 1924 was the one I had known in Pontigny, the universally admired prince of Letters. Yet at the height of his fame he chose to make a confession that would, he believed, ruin him—even as Oscar Wilde had been ruined. "I consider it much better to be hated for what one is than loved for what one isn't." Then he waited for the storm and scandal. None came. On the one hand, his prestige allowed him anything; on the other, readers had been prepared by Proust and Freud to accept anything. Proust, however, only depicted inversion; he didn't glorify it. Gide found fault with Proust and wanted in his own work to demonstrate the nobility of homosexuality. Young people read and were not roused to indignation. Henri Béraud attacked him brutally. "Nature abhors a Gide"; Massis opposed him in forthright fashion. Not only did Gide not suffer from these attacks, he actually took pleasure in them. They prompted him to show aggressiveness in other areas. In his *Voyage au Congo* (*Travels in the Congo*), for instance—a forceful attack on certain forms of colonialism—and later in his turn toward Communism.

In 1926 he published *Les Faux-Monnayeurs*—"my first

novel," he said. It was an original piece of work. He put into it everything he knew about youth and all his aesthetic theories besides—for one finds within the novel a description of the novel in process of creating itself, the main protagonist, Edouard, being a writer who is writing *Les Faux-Monnayeurs*. His use of his *Journal*, in barely transposed form, is considerable. *Les Faux-Monnayeurs*, says Claude Martin, is "the successful novel about a novel that fails." This is a Proustian idea. *A la Recherche du Temps Perdu*, however, is the successful novel about a novel that is successful. *Les Faux-Monnayeurs* has had an obvious influence on other writers; Aldous Huxley dedicated *Point Counterpoint* to Gide. As for being a very great novelist, Gide lacks the sweep and scope of a Balzac or a Tolstoy. His satire is everywhere in evidence and makes his characters squeak, but intellect is the controlling factor. *La Symphonie Pastorale* (*The Pastoral Symphony*), another novel about unconscious hypocrisy, has more humanity. A film was made of it, the success of which brought the book to the attention of a very large audience.

The swerve toward Communism, which began around 1932, is accounted for by Gide's desire to defy middle-class society (to which, unconsciously, he was attached by a great many ties), by his wish to remain close to the "progressive" element among the young, by a reaffirmation of the freedoms of *Les Nourritures*, and finally, by a need "to unite with something larger than himself." The idea of a society without family and without religion aroused his enthusiasm. He was joyously welcomed by the French Communists. They had acquired a great writer, one with enormous prestige at his command. He enjoyed attending their congresses and meetings, where he was treated with great respect.

In 1936, at the invitation of the Soviet government, he went to Moscow. It was a disillusioning visit. Stalinism was at its height. Gide was struck by the lack of freedom, was painfully shocked by the measures taken against homosexuals,

and didn't find what, without knowing it, he had come looking for: an evangelical poverty. In point of fact, no one was
further from that asceticism than Gide himself, who was a
creature of comfort, who knew nothing of the realities of
poverty, and who, although sincere in his desire to make
everyone happy, was incapable of conceiving the paths that
would lead to such happiness. His *Retour de l'U.R.S.S.*
(*Return from the U.S.S.R.*) was a statement of disengage-
ment, but had the chatelain of Cuverville really ever been
engaged?

His whole life was one long series of engagements and dis-
engagements. The only dogma to which he remained faithful
was the rejection of all dogmas. From this time on, he was
to preach a wisdom inspired equally by Montaigne and
Goethe. His *Thésée* (*Theseus*), written during the Second
World War, is reminiscent of Faust, Part Two. "If I compare
my fate with that of Oedipus," says Thésée, "I am happy.
. . . I come to a solitary death willingly. I have tasted the
fruits of the earth. It comforts me to think that after my
death, thanks to me, men will be happier, better, and more
free. I have created my work for the good of future humanity.
I have lived." It is Gide who speaks.

In 1938 Madeleine died. This caused little change in the
life of Gide, who lived in Paris, rue Vaneau, and traveled.
The young aesthete of 1900, constricted by family and
religion, had become an elderly Prospero, but he was not
burying his wand. Honors showered over him—the Nobel
Prize, a doctorate from Oxford, a highly successful production of *Les Caves du Vatican* at the Comédie Française.
Friends surrounded him in age: old friends (Jean Schlum-
berger, Martin du Gard) and newer ones (Amrouche, Delay). During his final illness Dr. Delay hardly left his side.
His heart had been failing for some time; a disease of the
lungs finished him. He did not suffer very much; he read
Virgil; and he had no fears. He had always said: "One must

live eternity with every instant." He was alive up to the last instant. His was, in short, a happy and triumphant life.

Young people read him less today. He who spent his life trying vainly to catch hold of some fixed point (Christianity, Communism) is not a fixed point to which a generation eager for action can attach itself. If he offers any philosophy, it is one of doubt. He succeeded through his method, however, in making a happy old age for himself. This existence, tortured though it was and warped by conflict, ended finally in serenity.

ALAIN

THERE ARE NOT a few of us in the world who think that Alain was, and remains, one of the greatest men of our time. I would not myself hesitate to say *the* greatest—and of his contemporaries would consider only Valéry, Proust, and Claudel of comparable rank.

I. THE LIFE

He was born Emile Chartier in Mortagne on March 3, 1868, and attended elementary school at the local *collège catholique*. His teachers found him universally gifted. If he had wanted to, he could have become a doctor, a poet, a musician, or a novelist. His only desire, however, was to remain free and to think clearly. After a brief glance in the direction of the Ecole Polytechnique, he decided to study literature at the Ecole Normale "because it was easier," and in order to prepare for it, he got a scholarship to the Lycée Michelet in Vanves. There he attended the philosophy classes of Jules Lagneau, "my great Lagneau, the only god, really, I ever acknowledged."

Lagneau was a profound thinker and wholly uncompromising man whose course consisted of but two parts, one on perception, the other on judgment. He marked his pupil for life. Chartier was admitted to the Ecole Normale in 1889. Brunetière, who was then in charge of the Ecole, warmly encouraged the philosopher's extreme, often radical views. Alain had no difficulty passing his *agrégation* examination and began his career as a teacher in the *collège* of Pontivy. He initiated himself into this exacting profession first at Pontivy and then at Lorient. His lectures were informal, improvised, and laced with illustrations from poetry, fiction, and everyday life that fired his students' imaginations. They soon came to revere him in the way he had once revered Lagneau. It was while he was at Lorient that the Dreyfus Affair thrust him into politics. He found he was a radical, that is, a dutiful but not respectful citizen—"the citizen against the powers that be." He spoke in the *universités populares*[1] and lent his support to the local radical newspaper by writing news stories. [Tr.]

Appointed to the Lycée Corneille in Rouen, he quickly won the same high regard. Sometime about 1906, he began, in *La Dépêche de Rouen et de Normandie,* to write, under the name of Alain, daily *Propos,* or "Observations," short articles of fifty lines which constitute the most astonishing phenomenon of journalism in our time. It is extraordinary that a political newspaper could, every morning for a period of years, print an uncompromising, often difficult piece of writing and not only not offend its readers but delight them. The style of the *Propos* was exacting, the thought lofty and unobliging. Still people read. More than one reader, from some vague presentiment of genius, cut out and saved these masterpieces. Later, the best of the *Propos* were collected in a volume called *Les Cent Un Propos d'Alain* (1908, 1909, 1911, 1914, 1928). At this same time Alain also contributed a number of remarkable dialogues to the *Revue de Métaphysique et de Morale.*

In 1902, his teaching success earned him an appointment to Paris, where he first taught at the Lycée Condorcet, then at the Lycée Michelet, and finally at the Lycée Henri

---

[1] Night schools for workers.

IV, where he filled the chair for the preparation of students for the Ecole Normale and shaped the minds of unnumbered generations of young Frenchmen. He also taught a class of young girls at the Collège Sévigné. His lectures there were so fine that a number of students from the Ecole Normale, and even a number of older followers, attended them. The most diverse persons emerged from his classroom; writers such as Simone Weil, Jean Prévost, Pierre Bost, Henri Massis, Samuel de Sacy, Maurice Toesca; politicians like Maurice Schumann; men of action and teachers like Michel Alexandre, who later became the editor of the *Propos*.

"Alain inculcated," writes Gilbert Spire, "in all the men he taught a certain number of principles, certain convictions free of any sort of attachment, any religious or political label. We learned from him that probity and courage are the primary virtues of the mind, that each individual has the powers of mind he deserves, that no one of us was excepted from the danger of stupidity through ill-temper, conceit, fear, or lack of faith in oneself; that the simplest questions are difficult if one examines them closely, that the knottiest problems become simple if one attacks them in an orderly and persistent fashion; and finally, that freedom is man's greatest attribute." It is important to keep in mind that Alain was, first and foremost, a philosophy teacher, and one who knew his business.

In 1914, Alain, no longer young, and exempt from military duty, wanted to enlist. He was opposed to all war, but felt that it was necessary to have fought in order to have the right to judge it. He refused to be an officer and served his entire tour of duty as a heavy artillery gunner. He wrote two fine books about this brief period of his life: *Mars ou la Guerre Jugée* (1921), and *Souvenirs de Guerre* (1937). It was during the enforced periods of idleness of this stint in the army that he wrote his *Système des Beaux-Arts* and his *Quatre-vingt-un Chapitres sur l'Esprit et les Passions*.

He had become a full-fledged writer. Michel Arnauld, a

friend, had taken a selection of his Rouen *Propos* to Gallimard; *Mars* and the *Système des Beaux-Arts* were submitted
to the same house and immediately accepted for publication.
Alain had resumed his teaching duties at the Lycée Henri
IV and the Collège Sévigné. Little by little, the rage of *Mars*
subsided: "I made my peace," he said, "with man. I loved
this poet in evil as in good. I began to understand how sorrow and happiness are transformed into poems and that
mythology, art, and religion serve as our everyday dress.
. . ." His teaching had become unfettered, wide-ranging,
and marked by great felicity of expression. *Les Idées et les
Ages* is the book that records this new-found calm; it is a
good-humored book which has the flavor of the "returns
from the wars" in Homer.

From then on, one great work followed another. In *Les
Dieux* Alain sets forth his ideas on the religions of the world.
He sees in them man's projection, upon a universe that requires nothing, of his own emotions, fears, and hopes. He
shows that the successive religions, from the earliest magical
tales up to Christianity, represent strata in man rather than
stages—for all of them still survive in each of us. In *Entretiens
au Bord de la Mer,* the most difficult but also perhaps the
most profound of his works, he sets forth his metaphysics. In
Idées, he studies Plato, Descartes, and Hegel, not by giving
an account of their work but by rethinking it. "Rediscover-
ing what the best have meant, that is itself to invent."

Alain always resisted the temptation of considering philosophy a discipline separate from other forms of human
thought—religion, art—and was throughout his life an avid
reader of fiction and a discerning literary critic. Complementary to his *Propos de Littérature* (1934) are *Stendhal, En
lisant Dickens* and, particularly, *Avec Balzac,* which is far
and away the best book ever written on the real meaning of
the *Comédie Humaine* and its less obvious beauties. It should
be noted that Alain made a point of reading only a limited
number of books, which he reread constantly and knew in

remarkable depth. He spent his life in the company of a few great minds; the rest did not exist for him.

He ranked Claudel and Valéry with the great masters of the past. Through the good offices of Henri Mondor, he became friends with Valéry, and he wrote commentaries consisting of a number of curious marginalia to *Charmes* and *La Jeune Parque*. I think that Alain was himself essentially a poet but that he chose to express himself in prose because this more severe form made it impossible to let song serve for thought. He was also a moralist; his *Aventures du Coeur* contains an analysis of the passions—love, ambition, avarice —which goes far beyond anything written by La Rochefoucauld, La Bruyère, and even Stendhal on the same subjects.

When he retired he had long since been suffering with rheumatoid arthritis. This illness worsened rapidly, and during the whole last part of his life he was obliged to live in reclusion in his little house in Vésinet, unable to move except from his bed to the table on which he wrote (or read) all day. He never complained and remained so alert mentally that his visitors left with a feeling of having themselves been revived and rejuvenated by this octogenarian. Many of his former pupils, now his disciples, visited him faithfully each week in Vésinet. Just as, in 1914, he had wanted to fight as a soldier because that was in keeping with his principles; and just as, at the time of the Dreyfus Affair, he had stood up for the Republic; so, in his extreme old age, sick, paralyzed, and in pain, he showed the stoical serenity of an Epictetus.

Throughout his life, Alain had shunned official honors. He had refused decorations, titles, and even chairs at the Sorbonne. However, three weeks before his death he was tendered and accepted a wholly unanticipated honor: the Prix National des Lettres, which was being conferred for the first time. The funeral services at the Père-Lachaise cemetery, were simple but moving. There were people of all ages present, but each shared the same feelings. The man was no more; the work had only just started upon its glorious future. The writer of the present book had the honor of speaking on that day on behalf of Alain's friends. This speech is reprinted here because it gives some idea of how people really felt about this great figure.

II. AT ALAIN'S GRAVE

"We are gathered at this place of mourning to honor our teacher and our friend. The dead cease being dead when, reverently, the living restore them to life. 'It is through the living that the dead again live, that they see and speak [as Homer so strikingly put it] by means of that fresh blood the shades drink and which for a time restores their memory.' We have, all of us, from our youth, been nourished by Alain's thought. The day has now come when Alain must be nourished by ours. Here—because he is present in each one of us—he enters into eternity.

"All that we loved him for, all we admired, remains. Our ideas, writings, feelings, actions, even our dreams carry his powerful stamp. Many of us here were personal observers of this great life; we will transmit the memory and example of it to the generations who will follow us. Socrates is not dead; he lives in Plato. Plato is not dead; he lives in Alain. Alain is not dead; he lives in us.

"Some men begin to live only when they are dead. Alain was fond of the word legend, legend being what must be said, the account of an existence after time and forgetfulness have purified it. But the life of our teacher was already his legend. We found that he always lived up to our highest expectations. The loftiness of thought, the beauty of style, the courage of his decisions never ceased to amaze us. 'Lagneau was loved by me,' he said of his own teacher. Alain was loved by us deeply. Disciples, though our own hair was already white, we chose to go to the house in Vésinet that was for us one of the temples of the mind and sit in the presence of the sage. Age had not been kind to him. His stiff and tortured limbs refused to serve him. Although in pain, he never complained. His welcoming smile was an affirmation of friendship of the most constant sort. The old master—faithful to the Socratic method—would, with an affectionate cuff, prod his visitor's mind, and sparks of ideas about the nature of things, ignited by his poetic genius, would begin to fly. The wonderful woman whose loving care and affection made this long-protracted torment more bearable, remained present during these exchanges, attentive and unobtrusive. Soon the illustrious shades came flocking—Descartes, Stendhal, Balzac, Auguste Comte. They were unforgettable meetings.

"Last Sunday when we entered the small bedroom, our teacher's body, wasted from long fasting, was stretched out on the bed. There was, about that face, forever stilled and molded in death, some strange aura of sharp-edged yet affectionate mischievousness. I believed for a moment that I was looking at the enigmatical and irrepressible young teacher who, almost fifty years ago now, in Rouen, came into his classroom and wrote on the blackboard: 'One must go to the truth with all one's soul.' I stood at the foot of his bed for a long time. It is natural that our musings should at such moments turn us to the dead who were our models for instruction and advice. What was required in this instance? What oath must one swear to this great soul?

"I think that the oath can be expressed in one word: hope. Alain asks us to have faith in man, which leads us to respect his rights; faith in man's mind to pursue, from one error to the next, the path of truth; and faith in man's will to find paths across that vast universe of forces which itself asks nothing. He who knows how, simultaneously, to doubt and to believe, to doubt and act, to doubt and will, is saved. Such was his message, such the figure we must keep alive in ourselves if Alain's spirit is not to die. The leave we now take of him is a promise. We swear, insofar as we are able, to be faithful to his teachings and to his example.

"This end will be the more easily achieved if we who were his pupils and his friends are able to maintain those ties of brotherhood which have today brought us to his side. We know that he liked commemorative observances, wherein the illustrious dead guide the living, and that he greatly approved of the reverent gesture of adding a stone to the mound over a grave. To be or not to be, Alain and us, we must choose. It depends on us whether Alain continues to exist. Today we lay the first stone of this spiritual monument."

III. THE *PROPOS*

Alain's output can be divided into two groups, which differ not in idea nor in method but in kind of composition. The first consists of the great mass of the *Propos,* the second of full-length books like *Les Dieux, Système des Beaux-Arts, L'Histoire de Mes Pensées,* and *Entretiens au Bord de la Mer.*

Alain invented the literary genre of the *propos.* The *propos* is a prose poem two pages in length, written every evening for a daily newspaper—"either with or without genius," Stendhal would have said. Of genius there was plenty. "If it had not been for the necessity of meeting a daily deadline, these succinct little poems would never have got written." Every writer, as every runner, has his distance. The hundred-yard dash specialist gets winded on longer runs. Alain found it easy to pace himself over the distance of the *propos.* He set a limit of two pages, no more and no less, believing that this limit would sustain him, just as the stanza keeps the poet going.

He had another rule, which was never to rewrite. Once any word had been written down in his large, bold hand, it was to be left. The next sentence just had to accommodate itself to what had preceded. Work done became the model for the work to be done; and the work pressed straight on toward its destination, keeping at a distance any and all extraneous ideas that might delay its progress. These latter ideas then remained on tap to lend color and substance to a given passage or metaphor. "This resulted," says Alain, "in a peculiar kind of poetry and strength. The voices that make up a fugue are even thus sometimes raised to a higher level of excitement in the stretto, which is that part of the fugue when all strands come together as if passing through a ring. Everything comes crowding in at once, and one must squeeze, and get through, and do so quickly. And that is how my acrobat's act works, so far as I can tell; moreover, I was able to make it work only once out of a hundred tries."

This steeplechase, ending each day with the clearing of a barrier, that of the last stroke of the pen, went on in the pages of *La Dépêche de Rouen* up until the war in 1914. No one had ever attempted to write newspaper fare of this quality; it is doubtful that such will ever be seen again. Readers were appreciative. Many read Alain's *propos* before turning to the news. After the war, the tone of the *propos* changed. His experiences as a simple soldier had left him heavy in heart and in spirit. Collected and published in books, the *propos* became more lengthy. Still, the acrobat remained faithful to his act, the philosopher to his themes. And to his style. For that was the end-all and be-all. "Our aim was to change philosophy into literature and, contrarily, literature into philosophy." Both of which goals were achieved. Alain always remained especially fond of the *propos* of the early years. In a dedicatory inscription, he wrote in my copy: "This lovely edition takes me back to the better days of the *Propos*. These latter are metaphorical. The reader has to guess at a great deal. I find in these pages a simplicity I no longer possess." And on a later volume he wrote: "I see here a diminution of poetry and more of the obviously serious. That is what is known as getting old, and there's nothing for it." Actually he was doing himself an injustice. The later *propos* give me as much pleasure as the early ones. They are more somber, but so were the times.

Indeed, I find that one of the beauties of the *propos* is the way they shift with the years and times. It is like watching Orion's belt rise and descend. One follows the seasons in their appointed rounds. Holidays come and go in sequence. Easter, Pentecost, Corpus Christi, All-Hallows, Christmas are each the occasion for ever-fresh reflections and meditation. And in the background one perceives seasons of a level different from those governed merely by the precession of the equinoxes, and The Great Freeze that will return the centers of civilization to Babylon and to Tyre.

The blasé reader who has too long pursued "that which in all the world most quickly palls: novelty" can well stand a dose of the classics. He needs to go back to those time-tested books that free one of choice and allow one to think. "Gymnastics as an antidote to the real war within," says Alain, "and add to that *The Iliad*." I say: "And add to that the *Propos*."

In the long series of *Propos,* Alain has his favorite subjects. He is interested in every manner of thing and speaks impartially of grooming horses and love's passions, the byways of politics, the painter's art, war, and God. But he buttresses each subject with a set of central ideas that serve as a framework for his thought and to which he constantly refers as the basis for a well-aimed thrust. Is he repetitious? Undeniably. "They say I repeat myself," wrote Voltaire. "Well, I shall continue to repeat myself until they mend their ways!" Alain, however, repeats himself in order to correct *himself,* in order to state more forcefully or with more poetry what he considers essential.

Always the reference is to the real world. A bird, a tree, a man at work, the sun looking larger on the horizon, an enchanting monster found in Retz or Saint-Simon—these are what he uses to bolster his thought. The world of things cannot exist without the mind. But, inversely, the real world is the sole regulator of our thoughts. The dialectician would like to live in a world apart, the world of ideas, but there is but one world, and we are, as Plato says, children of the earth, bound up with trees and rocks. Except for Plato, no other thinker is as thoroughly at home as Alain in the arts and crafts. He loves to explain thoughts in physical terms. He is aware that a man's irritation sometimes stems from the fact that he has been standing up too long. "Instead of arguing against his bad temper, offer him a chair." He notes that men who wear glasses run the world because it is impossible to look them in the eye. "One gets fooled by the reflections of the glass. That gives them time." He was delighted when I told him that Disraeli, who didn't smoke, accepted from Bismarck the offer of a cigar so that Bismarck would not be the only one to have the advantage of the pauses between puffs. He believed that poetry never follows when thought walks ahead.

The body expresses character. When Alain looks at a mouflon or a billy goat, he thinks: just as a mouflon will always be a mouflon, and a billy goat a billy goat, so will a miser always be a miser and a courtesan a courtesan. Gobseck has no need of Popinot's virtue, and is, moreover, incapable of it. However, Gobseck is capable of his own kind of virtue. Thus, Alain concludes, since the natures of things are immutable, one can put one's trust in them. Like Balzac, Alain excels in demonstrating that the métier makes the man; and, like Montesquieu, he excels in describing the mechanism whereby peoples take on the characteristics of the land they live on. The deep English estuaries, in comparison with the lagoons of Venice, betoken superior sailing ships and bolder sailors. "So it is that the mainland drives herds of nebulous ideas towards the sea-laved islands; and it is the mariner Darwin who shears them."

Like the sea, the human body has its tides on which

thought must rise and fall. After anger comes the ebb of fatigue. That is the way things are, and nothing can make man have no passions. This does not mean that he cannot govern himself through small and momentarily adequate actions. If a sailor knows how to sail, his sailboat is able to take advantage of wind and tide to reach a given destination. Political power is perfectly aware of the blind fury of the mob and takes care not to confront it head-on but beats to windward and runs close to shore. "One must stand firm between two kinds of madness, that of believing one can do anything, and that of believing one can do nothing."

"All of these *propos* are both of the will and on the will." *Of the will* because of the firm intention of beginning afresh each morning and not going back to anything that has been done. *On the will* because of the recurring evidence of man's power over things and over himself. The vast universe about us is neither hostile nor friendly. Any man can act in it if only he knows how to will. And there is only one way to act, and that is to act. To will means to begin afresh and to continue. "I will do" is nothing. "I do"—that is a decision. The only kind. The farmer doesn't groan about the thistles; he cuts them down. A work merely started speaks volumes as compared with intentions and desires. "Happy the man who sees in the work of the previous day signs of his own will."

Not long since, a treatise on happiness was extracted from the mass of the *propos*. There was nothing wrong with the idea. The *"Propos* on Happiness" rescued a goodly number of readers from despairs for which no real evils could satisfactorily account. In isolation, however, these *propos* on the conduct of life took on the air of recipes. They are more beautiful when seen as part of a huge landscape of ideas. Saturated in ancient myth, inbued with Christianity, they blossom forth. Alain's numerous remarks on appearances make us see more clearly how imagination dupes us and how, for instance, it is false to say that we think of our deaths with fear—for such a thought has no object: we cannot think of ourselves as other than alive. That the pain of the imagined accident is almost always worse than that caused by the actual accident, that the sick man's suffering is different from that of the man in good health—and of a kind the latter cannot possibly imagine—these are all nails to be driven deep, for they contribute to peace of mind.

One remarkable aspect of the *Propos* is that Alain, who is so quick to expose appearances for what they are, is equally careful to point out the truth they contain. Religious doctrines, Christianity especially, are here described by a fearless but not faithless mind. Is there, after all, any more effective antidote for the follies of the imagination than ceremonies of worship? "The catechism is the first expression of the universal school. And although it expressed itself in figures, the doctrine was stirring and persuasive because of the idea buried within it—which is none other than the idea of the human spirit. Our customs are still, happily, suffused and quickened by that powerful idea—to which we owe the dignity of womankind, the spirit of chivalry, and the idea of a spiritual power greater than kings and nations."

IV. ALAIN'S POLITICAL THEORY

But wait! This same thinker who accepts and extols the value of ceremonies is intent above all on keeping his freedom of thought intact. Many of the *propos* are political. Alain had very strong views on politics. If his emotions had prevailed, he would have become a Julien Sorel, fuming about The Establishment. But his common sense led him to recognize the exigencies of power—although never to succumb to them. A society must be governed. Otherwise it will perish. And one must begin with obedience. All disobedience, even in the name of justice, only makes the abuses of authority last the longer. "Do you like doing police work?" is one of

the questions asked in *L'Otage* (*The Hostage*). "No," replied
the prefect, "but one must do what one does." Although
Alain admired Napoleon, he notes that Napoleon kept a
close watch over the treasury, carefully guarding it against
thieves, but helped himself to it. The fact is that the Ogre
of Corsica had a kick ready for any and all—marshalls,
bishops, ministers of state, fashionable ladies—and that
Alain the common soldier saw a kind of justice in that.

Politics, whether practiced by Turelure or Napoleon, is
a trade just as grooming horses is a trade. The politics of the
mind, on the other hand, retains freedom of judgment and,
while it grants obedience, withholds respect. A Revolutionary? No, he couldn't be called that. He believed that after
every upheaval the same basic power elements re-emerge
unaltered and that any leader of The Establishment, given
his head, will incline to tyranny. To which the sole remedy
is a watchful citizenry properly mistrustful of its mandatees.
Even the executive power should defend the citizenry against
those powerful ruling agencies which, if allowed, would
destroy the State. Alain is wary of anyone who spends other
people's money. One of his favorite protagonists in the *Propos*
is Castor, the careful, somewhat grasping businessman who
does everything for himself. There was something of Castor
in Napoleon, who counted the shells in his ammunition-boxes.

Letting a manager or intendant run your business will ruin
you every time, says Castor. He will sell short because he has
a deal on with the buyer; he will pay long because he gets
a cut for agreeing to buy inferior goods. "You will be ruined;
you are ruined; your money dwindles away. The alternative
is to adopt the miser's method of taking care of everything
himself. And one manager is really nothing in comparison
to a multitude of managers forming a well-paid and badly
supervised bureaucracy—for in that case the inexorable law,
which says that the lazy proprietor is certain to be ruined by
any intendant, is able to operate in the awesome name of the
State. "One fine day your many-faced manager announces

that you have lost four-fifths of your money and that he, as manager, is to be paid five times as much, as is right and proper."

Such was Alain the political economist—the Balzacian observer who entirely understood why the Général de Montcornet is gouged by his peasants whereas Grandet gets richer and richer. He obtained from Marx the idea that economics governs politics. "The primary concern of the salaried man is his salary." Alain often speaks of the bourgeoisie and the proletariat, but not in the same sense as Marxists. For him, the bourgeois—the merchant and the lawyer, for instance— is the man who lives by pleasing and persuading; the proletarian—the bricklayer, the weaver, etc.—is the man who lives by *doing*. The funeral director, who deals in nothing but signs and symbols, is the perfect example of the bourgeois. By contrast, there are manual skills which altogether forgo signs and symbols. "Lofty looks are clearly of no help whatsoever in turning off a faucet or making a watch run." Or in running a factory. An engineer becomes less bourgeois to the degree that he knows his trade. Neither Louis Renault nor Aristide Boucicaut were ever entirely bourgeois.

When, as a very young man, Alain saw a much older man of whom he was fond, greet in hollow flattering fashion a group of devious administrative types, he told himself: "Now you listen to me, young man; you will never greet anyone thus. You must so solemnly swear right now." Most people will, enthusiastically, even proudly—as in the story of William Tell—bow to a hat on a stick. Alain never bowed to Gessler's hat. That was the nature of his irreverence. I have already noted the manner in which he was reverent. The "solemn oath" is characteristic. "One must swear" he would say. "If one's ideas shift with events, then thought is nothing but a prostitute."

This mélange of obedience and irreverence was hard to maintain when the philosopher became an artilleryman. Nevertheless he preserved it. A willing and disciplined soldier, judging and not flattering his superiors, he learned to hate war, not so much because of its dangers (he was courageous by nature and by conviction) as because of the state of servitude it forced upon citizens who believed themselves free. He came to believe that war and war preparations were the greatest evils of society. In wartime tyrants are not subject to control of any kind. And even in peace time, who decides to stock armaments? Build up military strength? Make treaties? A small circle of men who are said to know best and who pontificate in commonplaces. Millions of other men, on reading a proclamation, will prepare to die.

The *propos* of the post-war period are suffused with a raging and righteous anger. It was important above all, Alain believed, to control the threat of war, lacking which all other forms of regulation would be meaningless. But aren't we dependent on money, on wealth? That is indeed true. But there is a distinction to be grasped. One can change masters; one can defy one's master; one can question. "The unions are powerful; which makes it clear that capitalist power is not at all comparable to the power of the military. What remnants of slavery survive in our time have their source in war and threats of war. It is on that area that free men should concentrate their efforts, and there exclusively." Free men, however, were unable to grasp this categorical imperative. The free nations wrangled idiotically among themselves and thereby allowed the eternal tyrant to rise again. Week after week, Alain never slackened in his defense of peace and of the Republic—"thrice denied, thrice cursed, thrice betrayed daily—and by their best friends—before cock-crow. So be it. But may the crowing of the cock now serve to warn us." He hoped for negotiators who were not tragic actors seeking applause and asked that public opinion discredit those so bravely prepared to do battle by proxy. "The heros are well aware that Messieurs the fifers and flag-wavers will play for them only as far as the last city policeman.

They are well aware that those who clamor loudest will fall back on Bordeaux."

The prophet was not heard. The clamorous were again seen in Bordeaux. May the crowing of these cocks be a warning to us all.

V. ALAIN'S *SYSTÈME DES BEAUX-ARTS*

To understand the role of the fine arts in the human community, one must take account of that skittish thing called man's brain, quivering like a thoroughbred's withers, so quick to unleash its emotions and fears upon the world. Imagination is parent to error, and revery without object dangerous always. The role of the fine arts is to furnish the imagination with real and solid objects. Many people believe that art has its source in some peculiar kind of delirium; that is true, but only when the delirium is controlled. The beautiful stands off from the convulsive even though it uses this excess of energy to impose a form on nature. A musical sound is a cry, but a controlled cry. The novel is a passion, but a directed passion. The rustic sculptor, frightened by a grinning tree trunk, fashions from it the form of a god and, in thus fixing it, delivers himself of it. One becomes an artist by making for oneself what one would like to see or hear. There is no way to bring a bison or a hut into being other than drawing the one or building the other. Moreover, giving one's reveries an object is healthy, because objectless thought is a greater evil than the notion of a rigid necessity. It is possible to consider and contemplate a solid object which, like the actual world, is neither loving nor hostile. It is also characteristic of the work of art that one cannot and does not wish to change it in any respect. Chartres cathedral and a Baudelaire sonnet are just what they are. That is how art is.

The artist, even as the viewer, is subject to the same neces-

sity—that he can only see the work if he creates it. Trying
to create a work out of revery alone always ends in disaster.
Ghosts of novels haunt the imagination of the novelist,
but one can no more count their chapters than one can count
the columns in a photograph of the Pantheon. The artist
needs the resistance of nature, just as the gliding dove needs
that of the air, and it is in that sense that nature is the master
of all masters. An actual event is for the novelist like those
blocks of marble Michelangelo would go to gaze at—blocks
that became subjects and first drafts for him. It is the resistance of things which, combined with emotion, give rise
to a work of art. Abstract ideas, as in the *roman à thèse*,
result only in manufactured literature. Here again, if one
starts from the bottom and works up, it works; if one starts
from the top and works down, never. The portrait painter
doesn't start with some pure idea; the idea comes to him as
he paints; it may even come to him afterwards, just as it
does to the viewer. Genius must astonish itself.

Thought in and of itself will not give rise to form. It is the
movement of the body, impelled by the emotions, which brings
the artist into contact with objects and experience and provides him with his block of marble. The man torn by passion
may grunt, groan, gasp, and scream; which is the musician's
way. Or he stirs about and hollows out a negative mold
for his form: the result being a cave, a house, a bed, a tier
of seats, or a stadium. "Art is man added on to nature,"
says Bacon. At bottom the arts are a discipline of the human
body and, as Aristotle says, a purging of the emotions. However, one can conceive of two different ways of disciplining
the emotions. One is through disciplining the body, its
motions and sounds, from which arises a first group of arts:
dance, singing, music, poetry; the other is by shaping
the world so as to provide the emotions with an object:
which results in architecture, sculpture, painting, and drawing. Between these two groups lies spectacle: processions,

ceremonies, theater, in which the body is simultaneously the observed and the observer.

The village dance is a good illustration of the Aristotelian idea of purgation. Love first expresses itself in a kind of shyness, which gives rise to the fear of rejection, which in turn becomes the source of great passion. If it remains unattached, this emotion can lead to despair and violence. In the dance, however, love is given form. Desired actions become permissible because they are regulated. A mutual understanding among all the participants brings animal desire into the human order. Through regulated and rhythmic movements, love allows itself time to think; it becomes more secure; it stops babbling. The dance excludes disorder and frenzy. There is an element of motionlessness in the most beautiful dances of love—as Spanish dance so clearly shows.

Similarly, a fine portrait distills the essence of the model by leaving out the shifting play of moods and expressions— retaining only the permanent. It isn't the portrait that resembles the model, but the model the portrait. In this Alain is in agreement with Kant. The beautiful, Kant teaches, is that element in the object which makes us aware of the harmony of the two parts of our nature—the high and the low, the intellectual and the emotional. A cathedral is absolute evidence that the believer understands without logical proof.

The sublime occurs when the false infinities of nature— thunderstorms, hurricanes, mountains, deserts—are mastered, measured by the mind. Pascal's thinking reed is sublime. Beethoven's and Wagner's chaotic outpourings, kept within bounds by rhythm, lit by bolts of recurrent themes, are sublime. But sublimity also occurs when the philosopher or novelist masters the storms of the passions. There is no single pure aesthetic feeling. All our passions—love, ambition, greed—become aesthetic through purification. Man should not be in an already purified state when he approaches the beautiful—for in that case, he will be an aesthete and not an artist. A man cannot appreciate or create the sublime if he doesn't find himself embroiled in a situation of misfortune to which he expects some awful outcome. The beautiful requires an accumulation of pent-up emotions, which first constitute a threatening turbulence, then subside into quietness and relief. Racine's tragedies are a fine example of this. *Candide,* in which violence and horror commingle beneath the *prestissimo* of the narrative is beautiful in the same way Mozart is beautiful. Oratory is beautiful if it gives order to men's inner disquiet. The funeral oration and the requiem mass require of orator and musician alike the same transcendence of grief.

Poetry throws further light on the mystery of the fine arts. The subject of poetry is not the beautiful; a bad poet can write a bad poem on Nausicaa. Nor is idea central: Hugo can make a sublime poem out of a commonplace. What makes beauty is the element of the unexpected that comes out of the song itself, of the meter, the rhyme. In all the arts, indeed, beauty is born in the execution and not in the conception. It is in searching for words that fit his meter that the poet hits upon memorable phrases and discloses his thought. That his means be resistant is also a necessity. The great poet does not break away from the strict rules of poetry. Valéry wrote metered lines, just as Michelangelo accepted blocks of marble. Limitations are a fact of nature and strengthen the spirit. Dull style is dull because it has nothing behind it but intellectual understanding and makes us forget the continuity of nature and the mind. That is why the poet is the best of thinkers. Absurdity awaits him who would seek truth from a height, through logic. Homer may properly be taught in a philosophy class. The truth of man through the harmony in man, that is the lesson of poetry.

As for the novel, Alain—the most sensitive reader Balzac, Stendhal, Sand, and Tolstoy have ever had—must be read to be fully appreciated. It need only be said that in the art of the novel, just as in the art of the garden, he makes us see a dual motion. The essence of all fiction is the will of a hero who has chosen his fate. Love in fiction is love that has been chosen. However, the dreams and feelings of the hero are not enough to bring a novel alive. Abstract reportings of feelings are boring. They need a solid exterior world to carry them. "How exterior forces get the better of the man who is bold, how his will becomes the fate of those less strong or more circumscribed by social custom, and how, given these elements, all the inexorable forces of society fall upon the fiction and tear it to shreds with their talons"—that is the subject of *La Chartreuse de Parme, Le Lys dans la Vallée,* and all great novels. That is why Balzac found it necessary at the beginning of his novels to take such pains in describing his houses and towns—Guérande is described before *Béatrix* really begins, Saumur before *Grandet*—just as it was necessary to include "automaton" characters of the Hochon, Cibot, and Listomère genre. These latter are objects. Only one character is seen from inside and thinks for the reader. Sometimes it is the hero, as in Stendhal. And sometimes it is the omniscient author. The following epigram is worth pondering: "The novel is the poem of free will."

What is the nature of the novelistic imagination? Does the novelist see, does he hear the beings he has created? There are no images without perception, and no perception without some basis in nature. It is a known fact, for instance, that Stendhal took the subject of *Le Rouge et le Noir* from the account of an actual trial, and that of *La Chartreuse de Parme* from an Italian news dispatch. Balzac used people he had met: Thiers, la duchesse de Castries, Liszt and Madame d'Agoult, Vidocq the police agent. However, these givens of nature are, to the novelist, what the block of marble is to the sculptor. The moment he begins to dress them down, he finds other figures emerging from nature's rough sketch; however, he finds in the exterior world, in other objects encountered in real life, other elements that lend themselves to being incorporated into this dough he is kneading. Imagination is able to create only by means of this work of the hands and of the pen. A novel projected in imagination is no more a novel than a statue merely visualized as a statue. The key to the fine arts lies in the simple fact that execution never fails to surpass conception. What we call inspiration is that movement of nature which exceeds our hopes.

It only remains to be said that Alain's work on art is a work of art.

VI. *LES DIEUX*

Just as science is a commentary on perception, so philosophy is a commentary on religion. What matters here as in all things is showing that each religion has its own kind of truth and that its lower forms are prerequisite to the achieving of its higher forms. "If I could conceive of all the gods in God, and like God, all the gods would be true ones." This sounds very much like Spinoza.

From what did the different religions arise? From the fact that we seek to find our emotions, hopes, and fears reflected in a world that cannot respond. "It is because of this that we invent that hidden and lurking presence which makes us believe that gods exist in everything. But the gods refuse to appear; and it is as a result of this miracle which never comes to pass that religion takes expression in temples, statues, and sacrifices. . . ." For it is urgent that something be made to appear. Thus, the invisible, by turning our appeals back upon ourselves, makes its presence doubly felt. The great structures, sanctuaries, cathedrals, where one has presentiments of some thing that is worth the trouble of divining, are also centers of prayer and pilgrimage. Works of language—when, like the Bible, they become the central object of a cult—are so many enigmas and not less worthy of contemplation than statues of the gods. Alain's reverent

method consists of assuming all religions to be valid and
of finding out in what respect they were valid.

One by one he reviews all of the stages of man, that of
Aladdin and magic, that of Pan and the rustic gods, that of
Jupiter and the gods of the city-state, that of Jehovah, and
finally that of Christophorus. Rustic religion and state religion
survive in all men, but after the advent of Christianity
occupy a subordinate position. Far removed from Jupiter's
power, one sees at the crossways a man being put to death
on two shafts of wood in the form of a cross. This tremendous
image, which became the primary symbol of the religion of
the spirit, requires explication. The initial and supreme
paradox is that the spirit has no being. The one great, vast
existence contains everything that is. The spirit has no power.
It is neither within nor without; it is the all of the all. The
spirit is one and indivisible. Those who perceive these things
without at the same time keeping them distinct from visions
and invisible powers, create the violent, exalted, and fanatical
religion of the Mind. Hegel termed the Jews the people of
the Mind. In the Bible, in the beginning there is nothing,
and the spirit creates in the same way one thinks. The false
gods are immolated, leaving the void of the desert, the
terrible absence that is everywhere. The only crime is of
forgetting that man is nothing with respect to the Eternal.
After this leap from the natural state to an empty god, to
whom, through a survival of state religion, is attributed
omnipotence, nothing further can be said. May thy will be
done, thy bitter will! Metaphor is essential to this religion of
the Mind which forbids idolatry and yet must needs bring
symbol to the level of perception. That need is the basis for
the metaphors of the Bible and of the parables of the
Gospels. The abstract word does not enter into man. The
event, the example, the image sustain discourse and make
us secure in and through all our being. Aside from the deep
tragic questions that catch us by the throat, we think easily
and smoothly about anything and everything.

The modern error, affecting perhaps four thousand volumes, is in trying to find out if religion was revealed, where and when, and the evidence we have for knowing it to be so. This proof can never be furnished, for all proofs of existence are proofs from experience, and there is no experience of the past. What matters is not whether Jesus said such and such a thing on such and such a day, but whether what he said is valid. One must begin by having faith, and then hold to it: "The intellect should follow faith, never precede it and never disrupt it." Ponder deeply the cross at the crossways. That is what I call praying. It is very important that a religion be idolatrous. Insofar as it consists exclusively of pure ideas it is no longer religion and amounts to little. The religion of the spirit expulses the gods of necessity: as for the gods of the belly, they must re-enter in the form of the devil. The devil of the thousand guises pursues us everywhere—as he pursued Faust—for he is within. That the devil, the lower gods exist, is obvious; they are, indeed, nothing but existence. Jesus said: "My kingdom is not of this world," but the empire of the devil is of this world, and it is so for all time, for the universe is now and has ever been without value. The spirit is misled if it believes only in itself. One doesn't do Christianity justice if one doesn't take into account all the murky religions it surpassed and doomed.

Marcus Aurelius and Epictetus had already carried to its limit the concern for not undervaluing the ruling part in man, but they are nonetheless pagans, for they consider and call themselves sons of the world. "Everything your seasons bring me is a fruit to me, oh Nature." By this expedient they were able to make shift with the gods of Olympus, who are the names of natural forces. But Christ is the son of Man. Christianity is human, not inhuman. Man and God are closely mingled in the free man. We must here refer back to the actual elevation that is the basis for all our thoughts. "Jupiter is a man but doesn't yet reach the point of being a god, except in reference to the snake, the cow, the wolf, the monkey, and the elephant. Jupiter is not sufficiently god; nor is he on the other hand entirely man, for he doesn't transcend himself and never passes judgment. He is good-natured as are all Caesars whose position is undisputed. And because he isn't enough man he is not yet worthy of being god. Jehovah, quite to the contrary, is no longer man at all, and his way of being incomprehensible is not man's, but rather that of the indescribable which hides itself in thickets or in clouds. This pure spirit can no longer take on flesh; it is cut off from man and reappears to him in the form of external marvels. It became urgent, given these oscillations from one extreme to the other, to come closer once again to the real man; and thus, religion came to take on flesh. . . . Such is the second stage of the spirit, which, by a dual motion, raises us from the athlete to the saint and brings us back from pure spirit to brotherly spirit. . . ."

Consider the child in the manger: "This weak thing is God. This weak thing which has need of everyone is God. This creature who would cease to exist without our ministrations is God. Such is the spirit in comparison with which truth is still an idol. The fact is that truth has found itself disgraced by power; Caesar enlists its aid and pays dearly for it. The child does not pay; he asks and asks more and more. It is a strict rule of the spirit that the spirit does not pay, and that no one can serve two masters. . . ."

VII

Ideas summarized are no longer ideas. Alain's ideas, especially, are valid not so much in their logical structure as in their metaphors, parables, the depth of their poetry. One should never forget that he always began his course, as did Lagneau, with three months of lecturing on sense perception, the source of our knowledge as well as our errors. Instead of

attempting to present these ideas within a systematic framework, I have tried to inspire the reader with a desire to in-
vestigate the laden orchards where this fruit was gathered
—and with the desire of changing his life by absorbing unto
himself a part of that wisdom which teaches men hope
rather than fear.

PAUL CLAUDEL

CLAUDEL'S SPEAKING VOICE helps those who know the man to enter immediately into his work. That voice is vigorous, harsh, dominating, and yet rich and cordial. It chews up words forcefully, cutting them into syllables, moving among sentences and their clauses like a plowshare among clods of brown earth. In the field of ideas it digs a deep and rigid furrow, but—within that straight line—the stones, and the beasts of the fields, and the uprooted plants, swarm with a chaotic life. It is a voice that is very French, but provincial—from Champagne—and peasantlike. "Any man who has tasted of the earth," says Claudel, "keeps the taste of it between his teeth."

I. THE MAN

Claudel has tasted of the earth. He was born at the edge of Champagne, in Villeneuve-sur-Fère-en-Tardenois, a village in the department of Aisne. The village's very name has beauty and could easily fit into a verse from *La Jeune Fille Violaine*. Claudel's maternal grandfather was a peasant, his father a commissioner of mortgages. As a child he was brought up at Villeneuve-sur-Fère. Seated in the fork of an apple tree, he would look out at the vast, white plain and at the royal road to Rheims. One day, the cathedral at the end of that dusty ribbon of road was going to be the destination of his thoughts.

To his country childhood, he owes his knowledge of the labors of the fields, the plants, the birds. When, later, he borrows images from sowing, from the harvest, from the village trades, they will be proper and precise. Claudel will never be a poet of the Parisian cafés, nor of the salons—not even Mallarmé's precious salon. He will know how to talk about bread, about soup, as a peasant's grandson who has done (or seen) the baking of one and the preparations for the other. Firmly tied to his soil, he will be able—without danger of alienation—to travel over the entire planet.

He has a cosmic mind. "The setting of this play is the world," he says at the beginning of *Le Soulier de Satin*. "He advances in spirit, like his Amalric, in the midst of continents."

> To the left Babylon with its bazaar, the rivers descending from Armenia; to the right the equator, Africa . . . and suddenly the great department store of the Louvre, crammed full of cloths and soap, it is India which is before us.

He never ceases to take an eagle's-eye view of the universe. "Like the Saint-Jacques of *Le Soulier* he gazes down from the top of the firmament at the wakes of ships on the oceans."[1] As a diplomat, he travels all over the globe. Everywhere, he will remain a Frenchman from Tardenois, cultured, wise, bold, but always, while measuring the world, keeping the standard yardstick of a brain from Champagne.

A Frenchman. A man of the soil. But also, and above all, a Catholic. Claudel's Catholicism does not date from his childhood. Although subject to the Catholic rites of baptism and first communion, that childhood was soon closed to faith. Born in 1868, Paul Claudel lived through his adolescence between 1880 and 1890. It was a period of scientific materialism. Taine and Renan were circling above the

[1] Marcel Thiébaut.

university hencoops. A mechanistic explanation of the universe seemed plausible. One day, thought certain professors in 1880, one day, it would be possible, by turning the wheels of a infinitely complex machine, to reconstitute a given moment in the past, and to prefigure a given moment in the future.

At the Lycée Louis-le-Grand, the student Paul Claudel had Burdeau—Republican moralist, Kantian Jacobin—as his professor of philosophy. Maurice Barrès would later draw a harsh portrait of him in *Les Déracinés,* under the name of Boutillier. Claudel adopted (temporarily) the philosophy of his master: "The powerful idea of the individual and of the concrete was obscured within me. I accepted the monist and mechanistic hypothesis in all its inflexibility. I believed that everything was subject to 'laws' and that this world was a rigid interlocking of causes and effects which science, the day after tomorrow, would succeed in unraveling perfectly."

Later, his rancor against this mechanistic theory would make him violent and unjust. Renan, whose *Vie de Jésus* he had liked at one time, became in Claudel's writing nothing more than "the revolting, the ignoble Renan."

Stay with me, Lord, because night is falling, and do not abandon me!
Do not lose me amongst the Voltaires, and the Renans, and the Michelets, and the Hugos, and all the infamous ones!
Their souls are with dead dogs, their books are buried in the dungheap.

How did the eighteen year old Claudel escape from what he calls "the materialistic prison?" First, through his meeting with Rimbaud in June 1886. "The first gleam of truth was given me when I met the books of a great poet—Arthur Rimbaud, to whom I owe eternal gratitude and who had a decisive role in the forming of my thought." Then there was the day, Christmas 1886, when he "met Christ."

Such was [he wrote] the wretched child who, the twenty-fifth of December, 1886, went to Notre-Dame to witness the Christmas services. I had then begun to write, and it seemed to me that in the Catholic ceremonies, considered from the point of view of a superior dilettantism, I would find its stimulation to be similar to some decadent exercises. It is in that spirit that, elbowed and jostled by the crowd, I assisted, with passing pleasure, at high mass. Then, not having anything better to do, I returned for Vespers. The children of the choir in white robes, and the pupils of the Little Seminary of Saint-Nicolas-du-Chardonnet who joined them, were in the process of singing what I later learned was the Magnificat. I was standing in the crowd next to the second pillar at the entrance to the chancel, to the right, on the side of the sacristy. And it is then that occurred the event which has dominated my entire life. In an instant my heart was touched and I believed. I believed, with such a forceful feeling of adherence, with such a swelling up of my entire being, with such a strong conviction, with such a certitude that left no room for any kind of the doubt, that ever after, all the books, all the reasoning, all the hazards of an eventful life, have not been able to shake my faith, nor, really, even touch it. I had suddenly the heart-rending feeling of the Innocence, the eternal childhood of God—an ineffable revelation. In attempting, as I have so often, to reconstitute the moments which followed that extraordinary instant, I find again the following elements which, however, formed only a single lightning-flash, a single sword, which divine Providence made use of to reach and to finally open the heart of a poor despairing child: "How happy are the people who believe!—But what if it was true?—It is true! God exists, he is there, he is someone, he is a being as personal as I am. He loves me, he calls me . . ." The tears and the sobs came, and the so-tender strains of the Adeste added to my emotion.

Claudel always remained faithful to that idea—that a conversion can only occur suddenly. And his heroes will always be saved by a shock which, by reversing the tapestry of the world will show them the sublime design, of which, until then, they had only seen the unintelligible side. In his writings he always returns to the image of the flash of lightning, which throws a brief white light over the court-yard of the farm, over the plain, over the dusty road. Grace, like the poet's inspiration, seems to him a complete and in-stantaneous turning over of the soul. The mind then follows, more slowly. Dialogue between Animus and Anima.

For Claudel, a few years passed between the illumination of Anima and the acceptance of Animus. Then Catholicism became the center of his life. This implies in him certain constant traits. The Catholic is always a realist—and we find in Chesterton's writings, as in Claudel's, that vigorous ac-ceptance of the real rejected by secular idealists. The Church is far from denying evil, the Church considers it as necessary and takes advantage of it. "Evil exists in the world," Claudel says "as a slave fetching water." The Catholic has clear points of reference. Enclosed in a framework of ceremonies and practices, he is sustained by them, and that framework constitutes an armor. Without the shadow of a doubt he knows what is right and what is wrong, what is white and what is black. He is privileged as an artist because men's spiritual dramas—pitiful animal adventures in the eyes of skeptics and cynics—become in the eyes of the Catholic the world's essential tragedy and *raison d'être*.

Claudel's originality is that in him Catholic realism takes as its object not only individual life, but social and economic life as well. After graduating from the School of Political Sciences he first entered the consular service and then the diplomatic corps.

He traveled over the whole earth—only the earth. He lived in New York, in Boston, in China, in Japan, in Hamburg, in Brazil. Toward the end of his career, he will be France's Ambassador in Tokyo, in Washington, in Brussels. And, a little like Walt Whitman, what he wants to sing in his verses is all this activity of man—these railroads, these ships, these banks, these wars mingled with the individual's passions, these labors of the land, these churches being built, this daily and surnatural life. He asks his muse, in one of the *Cinq Grandes Odes,* to grant him this rough, earthy, sensual, Catholic poetry.

> Let me be necessary! Let me fill a place recognized and approved,
> Like a builder of railroads, one knows that he is not useless, like the founder of a corporation! . . .
> Let me sing the works of men and let each one find again in my verses those things which are known to him,
> As from a height one has the pleasure of recognizing one's home, and the railroad station, and the city hall, and the man with his straw hat, but the space around oneself is immense!
> For of what use is a writer, if it is not to keep accounts.
> Whether they are his own, or those of a shoestore, or those of all humanity. . . .

Claudel's objective as a poet will be to become a good bookkeeper for the whole of humanity—while Claudel, the consul, will write precise reports on the commercial activity in Hamburg and Rio. These will earn him the respect of the Quai d'Orsay and of his chief, Philippe Berthelot—a strange, cynical, and tender man who was loyal to his subordinates, a great administrator, and a giant in the breadth of his intelligence and his pride. But there is no contradiction in this Catholic poet being a precise economist. "My desire is to be," said Claudel, "the gathering together of God's earth."

II. THE INSTRUMENT

To be the gathering together of God's earth . . . To sing the praises of God's vast empire . . . This is the theme. But what will the means be? Claudel's instrument will be a new

one, invented by him—an original form of drama and poetry.
However, like everything created by a mortal, this Claudelian drama has ancestors. What did Claudel admire when he began searching for his true vocation? First of all—Rimbaud. But also the greatest of the Ancients, the Bible (in particular the Prophets and the Psalms), Aeschylus (he will translate the *Oresteia*), the Latin of the Church and the Catholic Liturgy, Shakespeare, Dante—and among the most contemporary Catholics, Coventry Patmore.

To the Bible, to the Church, and to Dante he owes the idea of writing poetry. And I wouldn't be surprised if the fact that he was a translator of Greek and English had aroused in him a certain fondness, and even a love, for the twisted, abrupt sentence, for the unexpected adjective, for awkward constructions. Mallarmé, another translator, confesses to the influence that the displacement of words in a foreign text had on his language. One can sometimes see, in Claudel's prose, the ghosts of Aeschylus or Ecclesiastes passing near Rimbaud's.

In the beginning, he wrote traditional poetry:

La rougeur de l'amour et celle de la honte
Couvrent ma face d'où j'ai retiré mes mains.
Je me tiendrai debout, bravant les yeux humains.
Comme un homme marqué de qui nul ne prend compte . . .
L'inexorable amour me tient par les cheveux.
Puisque je suis à toi, découvre-moi ta face!
Puisque tu tiens mes mains, que veux-tu que je fasse?
Toi qui m'as appelé, dis-moi ce que tu veux.

The blush of love and that of shame
Covers my face from which I have taken my hands.
I will hold myself erect, braving human eyes,
Like a marked man no one pays attention to . . .
Inexorable love holds me by the hair.
Since I am yours, uncover your face for me!
Since you hold my hands, what do you want me to do?
You who summoned me, tell me what you want.

Those *Vers d'Exil* are not without beauty, but the clumsy cuts, the painful caesuras on the reader's lips make one imagine a constant struggle between the workman and his tool. Claudel was exasperated by the regularity of classic verse, and even by the regularity, which trys to be irregular, of romantic verse. He is not displeased by Hugo's lyrical flow, but he doesn't understand why Hugo feels obliged to tie it to the rhythm of the Alexandrine or of any other regular poetic form. Claudel thinks that the whole problem for the French poet, classic or romantic, seems to be finding words to fill all the rows of syllables, sound all the notes in the military march of sentences.

Taratata, Taratata, Taratata, is a correct alexandrine—and, in many cases, what Hugo puts in place of *Taratata* is no better, and even worse. (At this point I must tell how, at the end of his life, I saw Mounet Sully—without any memory any more, or even enough hearing to catch the prompter's voice—play Ruy Blas. With admirable dignity, in a superb voice filled with fierce passion, Mounet Sully roared every three or four lines: "Taratata, Taratata, Taratata!" or then, "Tarata, Tarata, Tarata, Tarata!" And it was very beautiful. It was even *as* beautiful. Which is a great and frightening lesson.)

What must the poet do if he is tired of formal poetry? Claudel thinks he should look for inspiration in the music of the French spoken sentence. For example, he says, "Listen to two ladies from the provinces or from Paris talking behind a wall . . . What interplay between those voices! What originality and what tartness in the attacks! What constantly novel uses of the language! What stops! What elegant undulations of the sentences, punctuated in defiance of grammar, ending in a warbler's cry! Ah! There's no longer any need for meter and counting feet! What a relief! How the mind enjoys the ear's deliverance! What will happen? There will be music that is always changing and always unexpected, and the joy of feeling oneself gracefully—one knows not how—carried over all obstacles! Compared to those birds' trills, the alexandrine seems to be something barbaric, something both childish and aged, something monitory and mechanical, invented to despoil the soul's vibrations—those sonorous impulses of the simple psyche—of their most artless accent and of their most delicate flower."

The reader who, in a literary sense, has remained in the age of crinolines and starched linens, frowns at the very name of liberty and I hear him saying: "But that is prose you are describing!" No, that is not prose, dear sir, it has nothing to do with it. Those are verses of which each is distinct, of which each has a different sound and contains within itself all that is necessary to be perfect, in a word it is latent poetry, still raw, but infinitely more true, and sprung from a source infinitely more profound, than all the mechanics of Malherbes. Prose is no more than the sculptural artifice of a thin-blooded man at his writing desk who no longer is conscious of his breathing and of the noises people make in speaking and who, taking advantage of the sleep of a silkworm, draws out of his body a long ribbon of coagulant thread. The apprentice of whom I speak will say to himself—how can I preserve that freedom, that liberty, that vivacity, that sparkle of the spoken language, and at the same time give it that consistency and that interior organization demanded by transcription on paper? How can I open up a path of roses for the Muse? How can I intoxicate her without ever filling her with music which has, at the same time, the fascination of the search and the sweetness of authority? How can I preserve the dream while avoiding sleep? How to sustain one's step at a pace as sensible and unfathomable as the heart? And to get rid of, for once and for all, that abominable metronome whose turnspit beat masks our playing as well as the voice of that old piano teacher who screams unceasingly at our elbow: one —two—three—four—five—six.

What does Claudel propose to the devotee of verbal music who refuses to accept the metronomelike classic cadences? He asks him to note certain facts: a) There exist natural rhythms of language, produced by heartbeats, by breathing —and it is natural that the cut of poetry, instead of being tailored according to prosody's rigid laws, take breathing into account. b) Unlike English and Latin, the French language is not accented and so cannot have the same kind of prosody as those languages. "The French sentence is composed of a number of phonetic parts, with the voice's stress being put on the last syllable." Example: *"Celui qui règne dans les cieux et de qui relèvent tous les empires, à qui senl appartiennent la gloire, la majesté et l'independance, et aussi le seul qui se glorifie de faire la leçon aux rois . . ."* Another example, which Claudel calls "a beautiful line," is borrowed from the Penal Code: *"Sera mis de plus, pendant la durée de sa peine, en état d' internement légal . . ."* c) A line of poetry is not a group of words having a set number of feet, but a group of words forming an entity and separated from the following group by an empty space in thought, as well as on paper. We think in successive leaps and the quantum theory is true for thought. Writing poetry—or the verses of the prophets or the Greek choruses—is to take those successive leaps into account. Writing prose, on the other hand, is to attempt to cement a structure of thought, to fill in the empty spaces and to bind the whole together with a layer of logic. A line of poetry, composed of a line and an empty space, is that twofold action, that respiration by which man absorbs life and gives back intelligible words. All spoken language is made up of raw poetry. The language that Claudel uses, is, he believes, the language of the man in the streets:

The words that I use,
They are the words of everyday, and they are not the
same.

You will not find rhymes in my poetry nor other magic.

They are your very own sentences. There are none of your sentences which I do not know how to make use of again.

Those flowers are your flowers and you say you don't recognize them.

And these feet are your feet, but see how I walk on the sea and how I trample, in triumph, the waters of the sea!

This is the origin of Claudelian verse which, for many readers, is a convention more difficult to accept than formal poetry, because they are less familiar with it, but which, when read aloud, carries along both the voice and breathing marvelously well. It is in such verses that all of Claudel's plays and most of his poems are written.

One day Paul Valéry told me, "Shakespeare is a dramatist who had the extravagant idea of having his characters, in the most pathetic moments, recite whole pages of Montaigne on the stage. That could have shocked, bored. Not at all. The spectators were flabbergasted and delighted." In the same way, it could be said of Claudel that, in certain scenes, he has his characters recite lengthy paraphrases of the Song of Songs or of the Pslams. But it would be a mistake to believe that Claudelian verse was Claudel's only means of communicating his thought. Read *Connaissance de l'Est, l' Introduction à la Peinture Hollandaise,* or *Positions et Propositions,* and you will discover a great prose writer.

III. THE THEMES AND THE WORKS

The first play of Claudel's youth, *Tête d'Or,* is a drama of death. Simon Agnel, a golden-haired Hercules, having lost the woman he loves, joins with an adolescent, Cebes, and with him undertakes the conquest of the world. An ancient empire is on the verge of being destroyed by bar-

barians. Simon Tête d'or takes command of the troops and saves the civilization, but Cebes dies at the moment of victory. As he has lost mistress and friend, Tête d'or becomes pitiless and attempts to dominate the whole world. Soon, Europe is conquered. Tête d'or encounters Asia in the Caucasus. And there again he is victorious. But he pays for victory with his life. On the battlefield, a commander speaks of the triumph of death in the last words of the play:

> Three dead kings! Strange events!
> Traditional laws broken, human weakness overcome, the obstacle of material things scattered! And our efforts, coming to a vain conclusion,
> Unfold themselves like a cloth.

Tête d'Or is a drama of violence, a drama of the Conqueror. Attending a performance of *Tête d'Or*, Marcel Thiébaut states how it suddenly seemed impossible to him that Claudel had not been thinking of Bonaparte. Alexis Leger, with whom he discussed this, told him that Claudel, in his youth, had been obsessed by Bonaparte. When the question, "Who is your favorite fictional hero?" was asked one day, Claudel is said to have replied, "Napoleon Bonaparte." The Conqueror Tête d'or—Bonaparte—Claudel seizes power. Tête d'or has his duc d' Enghien: the old king. There is violence everywhere in Claudel's work. "In my family," he says, "we were violent, quarrelsome." As to his own behavior, he limited his violence to verbal aggressiveness. "He looks like a pile-driver," said Gide. And Henri Mondor: "No one ever questioned his courage in attacking others."

Schematically, *La Ville* is a difficult composition. The forces that constitute a city are represented by four characters: the two brothers Besme, who are the Magistrate and the Engineer—Avare, the Leader—Coeuvre, the Poet. At their side is Lala, the Woman. Avare, while preaching liberty, incites riots. The town is destroyed along with the brothers Besme. It will take fifteen years for the town to rise again from its ruins and for a benevolent hierarchy to be created. At its head will be the son of Coeuvre and Lala, now a Christian.

La Jeune Fille Violaine, later rewritten by Claudel under the title, *L'Annonce Faite à Marie,* is one of the two or three plays by Claudel which has reached and affected the theater-going public. It takes place in a stained-glass-window Middle Ages, in the Fère-en-Tardenois region where Claudel himself was born. The sweet Violaine is one of the two daughters of the old Anne Vecors, master of Combernon. She loves a neighbor, Jacques Hury, who returns her love, but who is also loved by Mara, her dark, wicked sister. Anne Vecors has decided to give Violaine to Jacques Hury, making him the master of Combernon, and to leave on a pilgrimage to the Holy Land. At this juncture, Pierre de Craon, an architect of cathedrals, a poet in stone, passes through Combernon. Alone with Violaine, he confesses to her that he is a leper, and in a moment of spontaneous sacrifice, she kisses him on the corner of the mouth. Mara, who has seen that kiss, denounces Violaine to Jacques Hury. Violaine is now leprous. Mara will possess the land and the man, while Violaine, blind, will live in a leper's hut. One day, Jacques and Mara's child just having died, the terrified mother runs to Violaine's hut, carrying his body. Then the miracle takes place, the miracle which is for the virgin, at the same time, "the sign of sanctity, the gift of motherhood, and the announcement of her approaching death." Mara— jealous to the point of crime—kills the sister who has just given her back her child. However, Mara will be forgiven.

"I am your wife," she said to Jacques Hury, "and you can do nothing to make me not be your wife.

"One flesh, inseparable, the contact through the center of ourselves, and the confirmation, that mysterious kinship between the two of us,

"Which is that I have had a child from you.

"I have committed a great crime, I have killed my

sister, but I have not sinned against you. And I tell you that you have nothing to reproach me with. What do the others matter to me? . . ."

L'Echange was written during Claudel's first stay in America and is a curious cheap lithograph of American-European life. Claudel's himself defines the subject. "The slavery in which I found myself in America was very painful to me, and I portrayed myself with the characteristics of a young male who sells his wife in order to recover his freedom. Out of the perfidious and multiform desire for freedom, I created an American actress—contrasting her with the legitimate wife, in whom I wanted to embody *the passion to serve*. All these roles spring in their entirety from the theme, just as in a symphony, one part is entrusted to the violins, another to the woodwinds. In short I am, myself, all the characters: The actress, the abandoned wife, the young savage, and the scheming businessman"—Louis Laine dies at the moment when he has just sold—to Thomas Pollock Nageoire—his wife Marthe, an honest peasant girl who gives back to Thomas Pollock Nageoire the dollars found in the dead man's pockets.

MARTHE—Take that back, Thomas Pollock, that belongs to you. See if it's all there . . .

THOMAS POLLOCK NAGEOIRE—I'll take back that paper, because it shouldn't be thrown away.

And money is for those who know how to use it.

The day is ended and another has begun.

I'm getting up. Oh, how heavy feel my legs!

Bittersweet, whatever the harm I have done you, forgive me.

What are you going to do now?

MARTHE—I'm going to make my mourning dress, for I'm a widow.

THOMAS POLLOCK NAGEOIRE—Can I help you in any way?

MARTHE—Thomas Pollock, I'm richer than you are . . .

No, I don't know what I'll do.

The present is sufficient, it's enough to live today, and
to do with care what one has to do.
I'll be sewing, working with the material I have on my
knees.

THOMAS POLLOCK NAGEOIRE—Will you give me your hand?
MARTHE—Help me to take him back to the house.

Partage de Midi has its roots in a searing and secret
episode of Claudel's life. During a voyage to the Orient, he
fell in love, with all his somber passion, with a woman who
was married and thus forbidden to a Catholic. He did not
let that stop him, feeling both a mixture of horror and joy.
It took him a long time to get over that storm. Through two
plays he exorcised himself of that memory. In *Partage de
Midi,* the first act takes place in the Indian Ocean, on
board a ship going to China. Mesa, a middle-aged man,
is on board this ship with Ysé, Ciz's wife. "Mesa, it is I,
Ysé . . ." This Tristan and this Isolde have drunk the potion.
But Ciz, "a handsome, slender, soft-eyed son of provence, an
unsuccessful engineer," is far from being a King Mark. And
there is a fourth character who is not in Wagner: Amalric,
the strong man to whom Ysé is attracted, not by love, but by
a need for protection. In China, in Hong-Kong, Mesa and
Ysé meet again. Ciz, as cowardly as is Louis Laine in
L'Echange, abandons his wife at the moment when he feels
her ready to fall into Mesa's arms, "What must happen happens at the appointed time." Sin leads to crime. Mesa, at
Ysé's suggestion, encourages Ciz to take a road which can
only lead to his death. But Amalric returns and effortlessly
takes Ysé away from Mesa because Amalric is strength and
life. In the last act, Amalric, Ysé, and Mesa meet again in a
besieged Chinese town. One pass can allow only one person
to be saved. Naturally, it is Amalric who will use it. Mesa
and Ysé will die together, united at last.

YSÉ—I am yours, Mesa.
MESA—All is consummated, my soul.

L'Otage, though the clearest of the Claudelian dramas, is also one of the most misunderstood. We are in the time of the Empire and of the secret police. The Pope, a prisoner of the Emperor, has just been kidnaped by Georges de Coûfontaine, a hero faithful to tradition, to his Church, and to his King. Coûfontaine has hidden the Pope in the ancestral family seat, where his cousin, Sygne de Coûfontaine, lives alone. Sygne and Georges, devoted to the same cause, love each other and by the feudal exchange of their gloves become engaged to marry. But the Baron Turelure, a prefect of the Empire, a plebeian—the son of Sygne's serving maid and a village sorcerer—a purveyor to the guillotine, the murderer of the monks of Coûfontaine, discovers the Pope's hiding place. He will hand over the Supreme Pontiff unless Sygne consents to become the Baroness Turelure. Sygne is horrified at the idea of deserting Georges de Coûfontaine in order to unite herself to what she most despises in the world. But her confessor makes her realize that saving the father of all men is the highest moral duty. She marries Turelure and has a son by him. But she never accepts the sacrifice with humility, with generosity, with her whole heart, and she dies hating Turelure. For this Claudel condemns her. If Sygne had loved her monstrous husband, she could have purified him, as Clotilde did with Clovis.

L'Otage is the first of a trilogy which also comprises *Le Pain Dur* and *Le Père Humilié.* Those two dramas take the history of the Atrides Coûfontaine-Turelure to the time of Claudel's childhood. The Baron Turelure, having become Count of Coûfontaine, is President of the Council of Ministers under Louis-Philippe. His son, Sygne's son—but more Turelure than Coûfontaine—marries a Jewess, Sichel, by whom he has a daughter, Pensée. And Pensée, half Jewish, will fall in love with the Pope's nephew. In *Le Père Humilié* there is great beauty of detail, but its design is less simple than that of *L'Otage.*

Claudel gave eight years of his life to the Coûfontaine trilogy. The whole period that followed was devoted to the *Soulier de Satin*. "I worked on that book for five years," Claudel said. "It is the summation of all my dramatic and poetic work. In it I unfold the life of a Renaissance conquistador. I consider the Renaissance to be one of Catholicism's most glorious periods—when the Gospel transcends time and space, when the Church, attacked by heretics in a small corner of the world, counters with the Universe, when the humanists rediscover antiquity while Vasco da Gama rediscovers Asia, when Christopher Columbus sees a new world springing up for him from the bosom of the waters, when Copernicus unlocks the Bible of the heavens, when Don Juan of Austria repels Islam, when Protestantism is halted at the White Mountain, and when Michaelangelo raises the dome of St. Peter's. *Le Soulier de Satin* is *Tête d'Or* under another form. At the same time it summarizes *Tête d'Or* and *Partage de Midi*. It is even the closing part of *Partage de Midi*."

And, in fact, *Le Soulier de Satin* is *Partage de Midi* with a Christian denouement. In it "order has been established. The separation of those who love each other is no obstacle to their love." Rodrigue and Prouhèze know that they will never be with each other again in this world . . . But Rodrigue, by living with his agonizing love, finds peace through sacrifice as well as grace. Woman is only a lure offered so that man may accede to perfect love, the love of God. The conflict begun by desire for one body ends in a struggle for "life or eternal death." At that point it would seem useless to the lover that his beloved be restored to him, because it could only be "the same thing likely again to escape him." And yet, in this world, no act ends in nothingness. "When two souls have been united, a trace of that union may remain in eternity."[2]

[2] Marcel Thiébaut

IV. THE PHILOSOPHY

What is the profound meaning of the Claudelian dramas? It is salvation through sacrifice. Violaine becomes a saint capable of performing miracles. Why? Because she has gone to the limits of sacrifice, because she was willing to do the most terrifying and unclean thing—to kiss a leper, because she sacrificed to divine love her earthly love for Jacques Hury. Rodrigue, the conquistador, the hero of *Le Soulier de Satin,* feels free only on the day that he becomes a captive: "The servile tasks are ended! Your tyrant members have been put in chains, and you need only breathe to be filled with God."

It is in that sense that *Le Soulier de Satin* is the true conclusion of *Tête d'Or.* Like Rodrigue, Tête d'or had temporal ambitions, but he did not know how to surmount them. He died without being forgiven, without forgiving himself. It is also in that sense that the philosophy of *Le Soulier de Satin* is the same as that of *Partage de Midi.* Mesa is freed from sin the moment he agrees to sacrifice himself so that his rival Amalric may live.

Thus evil is not an obstacle to salvation. Quite the contrary. "Evil contains its good, which must not be lost." In each one of Claudel's dramas there is a villain whose viciousness becomes an instrument of salvation for the hero. If Mara had not been so evil, Violaine would not have had the means to reach sanctity. If Amalric had not been an adventurer, he would not have accepted Mesa's sacrifice. If the American actress, Léchy Elbernon, did not entice Louis Laine, the latter would not have sold his wife, and Marthe would not have had the opportunity to be so nobly Marthe.

In addition, we must believe that love, and even lust, are steps on the path to perfection because they are the apprenticeship of sacrifice. A human being who loves another with all his heart is prepared to do for the loved one what he will later on do for God.

One cannot hope or wish to eliminate evil from the world. One does not begin the Creation over again. But we must try to overcome base instincts *within ourselves*. How? Through discipline, through constant, fierce and joyful courage, through fixed concentration, through obedience, through acceptance. "Thy will be done and not mine" is perhaps the essence of all wisdom, and on that subject the philosophers are only repeating the word of God. "I have developed the habit," said Descartes, "of triumphing over my desires rather than the order of the world, and of believing that what has not occurred is, in reference to me, absolutely impossible." We all have the duty to be saints. "Be perfect, as your father in Heaven is perfect." *We all have the duty to push ourselves to the limits of sacrifice.*

As with grace and inspiration—the unexpected turnabout, the sudden illumination which lead to sacrifice happen in a flash of lightning. There is "the crucial moment for the saint." Did Violaine know, a second before, that she would give a kiss to Pierre de Craon that was going to determine her whole life? Man's natural impulse is to run when faced with sacrifice, but the Law pursues them to the darkest hiding places.

I fled in vain; everywhere I found again the Law.
One must yield at last! O door, the host must
be admitted; O quivering heart, the master must be accepted,
Someone who is in me more myself than I am.

But sacrifice, in order to be salutary, must be accepted, wanted, loved. Sygne de Coûfontaine, although she had agreed to marry Turelure to save the Pope, remains dissatisfied with herself and dies sadly. This is because she consented to the act, but not to the total gift of her love. "After all," wrote Claudel, "if Sygne did not accept her sacrifice, it is because her destiny was fulfilled. If she had

had more generosity and more strength, she could have created a new race. Essentially, it is Turelure who is right." The old order finished, and without hope of recourse, Sygne's duty was to bring to the new regime all that could be saved from the old. She could only do it by bringing herself, that is to say, by forgetting herself. In her, pride conquered faith.

Pride cannot give joy. Power only finds peace and joy in its own defeat. Joy is the reward of those who have accepted the real world and have surrendered into God's hands. The decision is always painful. "I know it—it is a moment of terrible anguish, but it must be. It is the question which is the theme of one of the last of Beethoven's quartets: *Muss es sein?* And that great soul answers on alternate notes: *Es muss sein! Es muss sein!*"

FRANÇOIS MAURIAC

FRANÇOISE MAURIAC is a great French prose writer who has a leading place in the line of Chateaubriand-Barrès. He is also a Christian moralist who has endeavored to live his faith. We will not separate the history of the man from that of the writer. The man, strongly influenced by his provincial bourgeois ancestors, little by little freed himself of their prejudices; the writer has plunged deeply into men's souls and has found there, under thick layers of filth, pure and flowing springs. "A man of letters," wrote Mauriac, "is like a plot of ground were excavations have been undertaken; he is always, literally, overturned and in the open." In the gaping trench which constitutes his work, we shall study the superimposed layers brought to light.

I. CHILDHOOD AND YOUTH

Born in Bordeaux, raised in Bordeaux, returning each autumn to Malaga, the vineyard-encircled family home in the vicinity of Bordeaux, François Mauriac has many of the traits of a Gironde bourgeois—and he is proud of them. He thinks, with some justification, that in order to know his country well a French novelist must remain a provincial in his ties. "France and Voltaire, the Parisians of Paris, do not deal directly with man. Paris removes all individuality from passion; there, daily, Phèdre seduces Hippolyte and even

Thésée doesn't care. The provinces let adultery retain its fictional quality. Paris destroys the types of people the provinces accentuate . . ." Balzac knew it well, and, while living in Paris, would go each year to the provinces to refresh his understanding of the passions.

But, unlike Balzac, who would go from Argentan to Saumur and from Angoulême to Le Havre, Mauriac is a man of only one region. All his novels are located in the Southwest of France, around Bordeaux. "My destiny was contained," he wrote, "in that city and its surrounding country." In the country even more than in the city, for the two families from which he sprang did not belong to that proud and closed business aristocracy which, in Bordeaux, controls the seaborne commerce and the wine trade—"that race of merchants and shipowners whose mansions and renowned warehouses are the pride of the *Pavé des Chartrons*" —an arrogant race whose *Sons*, ever since the Black Prince, have retained their English features and speech. These *Sons*, with their Anglo-Saxon first names and their naïve sense of protocol, will be one of the targets Mauriac will spear with sharp shafts in his first books. But he has only the tenderest feelings for the beautiful stone city which, more than any other, evokes classic France: "The houses, the streets of Bordeaux are the events of my life. When the train slows down on the Garonne bridge, and in the dawn I catch sight of that enormous body which stretches itself out and embraces the curve of the river, I search for a belltower, for a church—signposts of a joy, of a sorrow, of a sin, of a dream."

Most of Mauriac's ancestors, on both sides, belonged to that rural bourgeoisie who at the end of the nineteenth century, denied their wealth by cultivating the vineyards in the Gironde Valley and by exploiting the pine forests in the Landes—that is to say, wine, mine timbers, and resin. As an industrialist from Rouen or Mulhouse was rated according to the number of his enterprises, so a bourgeois from les Landes was ranked according to the number of his pine trees. Strange people those landowners of the southwest. Mauriac's work portrays them without indulgence; what is important is not to condemn them but to understand them. Their vineyards and their forests were the flesh of their flesh. They had to protect their lands against division by inheritance, against taxes, against fires and storms. This was the duty bequeathed by centuries of patient peasantry. A narrow duty, often contrary to generosity, to charity; but if thirty generations had not respected that code, the French soil would not be what it is. All his life, Mauriac, squire of Malaga, will watch the storms circle around the crops, in the vast Gironde Valley, like beasts surrounding a tender prey, and he will anxiously look for the fragrant smoke rising from burnt pines.

He was twenty months old when he lost his father and had no recollection of him. The four children were brought up by the young widow, a very pious Catholic. Religion, closely tied to politics, was a constant source of discord for the bourgeois of the southwest. Anticlerical and devout families would defiantly face each other, and sometimes both tendencies were represented in the same clan. For François Mauriac and his brothers, when they knelt at night around their mother's skirts, there was no room for doubt. In unison they recited a beautiful prayer which began with these words: "Prostrate before you, oh my God, I offer thanks that you have given me a heart capable of understanding you and loving you," and whose last sentence was: "Not knowing whether or not death may take me by surprise this night, I commend my soul to you, oh my God. Do not judge it out of your anger . . ." Whenever the little François thought of this prayer, he would always hear: "Not knowing whether or not death may take me by surprise— ah!—this night . . ." It was his first sigh as an artist. What a remarkable brood they were—those four sons watched over by that strong and solicitous mother! The eldest, a lawyer, would one day write a novel under the pseudonym Raymond Houssilane; the second was destined to become a priest, chaplain of the Bordeaux Lycée; the third, Pierre, a famous physician in his region; the youngest François, one of the great French writers of his time.

The youngest of the family was a sad and overly sensitive child. "I looked," he said, "pitiful and puny." Has he, in his recollections, exaggerated that sadness? Perhaps. But he certainly didn't invent it. When he went to school, first at the Sisters of the Holy Family, then at the Marists, he had a feeling of frailty and of fear. "The terror of lessons not learned, of assignments not completed, of being hit in the face while playing ball . . ." He needed, like Charles Dickens, major successes to reassure him about himself. As a child, he found peace and happiness only beside his mother. The smell of gas and of the linoleum of the family stairway evoked security—sweet pleasures of reading, love, warmth, peace.

"François devours books. We don't know what to give him anymore . . ." At night, when the family sat down around the heater, he read the Bibliothèque Rose, Jules Verne, but also *The Imitation of Christ,* whose "flaming words would brand a heart for life," and a great deal of poetry. The poets he was allowed to read were not the best. In his anthology, Sully Prudhomme, Alexandre Soumet, even Casimir Delavigne, supplemented Lamartine, but a child born to be a poet can extract a measure of poetry from everything. Even more than to the poetry of poems, François responded to the poetry of nature, to the poetry of the vineyard—enchained martyr delivered up to the monstrous sleet storms in the great circus of the sky, to the poetry of the ancestral houses, "where the tide of each generation has left its shells, scrapbooks, small chests, daguerreotypes, Carcel lamps," to the poetry of children's childish voices singing in unison in the night, beneath the pines. From the moment he read the legend of Atys, the beautiful young man beloved by Cybele

and transformed by Zeus into an evergreen tree, he saw
flowing locks in the leaves stirred by the wind, and in the
sound of the pines he heard whisperings which slowly became a poem:

> My artless child's heart already had a sense of you,
> O unknown music, love, sweetness of life . . .

This phase of paganism could not be lasting in an adolescent so profoundly influenced by a Christian education
and whose Sundays, at the Marists, were divided this way:

> 7 o'clock: Communion Mass
> 9 o'clock: Solemn Mass
> 10:30   :   Catechism
> 1:30   :   Vespers and Benediction.

The beauty of the liturgy enchanted him, but if his
teachers initiated him into the practices of a cult, they did
not teach him its doctrines. Later he would reproach them:
"I apologize to the Marists who raised me, but I must
affirm that at our school, around 1905, religious instruction
was almost nonexistent . . . I must affirm that in their
school not one of my classmates could have identified, even
roughly, the kind of objections a Catholic would have to
answer. To compensate, my teachers excelled in surrounding
us with a celestial atmosphere which bathed all the hours of
the day. They didn't form Catholic minds, but rather Catholic sensibilities . . ."

It must be noted that, since adolescence, Mauriac revealed,
along with a solidly grounded faith, some irritation with what
appeared to him to be, in certain devout people, less a
religious emotion than an instrument for domination. Later,
as a novelist, he will portray saints and noble priests with
respectful affection, but he will harshly mock the unction of
easygoing priests. All his heroes have a horror of Tartuffe,
"of that strange, suspect kindness prowling about, still sug-
gestive of the Inquisition. . . . The divine hunter's helpers
are not always skillful and they often frighten the very game

they are charged to drive toward the Master . . ." But those negative gestures, that anger, are superficial; in Mauriac, the central core, the bedrock, is Catholic: "The more I shook the bars, the more I felt them unshakable."

He continued his studies first at the lycée, then at the University of Bordeaux, where he obtained a *licence ès lettres*. There he read Baudelaire, Rimbaud, Verlaine, combining these new enthusiasms with those he already felt for Racine, Pascal, Maurice de Guérin, and discovering that the proscribed poets were not very different from the approved poets. Now it was necessary for him, in order to become the chronicler of Bordeaux to escape from Bordeaux. He left for Paris, "a town of individuals, where each man can act without any fear."

Once there, he half-heartedly attended l'Ecole des Chartes, but writing was his true vocation, his only desire, and his gifts were so evident that his success was never in doubt. This young provincial immediately conquered Paris. The sickly child had become a young man of rare and striking beauty, with the head of a Spanish Grandee transfigured by El Greco. He had wit, humor, and a certain satirical malice which Paris far from condemned. His first poems were circulating among his admiring companions. In 1909 he published a small collection of poems: *Les Mains Jointes*. "I entered the literary world like a Cherubim from a sacristy, playing on his little organ."

There was only one writer, among those of his elders whom he admired, to whom he did not dare send his book— Maurice Barrès, and that was because he loved him more than all the others. But Paul Bourget had Barrès read Mauriac's poems, and soon Mauriac would see, in a Barrès' article: "For twenty days, I have been enjoying the charming music of this unknown about whom I know nothing, who softly sings of the memories of his childhood, the whole easy life—protected, puritanical, dreamy—of a Catholic child . . . It is the poem of children from happy families, the poem of the good little boys, delicate, well brought up, whose light has not been obscured by anything, but who have too much sensitivity, and a crazy touch of sensuousness . . ." To Mauriac himself, Barrès wrote: "Be at peace; be confident that your future will be easy, open, assured, glorious; be a happy child."

II. HELL

No, he was not a happy child, the thin-faced, triumphant young man whose first novels: *L'Enfant Chargé de Chaînes, La Robe Prétexte, La Chair et le Sang, Genitrix, Le Baiser au Lépreux,* were conquering, with miraculous ease, the most demanding public. He was a man divided against himself, and the picture he painted of the devout, well-to-do peasant bourgeoisie from whom he came, was a black and tormented canvas. The "Cherubim from a sacristy" did not sing for long of his childhood dreams in a lyrical and tender manner. What he now played, on already powerful instruments, was the funeral march of the social group to which he was bound by ties of the flesh and of the soil.

That group was also burdened with chains, of which the heaviest was money. Because these men and women were descended from peasants, because their ancestors had for centuries coveted and ransacked that soil, their vineyards and their pine forests were more precious to them than their salvation. "Cybele has more worshipers than Christ," Mauriac wrote harshly. He portrayed the sinister maneuvers of unfeeling monsters who, in order to save an estate, forgot all pity, all shame. One of his heroines, Léonie Costadot (*Les Chemins de la Mer*), on learning that the notary, Revolou, has been ruined, dishonored, driven to suicide, goes unhesitatingly, in the middle of the night, to wrest from the unhappy Lucienne Revolou, her best friend, a signature which will protect at least a part of the Costadot children's fortune. Marriage, in these families, is not the union of two human beings, but the addition of one number to another, the reuniting of two parcels of land. Bernard Desqueyroux does not marry Thérèse; some pine trees are united to other pine trees. A poor and beautiful girl, coveted by a hideous and crippled bachelor who is, however, the owner of large estates, does not even conceive of the possibility of refusing herself, and she grants the leper the kiss from which she is going to die.

Within the family itself, money eats away at all innocence. Because they are lying in wait for an inheritance, children take note of the wrinkles, the fainting spells, the labored breathing, while their father, aware of this spying, tries to disinherit the worthless children through painstaking and ingenious proceedings. The noblest natures end by yielding to that contagion of greed and hatred. Those who at first think themselves immune soon reveal that small mark of rot which is going to spread. Thérèse Desqueyroux had dreamed of another life. In spite of herself she becomes passionately interested in the exploitation of her properties; she likes to stay with the men, intrigued by their talk about share-croppers, mine timbers, resin, turpentine. Although his fiancée is financially ruined, Robert Costadot half-heartedly wants, at first, to remain true to his vows. But his mother, a bourgeois Catherine de'Medici, upholds dynastic marriages. "It is a question of morality which prevails over everything; we are protecting the patrimony." And the instinct for conservation, the fear of taking risks, prevail over love.

That cult of Mammon has its voluntary martyrs. A matron, victim of cancer, elects to die more quickly, in order to spare her family the expenses of an operation. Feelings beat a retreat in the face of interests. An old landowner, at the bedside of his dying son, thinks: "If only my daughter-in-law won't remarry!" Kneeling beside his wife, at his father-in-law's death bed, a man leans over and, between two prayers, whispers to her, "Is the farm community property, and is your brother of age?" By instinct, by heredity, Mauriac's Gallo-Romans are litigious, clinging to their rights, and fiercely jealous of their possessions. The young people, who believe they can escape that atavistic madness, are, in turn, afflicted by it against their will: "Their dirty money! I hate money because it holds us. There is no way out. I've thought it all out: we will not escape the power of money; we live in a world whose reality is money!"

With money, another idol is raised up within these ravaged hearts: Social Position. A bourgeois family must "maintain its Position." Of what does this Position consist? It seems mysterious to an outsider, but the initiated are not confused about it. A man, so completely ruined that he is dying of hunger, has his dead sister brought, at great expense, to the family vault—because burial is part of Position. Maintaining Position requires that poor relatives be helped, "on condition that they don't have the audacity to keep a servant or have a drawing room." Family life "consists of the surveillance of each member by all the others." In the provinces, a family which upholds its Position with dignity must have a "guest room," and a fading daughter renounces a marriage which would have been her salvation because the newly-weds, lacking money, would have had to occupy the guest room—which would have been a disgrace. How many human sacrifices are made on the altars of Money and Position! Religion itself, for many rich bourgeois, is no more than one of the elements of Position, and is shamelessly mixed up with money. "Wild-eyed," says Mauriac of an old woman, "she was thinking of agony, of death, of God's judgment, of the division of properties . . ." An enumeration whose terms are arranged in order of increasing power.

What do these sad fanatics live for, beside Money and Position? Passionate love is rare among them, but they are human, and the demands of the Flesh torment them. Old bachelors, heirs to vineyards and pine forests, buy themselves young and fresh brides, or hide a mistress in a secret apartment in Bordeaux or Angoulême, whom they keep in a miserly fashion and treat with scornful harshness. Adolescents themselves are torn between the temptations of the Flesh and the terrors of Sin. They enter life with an ideal of Purity, but are incapable of remaining faithful to it: "Must the sweetness of loving, caresses, banquets of the flesh, be sacrificed to an ancient metaphysics, to hypotheses?" And are those who succumb to temptation happier? Mauriac, with the harshness of the Christian moralist, turns the raw light of his insight on two emancipated people he found in one of Lawrence's novels: "How sad they are! . . . They roll about, right on the ground, among poultry droppings . . . Why avert your eyes? Look at them, my soul: in the game-keeper's side, in the woman's side, the old original wound is bleeding."

All sensuality is deceiving. Women vainly search in it for some mysterious unity. "We use the only possible route," says Maria Cross, "but one which has not been cleared in the direction of what we are looking for . . . Always between those I have wanted to possess and myself, there was that rank countryside, that swamp, that mud . . . They did not understand . . . They believed that I had summoned them so that we could sink together . . ." And Thérèse Desqueyroux, speaking of her husband: "He was enclosed within his pleasure like those charming young pigs who are so amusing to watch through the fence, happily swilling at their trough . . . I was the trough," thinks Thérèse.

Possession is impossible for the sensualists: "They only find this wall, this closed breast, this sealed world around which we, as wretched satellites, revolve." And the sensual Christian is more disappointed than all the others, being torn as he is between concupiscence and the desire for grace. "I am not hurting anyone," the Flesh says. "Why should pleasure be Evil? . . . It *is* Evil, as you well know. Take a seat in a sidewalk cafe; watch the passing stream of faces. Oh shame-

ful faces! . . ." Virgins themselves vaguely feel that everything that has to do with the Flesh is bad. "We are not
doing anything evil," says the sweet Emmanuelle of *Asmodée,*
"or then is that the Evil?" And one fears to hear *Asmodée,*
from the depths of the garden, answering her in the mur-
muring of the pines: "Yes, it is the Evil."

But, as an escape from the dreadful solitude and the curse
of lust, don't legitimate affections exist: family, friends? "I
appreciate that fact, but those affections are not love, and
as soon as they resemble love, they become more criminal
than any other: incest, sodomy." The most monstrous temptations rear their ugly heads in all the families portrayed by
Mauriac. Brothers and sisters lie in wait for each other,
sniff about each other. Husbands and wives chained together, exasperated and hostile, slash at each other's souls.
"In the end, no one interests anyone; each one thinks only
of himself." And when a father, a mother, try to cross that
barrier of silence, reserve and habit paralyze them. They
return from that walk, on which they intended to tell all, to
talk of their son about whom they are worried, without having said anything. Read over this wonderful scene from *Le
Désert de l'Amour!*

> At that moment Madame Courrèges was dumbfounded
> because her husband had asked her to take a walk in
> the garden. She said she was going to fetch a shawl.
> He heard her go up the stairs, then come down with a
> haste unusual for her.
> —Take my arm, Lucie, the moon is hidden and one can
> hardly see . . .
> —But the alley is white.
> As she was leaning a little against him, he became aware
> that Lucie's flesh had the same odor as in the past, when
> they were engaged and they would, those long nights in
> June, remain seated on a bench . . . This odor of flesh
> and of shadow was the very perfume of his engagement.
> He asked her if she had not noticed a great change

in their son. No, she found him always as sullen, peevish
and stubborn. He insisted: Raymond was less careless; he
had more self control—even if it was no more than the
new care he took of his own appearance.

—Ah! yes, let's talk about that; Julie was grumbling
yesterday because he demands that she iron his pants
twice a week!

—Try to realize that Julie, who saw Raymond being
born . . .

—Julie is devoted, but devotion has its limits. Whatever
Madeleine says, her servants don't do anything. Granted
that Julie has a nasty disposition, but I can appreciate
that she's furious because she is obliged to clean the servants' stairs, as well as part of the main staircase.

A miserly nightingale sang but three notes. They were
surrounded by the bitter almond perfume of the hawthorn.
The doctor began to speak again softly:

—Our little Raymond . . .

—We'll never be able to replace Julie, this is what we
must remember.

—You'll tell me that she's the cause of all the cooks
leaving; but very often she's the one who's right . . .
For instance, Léonie . . .

He asked resignedly:

—Which Léonie?

—You know very well, the fat one . . . No, not the last
. . . the one who only stayed three months; she did not
want to clean the dining room. And yet that wasn't
Julie's work . . .

He said:

—Servants today are not like those in the past. He felt
a tide sweeping through him—an ebbing which carried
away with it confidences, confessions, freedom, tears.

—We'd better go in.

—Madeleine keeps telling me that the cook is always making a long face, but it isn't because of Julie. That girl
wants a raise; they don't have as many advantages here
as in the city, although we have a very large food budget,

which brings them commissions; without that, they
wouldn't stay.

—I'm going in.

—Already?

She felt that she had disappointed him, that she should
have waited, let him speak; she murmured:

—We don't talk so often—

Beyond the wretched words that she accumulated in
spite of herself, beyond this wall which her patient vulgarity had built day by day, Lucie Courrèges was hearing
the stifled call of one who has been buried alive; yes,
she was conscious of that cry of the buried miner and,
deeply within herself, a voice was answering that voice,
and a tenderness was stirring.

She started to lean her head on her husband's shoulder,
sensed the recoiling of his body, his closed face; raised
her eyes towards the house, and could not refrain from
saying:

—You left the lights burning again in your room. And
immediately regretted the word.

Those two could not, that night, cross the desert of love.

III. FALSE SALVATION

Some of Mauriac's readers reproach him for that pessimistic view of the world. He reproaches them those reproaches: "Those who profess to believe in the original fall
and in the corruption of the body, cannot tolerate the works
that bear testimony to it." Others criticize the writers who
combine religion with sensual conflicts. "Those writers," answered Mauriac, "do not try to spice their stories with a dash
of cloudy mysticism, nor to use heavenly things as condiments.
But how can one portray the movements of the heart without
speaking of God?" Isn't that "hunger for the absolute" that
some of his heroes showed when in love, of Christian origin,
as are their scruples? In order to ignore the Flesh, and to

write novels in which nature's corruption wouldn't appear, the writer would have to learn to turn his attention away from each thought, from each look, and cease trying to discover in them embryonic desire, potential impurity. One would have to stop being a novelist.

How could a novelist, or a painter, if he is sincere, change a style which is only the exterior form, the projection of his temperament? No one reproaches Manet to have painted Manets, El Greco to have painted Grecos. "Don't speak to me of nature," said Corot, "I only see Corots . . ." And Mauriac: "As soon as I start working, everything takes on the coloring of my eternal colors . . . My characters enter into a sulfurous light which is proper to me, which I do not defend, but which is singularly mine." Every human being, under François Mauriac's pen, becomes a Mauriac character . . . "A certain type of literature of edification," says Mauriac; "falsifies life. Here the set purpose to do good runs counter to the goal which is sought." And another great Catholic critic, Charles du Bos: "Human life is the material with which and on which the novelist works and must work . . . Living matter in which swarm impure elements . . . And the first task of any novelist is to reconstitute this living matter, this impurity of elements, this human weight as they are in their truth."

But is it truth that Mauriac paints? Are we Mauriac's characters? Are we the brothers of those monsters? An essential part of Mauriac's art consists in showing us that the elements present in those monsters are present in each one of us. Crime doesn't exist outside of humanity. Crime is universal, daily, banal. "Our first impulse is to kill," said Alain. Monsters are also men and women. Thérèse Desqueyroux is a poisoner, yes, but she never said to herself: "I want to be a poisoner." The monstrous deed grew slowly within her, out of her boredom, her disgust. Mauriac prefers Thérèse to her victim, to Bernard Desqueyroux, the husband. "She may die of shame, of anguish, of remorse, of lassitude, but she will not die of boredom . . ." When a real poisoner, Violette Nozière, is arrested for having killed her father, Mauriac writes an article about her in which he tries to be charitable, fair toward the accused. She doesn't surprise him and he is surprised that this should be surprising.

All of us, readers living quietly, protest in all good faith, "I have no crime on my conscience." Are we really sure of that? We haven't killed with a firearm, we haven't throttled a gasping throat. But have we never pitilessly put out of our lives people whose lives might hang on a word from us? Have we never refused the help which could have been the salvation for one—or for several—people? Have we not written words, books which were sentences of death? When the Socialist minister Salengro, following a newspaper campaign, committed suicide, Mauriac, as a great novelist, exposed in an article in the *Figaro* the human drama which lay beneath that political drama. He showed the unhappy minister, alone in his kitchen in Lille, deciding to die in the exact place where his beloved wife had died the preceding year. Did the man who had engineered the campaign, and who was responsible for that death, think of himself as an assassin? Undoubtedly not, because he wasn't clear-thinking enough to measure his responsibilities, but in the eyes of God, was he less guilty than others who pay for their crimes on the scaffold? And how many crimes in the affective life! "How could loved ones escape their role of tormentors?" Every human being who, consciously or unconsciously, incites a passion which he doesn't feel becomes, willingly or not, an instrument of torture.

Couples who travel through the deserts of love, do not cease, in their frenzy, to tear each other apart. The man of letters who, in his dangerous obsession, considers that he has no obligations and that everything is owed him, is a man as dangerous as the outlaw. He considers himself above ordinary morality. "That elite feeds on everything, except on daily bread." He doesn't hesitate, if his work demands it, to torture those around him to force from them the cries he needs for his bizarre harmonies. Why should that vivisection be innocent? The truth is that every soul possesses, in relation to any other, a frightening capacity for harm. Love of neighbor is in us forever numbed by the poison of desire. Who are we, then, to judge others? Being bad ourselves, the only feelings we have the right to have in the face of Evil are humility and pity.

"And yet," protests the Optimist who could also be called the Angelist, "and yet, there are good people, there are pious people." There are, answers Mauriac with his lucid incisiveness, people who believe themselves good, who believe themselves pious, but if they believe it too easily, it is possible that they are mistaken about themselves and that they are the blackest of all. Mauriac, in all his work, pitilessly pursues the false devout. We find him in his theater, and it is Monsieur Couture, disruptive member of a religious third order, who prowls around women and masks his lascivious advances behind religious exhortations. We find him again in *La Pharisienne:* Brigitte Pian. That proud Christian woman believes she is a great soul. She weaves around her a cloth of perfections. Incapable of love, she follows the course of other people's loves with unrelenting rancor. "Thus that frigid soul glories in her frigidity, without reflecting that at no time, even at the beginnings of her search for the perfect life, had she felt anything which resembled love, had she ever addressed the Master except to ask him to bear witness to her singular merits."

La Pharisienne herself tries not to see the feelings of hate and cruelty that appear in her heart. Others don't fail to see them: "An astonishing woman," says a priest, "A miracle of distortion . . . A profound nature, but one in which— like a fish pond where the eye follows all the movements of the fish—the most secret motives of Madame Brigitte's actions are apparent to the naked eye." But, as we all do, she finds the means to reassure herself and to interpret her worst passions in an angelic light. Sometimes, it is not easy: "What troubled her was the fact that she could not hide the joy she felt at that sorrow, a joy which ought to bring her shame and consternation . . . She had to find a reason which would explain her pleasure, and to make it fit into her system of perfection . . ." Alas! she found it as *we* find it when it is imperative to save from destruction the angelic image of ourselves which we carry so preciously in front of us.

It is the same with Landon, the filthy and mysterious Landon of *Les Chemins de la Mer*: "As with all his other passions, the hate he felt took on the aspect of duty; his penchant for virtue forced him to that disguise. All the horrible signs which could have put him on guard against himself, were seen only by others: in his shifty look, in his walk, in his voice. But within he was bathed in virtuous sentiments which deceived him . . ." In many ways, in this instance, the perception of the Catholic moralist recalls that of the psychoanalyst. Each know how to translate into real feelings the gestures and words that are only their exterior signs. "None of our abysses escapes me: A clear self-knowledge plays into the hands of Catholicism . . . Ah! poet, you are God's quarry."

At the beginning of his career, Mauriac felt obliged, at the end of a novel, to bring back to God, through a fairly obvious device, those kept away from him by concupiscence or avarice. "All those nice people have been sent to Paradise," said a critic. Later, Mauriac lost his tolerance for that *false salvation*, a formality devoid of real penance, devoid of that profound change in the soul which alone would be the sign of Grace. He is less critical of the extreme decadence of a young rake than of those who are "the caricature of what is most sacred in the world." The atheist himself sometimes seems to him less remote from God than his devout spouse whose every word, every action denies Christ: "There isn't one of the Beatitudes of which you haven't preached the opposite," writes the hero of *Le Nœud de Vipères* to his wife.

The more Mauriac advances in the mastery of his soul and in the knowledge of men, the more he hardens himself against false virtue. He judges himself, and his worldly success, with as much relentless clarity as he judges others. He writes, at the time of his triumphs: "Let us have the courage to recognize that success is the measure of true ambition; the one that is clever enough not to acknowledge itself. Those indiscretions, that openness of heart, that foolhardy abandon, those professions of faith, that taste for dangerous subjects—isn't all that apparent folly the characteristic of a man who, knowing the ephemeral quality of elaborate designs which reality always frustrates, trusts an instinct within himself—that instinct of mules in the mountains, who peacefully plod along on the very edge of the abyss?"

Here the instinct for conservation is continued and flowers into an instinct for advancement, and manifests itself by reflexes of an astonishing sureness. Furthermore, it is not incompatible with a kind of detachment, once the goal is attained. Reaching for everything, not in order to enjoy it, but in order not to have to think about it, this is the method used by certain Christians who want to cure themselves of ambition; they believe they are not ambitious because they only consider the high places they have obtained as no more than a dismissed preoccupation. To reach honors naturally, without intrigue, in such a way that no pretext any longer diverts us from the only necessity. No saint, to our knowledge, has followed this route to reach God. But perhaps a Bossuet, a Fénelon, or even a Lacordaire?

Thus, Bossuet, Fénelon themselves . . . But yes, certainly, they were men and marked by original sin. In each of us, bishop, merchant, poet, one finds "a ferocious beast and a pathetic heart." In each one of us . . . And, for a long time, Mauriac was content to show us, without judging them, those human beings who struggle between a confused desire for purity and the powerful assaults of temptations. He said to himself, "It is impossible to portray the modern world as it is without showing a holy law violated." It seemed to him that this ignominy of souls, deprived of grace in an atheistic world, was the best of apologies for Christianity. Then, toward the middle of his life, a ray of sunshine pierced the tenebrae of his work.

IV. NEL MEZZO DEL CAMIN

"Rarely does the shape of our interior universe reveal itself to us in our youth, and it is the joy of middle age to see emerging the finally completed person—a world of which each one of us is the creator, or, more precisely, the organizer. Undoubtedly, it will come about that this achieved world will be further modified. Storms and tidal waves sometimes alter its appearance. Human passions, divine grace intervene; devastating fires, fructifying ashes. But after the cataclysms, the mountain tops reappear, the same valleys are filled with shadows, and the seas no longer sweep across their boundaries."

Mauriac has always loved this image: "the ebb and flow around a central rock—which at the same time expresses the unity of the human character, its changes, its repetitions and its eddies." In his mind, the central rock remains "the Catholic sensibility," and though his faith stayed intact, he had also formed the easy and rather pleasant (in spite of its apparent bitterness) habit of intermittent compromises between the Flesh and the Spirit. Their conflict nourished his work. If the Christian had wished to end it with a victory of the Spirit, the novelist and the poet would undoubtedly have whispered sophisms in his ear. And so, as a pious aesthete, the writer accepted to live under an armed truce, but he was not satisfied with himself: "Without doubt," he wrote, "there is no worse attitude than that of the man who partially renounces . . . Lost to God, lost to the world." The great upheaval of his interior universe occurred in the most unexpected manner. In 1928, André Billy, who was editing a series of "sequels to famous works" for a Paris publishing house, asked François Mauriac to write a sequel to the *Traité de la Concupiscence* by Bossuet. From this came a short but intense little book: *Souffrances du Chrétien,* which Mauriac later entitled: *Souffrances du Pécheur,* in which he dealt with "a rather base demand, the demands of the Flesh." Base? I don't know, but certainly pathetic. This text contains great beauty and the theme is Christianity's terrible harshness toward the Flesh. Christianity does not grant the Flesh its role, it abolishes it. In Tunisia, Mauriac had observed Islam, "a practicable religion, which doesn't ask for the impossible, which doesn't turn away the poor cattle from its drinking troughs nor from its manure which keeps them warm. No more of those Christian requirements . . ."

And yet, he had also seen that the people of Islam were tormented by their base instincts. Where is truth? "Prove to me that all those dreams are in vain," says the Flesh to the Spirit, "so that I may fornicate in my corner without fear of offending anyone . . ." And can't the sufferings of sensual love be redemptive? "After his passion is spent, after having passed through furnace and fire, his feet burned by cinders, dying of thirst," perhaps the carnal man will end by reaching God. Alas! In order for that to happen it would be necessary for him to sincerely desire to terminate his suffering, but isn't that suffering his life? "Concupiscence, out of which a battered humanity is formed, can only be vanquished by a more powerful joy, what Jansenism called the interior joy of Grace . . . How can concupiscence be cured? It is not limited to a few acts: it is a general cancer; infection is everywhere. And that's why there exists no greater miracle than conversion."

And it is exactly this miracle which then takes place in Mauriac's mind. *Souffrances du Chrétien,* welcomed by critics as a masterpiece of style and vigor, had seriously disturbed Maruiac's Catholic friends. In it there was a self-indulgent despair, a sensuality combined with religious feeling, which to them seemed dangerous. Under the influence of Charles du Bos, and later of the Abbé Alterman, Mauriac entered into a period of retreat and meditation. He came out of it "shattered." Soon he will answer himself and publish *Bonheur du Chrétien*. In it he will condemn the "pitiful anguish," the "latent Jansenism," of a man divided against himself who has chosen to live in that condition. To the lugubrious monotony of concupiscence, he will oppose the joys of entering into Grace. To human love, which wears out and is altered by presence, the eternal and renewing force of divine love.

Until that day, Mauriac had hardly been a solitary man. In Paris he had been largely unable to resist the attraction of friendships, meetings, confidences. Now, at Malaga, in the old house, which was closed except for one room, he welcomed a thoughtful solitude. "I had lost," he said, "I was saved." How pleasant it is not to fight, but to accept. Of course, he continues to recognize the difficulties of Christian life. "The Christian sails against the current; he goes upstream, on river of fire: concupiscence of the flesh, pride of life." But Mauriac knows now that the fight can be won, that the Christian can find peace of mind, and even joy. And it is then that he changes the title of *Souffrances du Chrétien* to *Souffrances du Pécheur*.

Another event completed the miracle of what must be called a conversion, although it was rather a return. In middle age, a terrible illness that was believed to be (and, fortunately, was not) cancer of the throat, put Mauriac at death's door. For several months his friends, his family thought him lost, and he—he who had so greatly doubted love—saw himself surrounded by so much love that he could no longer doubt. "More than one critic and reader have criticized in me—as if it were a crime—that pessimism which made me portray such black characters. And during my illness, I criticized myself for it, seeing myself surrounded with such good and devoted people. I admired my physician. I thought of those who had loved me since I came into the world. And I no longer understood how I could have depicted a humanity so cruel. From those moments was born the desire to write the book I am now working on."

That book, *Le Mystère Frontenac*, is indeed the most tender, the freest, the freshest of Mauriac's novels. It pictures the glowing and gentle side of family life, it pictures a brood of brothers and sisters huddled in the shelter of a mother who defends her young with self-denial and nobility. In it one can believe one recognizes Mauriac himself, as the adolescent poet, and his brother Pierre as the admiring and affectionate first-born. The dawn of glory illumines young foreheads; the undergrowth is lighted; the wind rises. "Into the hideous order of the world, love brings its delightful happiness."

Love? Can it ever be pure? And can we be saved from the corruption of our nature? Yes, answer Mauriac's last books, if we begin by being aware of that corruption, if we honestly recognize all our weakness as carnal people. "God loves us when we know ourselves in our cruelty. His anger against the Pharisees is evidence that he rejects us when we refuse to see ourselves as we are . . ." "The saints understand their misery, despising themselves because they see themselves, and that's why they are saints . . ." As an epigraph in one of his books, Mauriac quotes Saint Theresa: "God, realize that we don't understand ourselves, and that we don't know what we want, and that we infinitely remove ourselves from what we desire . . ." And Verlaine:

> *Vous connaissez tout cela, tout cela,*
> *Et que je suis plus pauvre que personne,*
> *Mais ce que j'ai, mon Dieu, je vous le donne.*

> You understand all that, all that,
> And that I am poorer than anyone,
> But what I have, my God, I give it to you.

Mauriac does not disown all those monsters he portrayed, all those black angels, and he continues to create them. "It is enough to purify the springs, I said . . . That was forgetting the fact that the purified spring would still have in its bottom the original mud into which the secret roots of my work are sunk. Even when in the state of Grace, my creatures come out of the most unclear part of myself. They are created in what continues to exist within me in spite of myself." Only now he thinks that the black angels can be saved no longer by the superficial denouement of an unexplained conversion, but by that conversion, by that deeply felt return, which will come to them out of the knowledge of themselves and out of the imitation of Jesus Christ. "The creation of opposition between Christians and unbelievers has nothing to do with the ability to make use of what is given, but rather with the presence or the absence of a model." If they renounce pride, if they humbly imitate the Master, the guiltiest participate in redemption. It does not depend on them to be freed from original sin. "The die was cast a long time ago, and from your birth." But monsters, if they know themselves as they are and disgust themselves, can become saints. And are even monsters, monsters? In one of his most beautiful books, *Le Nœud de Vipères*, Mauriac portrays an old man—filled with hate, suspicious, secretive, and besides, violently anti-religious—who, suddenly, towards the end of his life, begins to understand that he could, at a single stroke, free himself from the vipers' knot which smothers him. And here, dying, he writes to the wife he so bitterly hated.

"Well, I must make a confession to you: It is on the contrary when I look at myself, as I have for the last two months, with a concentration stronger than my disgust; it is then when I feel myself the most lucid that the Christian temptation torments me. I can no longer deny that there exists in me a road which could lead me to your God. If I could succeed in pleasing myself, I could better fight against that exigency. If I could despise myself without a second thought, the cause would finally be won.

But the hardness of the man that I am, the awful nakedness of his heart, the gift that he has to inspire hate and to create a desert around himself, none of all that prevails against hope . . . Are you going to believe me, Isa? It is not, perhaps, for you, the just, that your God has come, but for us. You did not know me, you didn't know who I was. Have the pages you've just read made me less horrible in your eyes? And yet you see that there exists in me a secret softness, the one that Marie, just by coming into my arms, awakened—as did little Luc, when on Sunday, after Mass, he sat on the bench in front of the house and looked towards the meadows . . .

"Oh, above all, don't believe I've formed too high an opinion of myself. I know my heart, that knot of vipers: suffocated beneath them, saturated with their venom, it continues to beat under that swarming. That knot of vipers that it is impossible to untie would have to be severed with the stroke of a sword: *I have not come to bring peace but the sword.*

"Tomorrow, it's possible that I may deny what I have here confided to you, as I have denied, tonight, my ultimate choices of thirty years ago. I seemed to hate with an inexpiable hatred all that you believed, and I no less continue to hate those who claim the name of Christian; but isn't it because many diminish a hope, and disfigure a visage, that face, that visage? You will say, what right do I have to judge them, I who am abominable? Isa, isn't there in my turpitude something, I don't know what, which resembles, more than their virtue, the sign you adore? What I'm writing is probably an absurd blasphemy in your eyes. You would have to prove it to me. Why don't you speak to me? Why have you never spoken to me? There may exist a word from you which would open my heart. Tonight, it seems to me it would not be too late to start our life over again. What if I was not waiting for my death to deliver those pages to you? What if I begged you, in the name of your God, to read them to the end? What if I watched for the moment when you would have finished reading them? What if I saw you entering my room, your face bathed in tears? What if you opened your arms to me? What if I begged your forgiveness? What if we fell to our knees before each other? . . .

"It is possible to achieve nobility," said Nietzsche, and Mauriac adds: "It is possible for a nature devoid of nobility to achieve it. There is no hopeless case for the Son of Man." La Pharisienne herself will be saved: "She didn't run away when I alluded to past events; but I understood that she stood apart, even from her faults, and that she had abandoned everything to Divine Mercy. In the twilight of her life, Brigitte Pian had at last discovered that one must not behave as a proud servant, anxious to astonish the Master by paying Him His due to the last farthing, and that Our Father doesn't expect us to be the meticulous accountants of our own merits. She knew now that what was important was not to *deserve* but to *love*."

How does Grace manifest itself to those who believe themselves to be still far from Christ? "A child who has not yet seen the sea comes near it and hears it roar long before he sees it, and he tries to find the taste of salt on his lips." By the direction of the wind, by the freshness of the air, the soul knows that it is traveling the roads to the sea. In spite of himself, the atheist catches himself whispering, "Oh God! God! If you exist . . ." Then he divines, at arm's length, and yet at an infinite distance, an unknown world of goodness. Soon he realizes that one gesture from him would be enough to tear off the mast that smothers him. "I have been a prisoner all my life," says the hero of Le Nœud de Vipères, "of a passion that consumed me. Like a dog baying at the moon, I was fascinated by a reflection. I had been such a terrible man that I didn't have a single friend, but I told myself, isn't it because I had always been unable to disguise myself? If all men went about thus without masks . . ." Does this mean that the cynic will be saved by his very cynicism, which is frankness? No, because he would still need to have the resolute desire to imitate the divine model. Is he capable of it? Can the monster of egotism humiliate himself, love, forgive? The whole sublime Christian paradox consists of the affirmation that that reversal is possible. It is almost as if salvation appeared to Mauriac to be "at the same time necessary and impossible." And yet it isn't impossible because it *is*. He writes: "As for me, I belong to the race of those who were born into Catholicism, and who, on just reaching manhood, understood that they could not escape from it, that it wasn't in their power to leave it or to enter it. They were in it, they are in it, they will always remain in it. They are bathed in radiance; they know that it is true." He thinks there is no hope for those who, respectful of Christianity, accept it merely as a symbol, a noble tradition, an ethic. That would all be without importance for Mauriac if he did not believe in the historical, living truth of the Gospels. But, in his eyes, there is no more certain *fact* than the Resurrection. "Love brings with it its own certitudes." The destructive and pessimistic analysis of a La Rochefoucauld is wasted on the saints, without ever getting to the essential charity of their nature; over the saints, the devil loses his rights.

Mauriac is the living proof of the moral efficacy of that faith. Without losing any of his vitality, or even his sense of humor, he knew how to become, in middle age, one of the most courageous French writers, one of the most devoted to causes he believed right, even if they were unpopular. One may or may not agree with him on his choices, but any reader in good faith must admit that Mauriac tried, in every instance, to say and to do what he conceived of as the duty of a Christian.

V. THE NOVELIST'S TECHNIQUE

The Anglo-Saxon novel is a country road boarded with flowering hedges—interrupted by fences and pastures where it loses itself—which twists and turns towards an indefinite goal that the reader sees only on arrival and that he may sometimes never discover. Like classic tragedy, the French novel of the pre-Proustian period was—not always, but most often—the story of a crisis. In it, characters were described, not from birth, like David Copperfield, but at a tragic moment of their life. Their past was evoked only through allusions, or through flashbacks.

This is the case with Mauriac. He read Proust, liked him very much, and, I believe, learned much from him about the analysis of feelings. But his technique is Racine's. His novels are novels of crisis. A little peasant renounces the idea of becoming a priest, leaves the seminary and returns to the life of the world; it is on that day that Mauriac seizes on him (*La Chair et Le Sang*). A rich bourgeois family, in which money plays a familiar role, learns that it is ruined; the novel begins with that catastrophe (*Les Chemins de la Mer*). By chance, a man sees a woman in a Paris café whom he coveted as an adolescent, but never possessed. This is the beginning of the book (*Le Désert de l'Amour*), and the remembrance of the past will come only after that leap *in medias res*.

The story moves rapidly. One feels it was written in one stroke, spurting impatiently, frenetically, from the mind, under the pressure of violent interior passions. "To write is to reveal oneself." Some writers have nothing to say; Mauriac writes because he has too much to say. The popular expression: "His heart is too greatly burdened" always makes him think of the novelist's art: "Under the crushing weight, the shattered heart explodes, the blood spurts out, and each drop of that spilled blood is the fertilized cell from which a book is born."

"Essentially, a writer is a man who has not resigned himself to solitude . . . A work is always a cry in the desert, a pigeon released with a message tied to its leg, a bottle cast into the sea . . ." Not that a novel is a confession. One could say, rather, that a novel is a confession of what we might have been and didn't become. "From every love rejected by that solitary, Jansenist child, a living embryo was formed."

Proust used to say that one moment of jealousy was enough to give a writer the elements necessary to create the character of a jealous man. Mauriac wrote: "Almost all our characters are born out of our substance, and we know exactly, even if we don't always admit it to ourselves, from which rib we pulled that Eve, from what mud we kneaded that Adam. Each one—deformed or transposed—represents states of mind, tendencies, inclinations, the best and the worst, those from the top and those from the bottom. Besides, it is always the same ones that are used, the same ones which are incarnated in characters of diverse backgrounds. Into a field of fictional possibilities, we release the eternal troupe of traveling actors of whom the poet speaks."

Concerning the creation of characters, one could say that there are two kinds of novelists—those who constantly explore new areas, discovering in them types which they study (this is the case with Balzac), and those who dig, always more deeply, into their memories in order to make use especially of themselves and of a few people they have known well (this is the case with Mauriac). Moreover, it is possible to combine the two methods, and one can imagine a writer taking out of one *milieu* the physical traits, the mannerisms of one person, and giving him the character of a close childhood friend, or enriching it from his own experience. "I am Madame Bovary," said Flaubert, and Swann, whose model was believed to be Charles Haas, is also, in great part, Marcel Proust himself.

Among the novelists who prefer to give the new roles to their interior and permanent "troupe," and who use few stars in a performance, one often sees again the same actors under other names. This is the case with Stendhal, in whom Julien Sorel, Lucien Leuwen, and Fabrice Del Dongo are three ribs detached from Stendhal.

In Mauriac's work, we soon come to know the troupe. There is the *grande bourgeoise* from Bordeaux—impassioned mother, vigilant guardian of the patrimony, alternately sublime and monstrous; there is the selfish old bachelor—hungry for new flesh, but still more prudent than passionate; there is the Black Angel—an incarnation of evil and sometimes an instrument of salvation; there is the woman without religion—cultured, skeptical, bold enough to commit a crime, unhappy enough to commit suicide; there is the forty-year-old woman—pious, virtuous, whose flesh has been weakened by desire for sweating, open-shirted adolescents who pass by; there are the young men—rebellious, hairy, mean, grasping and—unfortunately—too charming! There is the male Tartuffe, who is Blaise Couture, and the female Tartuffe, who is Brigitte Pian. There are a few daring and wise priests, a few clear-eyed girls. What more is needed to give life to a world and to play a divine comedy? In Mauriac, what changes is not the sets, nor the troupe, but the analysis of the passions. He always digs the same plot of ground, but each time more deeply. The discoveries that Freud and his disciples thought they had made in the unconscious, had been made a long time before by Catholic confessors in the darkest corners of the conscience. They were the first ones to drive out, from the swamps of the soul, the barely glimpsed monsters. Following their example, Mauriac tracked down those monsters, and drove them into the light of the novel.

The style is admirable. Mauriac is a poet who owes his poetry partly to the profound and passionate knowledge of a country, the France of pines, wood doves, and vineyards which provided him with so many images; partly to a profound knowledge of the Gospels and the Psalms, fountains of poetry, as well as of a few writers, such as Maurice de Guérin, Baudelaire, Rimbaud, who were dear to him. From Rimbaud he took many of his titles, and perhaps a portion of

that searing vocabulary which lights up his sentences with a
sinister glow, like a fire which lays waste to les Landes.

It is important to add that Mauriac, after the war of
1939–45, became a great journalist, the best of his time, and
a formidable polemicist. Although he still published a few
novels (*Le Sagouin, l'Agneau, Galigai*) he particularly poured
his talent into a newspaper which was, at the same time,
both personal and political: *Le Bloc-Notes*. Since 1936 he
thought that it was the duty of the Christian to commit himself. He did it with passion. The sentiments that inspire
him are complex: a violent hostility toward a certain bourgeois hypocrisy; a horror of the falsely devout who exploit
religion more than they respect it; a warm attachment to
certain men: Mendès-France, and later General de Gaulle;
a scorn for those who oppose his heroes. This journalism
in the grand manner is akin to Pascal's *Provinciales*. The
style is in the tradition of Barrès, with ancient and solid
influences from Port-Royal. The political fires are tempered
by childhood memories, by the thought of death. The lilacs
of Malaga and religious feasts carry with them a perfume
and a tenderness which soften the harshness of judgments.
The mixture is irresistible and certain pages will, in antholo-
gies, long outlast forgotten controversies.

VI

François Mauriac is the most profound of the Catholic
novelists. But it is not that he constructs novels in order to
make them instruments or symbols of Christian virtues. Accepting man as he is, in his misery and his savagery, he has
pitilessly portrayed the conflict of the Flesh and the Spirit,
of Pride and Charity. And yet, because he believes in Redemption, he has shown that through humility, through self-
renunciation, through the imitation of Christ, salvation is
possible for everyone. "Man is neither angel nor beast."

Mauriac did not tolerate that the creatures born of his mind try to be angels. He wanted them to be conscious of their fall and has demanded from them, as from himself, not partial honesty, which is so easy, but complete honesty. And because of this his tragic works illuminate his life and our own.

GEORGES DUHAMEL

WHERE MAURIAC's thin, dark-skinned face and feverish eyes evoke El Greco's subjects, Georges Duhamel's round, pink-complexioned face, his expression sharp and gently mocking behind tortoise-shell glasses, are rather reminiscent of Holbein. A painter would have to be highly skilled to suggest all the complexity of that model. He would have to combine irony with an almost monastic blandness. Duhamel has sometimes been compared to Dostoievski; and it is true that certain of his characters have strange manias that bring to mind the heroes of *The Possessed*, but Duhamel dominates and judges that which Dostoievski endures. A Frenchman can hardly describe insanity except as a way of praising reason. The shuddering is there, and sometimes a sacred anger, but both are controlled by an acquired wisdom. Like Mauriac, Duhamel tried to find, through his work, a release for anxiety. But while Mauriac finds his salvation in Catholicism, it is from a sentimental stoicism and an acceptance of the human condition that Duhamel expected peace of mind. I'm not sure he found it.

I. THE FORMATION

Duhamel's biographers tell us that he had peasant ancestors and allege that it is to them that he owes his patience, his love of work well done. But almost all Frenchmen come from the soil. That's the characteristic of a nation, not of a man. At the time of Georges Duhamel's birth, his family belonged to the Parisian *petite bourgeoisie*.

> In spite of so many migrations, I learned very quickly [he wrote] that my fatherland was to be found in that section of Paris elliptically called: the Left Bank. From time to time we returned to it, between trips to Normandy and expeditions to Nevers; we came back to put up our tent and more than once, perceiving the rambling Seine through the open door of the carriage, I cried, "Thalassa!" in my childlike fashion. From earliest childhood, I have come back to that native landscape and, the Left Bank then still prominent and my feelings for it still unresolved, I saluted, then celebrated, in the *Montagne Sainte-Geneviève,* my fatherland *par excellence* . . .

Many of the streets of the Left Bank—those that surround the Panthéon, as well as those which lead to the Jardin des Plantes—run through Duhamel's work, with their particular appearance, their amiable or unpleasant character, their sentimental implications. Mauriac is the novelist of Bordeaux and of the Landes—Duhamel is the novelist of certain corners of Paris and, later, of some of the gardens in Ile-de-France.

Early in life he came to know Paris, his family changing domicile twice a year. His father, who was fifty-one years old when he finally completed medical school, practiced that profession in an offhand way, and could not remain in one place for any length of time. His mother was a marvel of patience and devotion. Bound to a proud dreamer who spent money he didn't earn, and who invested the meager and pitiful inheritance which came to his family in crazy enterprises, she had to accomplish a daily miracle to feed, clothe, and educate her children. Duhamel is full of tender respect for the courage of those housewives of the Parisian *petite bourgeoisie*. One imagines that the Pasquiers' life gives, with all the transpositions implied in imaginary memoirs, some idea of his childhood.

His childhood was difficult. If he knew the protective warmth of maternal love, he suffered from the poverty, the confusion created by the whims of a father who never grew up. Family quarrels, quarrels over money or prestige, quarrels for the possession of a room, or the assignment of a bed, hold no mysteries for him. From the need to escape these conditions, there came a poetic adolescence and, as happens to so many intelligent and unhappy young people, a despairing adolescence. If Laurent Pasquier represents, in part, the author himself, Duhamel felt at that time a passionate desire to flee from the family circle and to remake a life more worth living somewhere else. How did he conceive that new life? He felt, it seems, two essential needs—a need for poetic expression, and a need for enthusiastic, warm-hearted companions, as determined as he to rebuild a better society.

> We were five or six friends. And none of us deprived, or naked, but happily poor. To get across icy fields, my brother had buttoned city boots whose anemic soles would spit out their nails. Each night I would patch up the tears in my pants with safety pins. Nevertheless, we went across the whole hunchbacked heart of Europe and we made, in Piedmont, a triumphal descent, breakfasting on a piece of unsalted cheese and sometimes dining on a little vermouth . . .

It is known that he undertook, with a few friends—Arcos, Vildrac, Albert Gleizes, Henri Martin (Barzun), to create a sort of phalanstery. At Créteil, near Paris, they found an old house, the Abbaye, and settled there. One of their printer friends was to teach them his trade and they thought they could earn enough by their manual labor to continue their intellectual pursuits. Duhamel's were of two sorts: he wrote poetry (the Abbeye Editions published in 1907: *Des legendes, des batailles*), and he was studying medicine. The physician's profession is one of those which facilitates the knowledge of man. It was going to form and then enrich

Duhamel's mind. As for the experiment in communal living, which was a failure, it confirmed Duhamel's pessimism about groups of people, which he had first felt in the family circle—and which was the initial reason for his compensatory need for charity and love.

A practicing physician in 1909, he continued to write poetry, became literary critic of the *Mercure de France*, where he had charge of the poetry section, and wrote plays (*La Lumière, Dans l'Ombre des Statues* . . .). It was thus that he met Blanche Albane, the beautiful and charming actress who was to become his wife. However, neither poem nor drama allowed him to explain himself as completely as he wished. He was looking for himself. Having lost, around fifteen, all religious faith, he needed mentors. He found them in Claudel, in Dostoievski, in William James. James's pragmatism answered, at the same time, his moral needs and his metaphysical denials. But it took the war for him to glimpse, with a sharp clarity, the two essential ideas around which he was going to build his work: the horror of a mechanical and murderous civilization, and the necessity for a spiritual and humanistic civilization.

In 1914, Georges Duhamel, a major second class, was put in charge of a surgical unit, then, at his request, of a tent for the gassed and gangrened. During four years of war, he lived with his patients, fighting with them, on the battlefields of suffering, the terrible struggle of life against death. There, he saw mutilated, bloody, innumerable Frenchmen of all classes—workmen, peasants, the middle class—and he learned to respect them, to love them. In their suffering most of them showed a shyness, a modesty which served as lessons for the artist as well as for the man. They were the martyrs of a religion, the religion of France, and they helped Duhamel to understand how much he was himself—before all else—a Frenchman. The notes that he took on his patients, at the time of this great suffering, formed the basis of two books: *Vie des Martyrs* and *Civilisation*. The Duhamel we know was born.

These are the themes that run through these stories. A despairing pity for the atrocious sufferings that the people behind the lines ignore and want to ignore. A fraternal admiration for the courage of the average Frenchmen. A horror of machines designed to kill and of the mechanical civilization which has made of war a collective torture more horrible than any invented by the Inquisitions and the torture chambers of the past. A contempt for those who only see in that suffering subjects for moral discourses, occasions for glory or personal advancement, material from which to draw administrative rulings. A need to go beyond the routine acceptance of evil and to try to attain love. The tone is at times that of tenderness, at times that of epic humor, which is always tragic. A harsh irony, softened by pity, and that vanity of the living which flowers among men who are about to die, or who are already dead, form two books worthy of Swift. Duhamel's stories remind one of Goya's terrible and comic drawings on the horrors of war. He seems to say to us: Civilization is not in the autoclave, nor in the radio, nor in the airplane. "It is in the heart of man, or it is nowhere."

Duhamel also owed to the war another apparently minor acquisition, but for him a major one—his flute. He had always loved music. It was the conductor of the military band of the 13th line regiment, who suggested the flute to him as a relatively easy instrument and one which would permit him to join musical ensembles. "When night came, I slowly became intoxicated with the simple sounds I had created . . . Purged of its miseries, lightened, freed from anguish, my soul rose weightlessly in a serene light . . ." The lesson of music complemented the lesson of suffering. Music is not made to be enchained by hatred. It rises above our quarrels and our rancors. For Duhamel it was going to be a paradise removed from the follies of mankind.

Civilisation, winning the Prix Goncourt, had given its author a large public. *La Possession du Monde,* where he formulated the ethic of his experiences, earned him friends and disciples. In it he showed that happiness is founded on possession, that is to say, on the perfect and profound knowledge of things. The possession of the world is in the knowledge of this world, of its flowers, of its animals, of its men. We are not poor if we learn to know our riches.

In a few years, Duhamel became one of the spiritual teachers of Europe. He traveled all over in the course of his lecture tours. He was loved, particularly in democratic and "friendly" countries, like Holland, Switzerland, Denmark. The horror of war seemed to bring him close to the parties of the extreme left, which at that time combined international pacifism with a degree of national belligerence. But he didn't greatly enjoy the Russia of that period, nor did he feel at home in the industrial, capitalistic America of the *Scènes de la Vie Future*. Mass civilizations were not made for him. His fight against the domination of the Machine, against mechanical art, against collective thought, gave him then, in the world, a position which some compared to Rousseau's after the *Discours*. But we will later consider the profound differences which separate Duhamel from Rousseau. However, he was patiently, methodically learning his writing craft. After minor works, he daringly undertook the Salavin cycle, then the Pasquier cycle—two of those grandly proportioned monuments loved by the generation between two wars.

Few writers have had as many unknown and faithful friends as has Duhamel. His everyday romanticism affected, as had Dickens' in the past, the sentimental reader—while his biologist's realism reassured the cynical reader. Many misled, anxious souls found their nourishment and their refuge in this ethic devoid of metaphysics. Effortlessly, with a skillfully used friendliness, Duhamel became famous and powerful while still young. After Alfred Vallette's death he reigned at *Mercure,* the publishing house he had loved. At the French Academy, which had at first welcomed him a little suspiciously, he made his place through his staunch tradi-

[5] *Alain*

[6] *Paul Claudel*

[7] *François Mauriac*

[8] *Georges Duhamel*

[9] *Antoine de Saint-Exupéry*

tionalism, his perfect knowledge of the language, his blend of courtesy and boldness. Physicians and surgeons, proud of a colleague who was a great writer, asked him to address their conventions, better than they could have done themselves, on a profession which had been his.

To an observer, around 1938, his life appeared to be the life of a sage. In a house in the rue de Liège, in the heart of Paris, near the St. Lazare station, he found the only valuable solitude, that "which is the conquest over turmoil." He spent the summer at Valmondois, in a beautiful country house, with a garden which bore for him flowers, fruits and fables. His beautiful children formed an orchestra, in which he himself played the flute—and a theater troupe created by Blanche Albane transformed the Valmondois garden into a Shakespearian forest. His work will show us that, before attaining that wisdom, Duhamel had gone through a painful period of interior conflicts, and that his hates were as strong as his loves.

II. HIS LIKES; HIS DISLIKES

More than anything else, Duhamel likes French civilization and the civilizations of people whom he calls "friendly." No one is more a Westerner than he is. As soon as he arrives in Moscow he says, "If I had to live here, either Russia would have to change or I would have to decide to die." New York and Chicago astonish him. He loves everything about France: her landscapes and her cities; her monuments, her paintings, her books; her language—whose words, if they are used with taste and precision, give him a physical joy; her cooking, of which he speaks as a passionate amateur; her wines and her cheeses, whose subtle perfection equals, in his eyes, the perfection of a beautiful style. He respects the French sensuousness because it remains delicate and measured. One day, when an overly scrupulous economist explains to him that there is no advantage in making jams at home, because factory labor costs are lower, he loses his temper. And what about the aroma which fills the kitchen when jam is being made? "Here, sir," he says proudly to the economist, "we make jams only because of the aroma."

Domestic rituals are precious to him. Having been brought up in an itinerant family, which recalls Mr. Micawber's, he knows the importance of a well-kept house. It pleases him to watch the life of a happy brood. Naturally, one finds in any family circle many sorrows, quarrels, lies. But what can be done? A family is like that. And, in spite of everything, there is love in it: "What could be done with so much love —and what could be done with all the love, and all the tenderness, and all the work of the world, if there weren't all the families of the world to feast upon it and, if need be, to die from it?" The family is a monster invented to devour all the world's excess of love. When the children leave, they say to themselves: "What will I do? Surely, the complete opposite of everything they did in that wretched house." Then they end by imitating the parents even in the faults they deplored, and one day come back to that home they cursed so much: "You can't imagine how indestructible a family can be." This is especially true in the French middle classes. And Duhamel loves the French middle classes, "because if they are average when it comes to money, they stand—in their intellect, their knowledge, their disinterestedness—in the front rank of a society which they shower unceasingly with masters, leaders, principles, techniques, insights, examples, excuses." The milieu he knows well is that of the scholars, the professors, the physicians. Like the family, that milieu has its faults. One finds in it unattractive conflicts of ambition— but what love of work, of profession, of research! What a sense of social obligation! What courage! And even, among some (although, being men, they are never free from jealousy) what sanctity!

Even more than scientific research, the essential occupation of Duhamel's heroes is the search for sanctity. They are poor and they don't desire possessions beyond those of the mind and of the heart. They understand literature and the arts better than the middle classes of any other country in the world. They would like to improve themselves. Few succeed in it, because they are plagued by desire and pride and envy. But such as they are, Duhamel loves them, those flawed and unbearable Frenchmen, as Péguy's God loved them.

As for what he doesn't like in this world, Duhamel hates it with a passion which colors his style and which, by moments, makes a pamphleteer of this apostle. Like Zola, he could write *Mes Haines,* and his principal, central hate is mechanical and industrial civilization—not so much for what it is but regret for what it has destroyed. The *Scènes de la Vie Future,* which has done much to make Duhamel famous, took, in European public opinion and entirely against the author's will, the aspect of an attack on America. This was not, at any time, Duhamel's intention. Of course, he had been exasperated, in the United States, by certain aspects of the United States' mechanical giantism, but no one was better qualified than he to appreciate the essential decency and the latent goodness of that country. What he criticized was only a mechanical and collective civilization such as he had attacked in Russia, and which he was later to fight against in Germany. A doctor of mores, he had observed subjects—patients—stupefied in the intoxication of comfort.

As long as we did not have a car, we did beautifully without it. Now the need has been firmly established. It has us in its grip . . . The whole philosophy of this industrial and commercial dictatorship ends in this impious plan: to impose on humanity needs and appetites . . . The beings who today populate the American anthills demand palpable, incontestable possessions, whose usage is recommended to them, better yet: *prescribed* by the national gods. They want, frenetically, phonographs, radios,

illustrated magazines, movies, elevators, refrigerators, autos
—and even more autos. They want to possess—as quickly
as possible—all those objects so wonderfully convenient and
of which they will immediately become—through a strange
turnabout—the anxious slaves.

What does he blame the mechanical civilization for?
Killing the culture of the individual, which he feels is the
only culture, and substituting for individual effort, which in
other eras had created so much beauty, a uniform rationing
of false beauty and false thought. Entering a Broadway
movie palace, he had been exasperated by "that flashy luxury
of an international whorehouse"—by "that false music, that
processed music, that musical hash,"—by the spectacle on the
screen, "entertainment of idiots, pastime of illiterates, of
wretched creatures, stupefied by their work and their cares."
Traveling around the country, he had been shocked by a conformity which, although it was most often conformity through
nonconformity, seemed to him, in fact, to suppress freedom
of thought—"Our institutions are not made to insure uni-
formity of opinion; if that was the case, we could abandon
all hope." He had watched football and baseball games, and
he had reflected that to watch men run around was no
more to engage in sport than listening to records was to make
music. Everywhere, he saw men slaves of their business, of
their automobiles, of their comfort—and he was sorry for
them, for himself, and for the future of the world. Where
was the Valmondois garden and the family orchestra?

His rage spent, Duhamel was the first to recognize that
he had been unjust toward the United States. In truth, if
he knew them better, he would have found, in out-of-the-
way places, the American equivalent of the Valmondois garden, of the family orchestra, of most of the things he loves.
Prohibition, which displeased him so much, has disappeared.
But I believe that he would compromise less than ever on
his condemnation of mass civilizations, and that in all countries. "The spectacle of collective man doesn't often inspire

confidence. The life of groups of people never resembles the life of admirable individuals. Groups of people still behave like prehistoric brutes. That frightful zoology speaks only of treason, massacres, betrayals, defeats, or crushing reprisals. And yet this, in man, sometimes has greatness, sometimes has beauty. But it does not give the true measure of man." He is certainly right when he says that the passive absorption of art does not make artists, and that ideas only have value to the extent to which they have been reflected on and assimilated by each of us. As Paul Valéry said so admirably, "The most important thing is not to find, but to add to ourselves what we find."

Duhamel also attacks mass civilization for its vulgarity. He addresses a message to a Head of State (whoever he may be) asking him to bring advertising back within the bounds of decency and honesty. He asks for the creation of a Ministry of Language, which would control the use of words and would insist on maintaining them in their correct meanings; also for the creation of a Ministry of Noise, which would banish unnecessary noises from the towns. He wants to establish the Park of Silence where the devotee of solitary thoughts wouldn't be subjected to the intrusive screechings of world-wide radio transmissions. He suggests a Truce of Inventions, because inventions, for a century, have come upon man faster than the human organism's ability to adapt to them. Duhamel is very well aware that all this is visionary. Hyperbole is there only to attract, to force the attention of the sheeplike reader.

In the *Lettres au Patagon*, he makes fun of modern orators, who talk without knowing what they want to say, and are solely concerned with keeping the favor of a public who wishes neither to learn or to understand, but merely to enjoy. Such speeches do not involve eloquence, but rather "shock, frenzy, ranting, fainting fits." He mocks scholars, each occupied with his own showcase—petty, jealous, and incapable of forgetting their unimportant selves in the contemplation

of infinite things. Finally, he distributes censure all around—
to "an insane humanity, futile and wretched, which learns
nothing from anything." And don't talk to him about progress: "The enthusiastic respect for the word *future* and all
that it conceals ought to be relegated among the most naïve
ideologies of the nineteenth century."

Is he then a contemporary Rousseau? Does he preach the
return to nature? Does he believe that man was born free
and that only later did industrial civilization put him in
chains? Not at all. Those who still see sprouting the seeds
that he long ago put in the ground, cannot doubt that
Jean-Jacques had false ideas. Rousseau used to say: "Never
forget that the harvest belongs to everyone and that the earth
belongs to no one." "Alas! Poor Jean-Jacques!" Duhamel
answers. "The harvest belongs, under penalty of injustice
and social decadence, to those who have made it grow."
And elsewhere: "The art of husbanding a garden demonstrates that nature must be ruled." A garden abandoned to
nature by its master ceases to be a garden and returns to
the jungle.

> They blame me [writes Duhamel again] for being a suc-
> cessor to Jean-Jacques. I put my fellow men on guard
> against industrial civilization and its effects. I have never
> told men to renounce their civilization, which would be
> fanciful, but have advised them to judge that civilization
> . . . Because for fifteen years, relentlessly, I have initiated
> this trial of mechanical civilization, unknown and far dis-
> tant friends perhaps imagined me in the guise of a hermit
> dressed in animal skins, grazing my flocks, living on milk
> and cheese, or even on the fruits of my hunting and fishing.
> In that case it would be necessary to destroy that pastoral
> myth. I use machines as much as any other man of my
> time. I do my best, and it is sometimes very difficult, to
> remain the master of those machines, and not become their
> dazzled servant. I am careful enough not to misunderstand
> nor to despise them, which would expose me to their

blind reprisals. And I am mature enough not to ever adore them, or expect from them what they cannot give. I know, in accepting it, that their service is impure, the good they do too often corrupted. They take away one care, but by bringing another. Summing up, I accept a *fait accompli,* but I am not one of those who, thinking of humanity, base any kind of hope on all that heap of scrap iron.

Duhamel never preached the return to nature, but he advised those who live far from nature not to be deceived by the phantoms of a civilization which, after all, ought to have been made for man. He reminds the individual that, if he loses his soul, and if all individuals like him lose their souls, the mass which they constitute cannot be saved.

Let us stop humiliating moral culture, the only assurance of peace and happiness, before the irresponsible and untamed genius who haunts the laboratories . . . It would be better to try hard to teach doubting men that their happiness does not consist of covering 100 kilometers in a hour, rising into the skies on a machine, or conversing above the ocean, but rather—above all—in being rich with a beautiful thought, in being content with one's work . . . Scientific civilization must be utilized as a servant, and no longer adored as a goddess . . . A spiritual culture is at the same time an expression and a result of an effort . . . All systems of civilization which tend to diminish the effort consequently weaken the culture . . .

True civilization is a state of very fragile equilibrium, which we must be careful not to upset when, miraculously, it appears in the world: "Physicians, who taught me everything, have taught me respect for equilibrium. They have a favorite axiom which clearly reveals their feeling on this subject: *Quieta non movere.* First of all not to harm, not to disturb the equilibrium. For, if the pendulum is moved from the vertical, it is sometimes difficult and time-consuming to bring it back." As a result of this belief Duhamel has a profound respect for tradition. One thinks, in reading him, of that axiom of a British statesman: "When it isn't necessary to change, it is necessary not to change." In his adolescence he may have been tempted by destructive doctrines. In his maturity he became a conservative, although a liberal conservative: "Because it is restrained in its promises—because it speaks not of destroying and rebuilding, but of maintaining—tradition rarely attracts ebullient souls—souls straining toward the future. One must have lived painfully to understand that, in the destructive turmoil of the world, to conserve is to create."

That beautiful sentence recalls Disraeli's, "To conserve is to maintain and to reform." Laurent Pasquier, the character who most resembles Duhamel, exercises the same restraint as his creator. He feels himself, little by little, becoming a "social" individual, tolerant and disciplined: "I never forget that I have to live in a society." That equilibrium between individual and society, as delicate as the body's chemical equilibrium that physicians rightly fear to upset, is the one finally attained by Duhamel's intelligence. Equilibrium between the public functions and the independence of the writer, between solitude and commotion, between the desire for sanctity and man's limitations. Salavin's epic is a lengthy commentary on Pascal's thought, "Man is neither angel nor beast, and the misfortune is that he who wants to play the angel plays the beast." Duhamel escapes, at the same time, from both the angelic and the cynical. "He places the sovereign good in the sure and full enjoyment of moderate sentiments."

What we must remember, what the study of his work will make us see, is that this equilibrium is a conquest. Duhamel's starting point was a failure, repeated failures: The family, the Abbaye, friendship, sainthood. He pities "lost men" because he felt himself one of them. He knew moral loneliness, but he overcame it. As Paul Claudel wrote, Duhamel was saved by the contact with the suffering flesh of the wounded.

Under his scalpel he found the soul. He understood that there is a key to souls and that one can, past the threshold, go beyond the flesh. Is this to say that he found religious faith and realized there could be a harmony between reason and faith? "No. I have an attitude respectful and hopeful, but above all honest . . . I wouldn't consider myself honest if I made gestures, mouthed words which would not spring from my profound conviction . . ."

"You have given us an ethic," a friend told him after *La Possession du Monde,* "Now you owe us the metaphysics . . ." He replied, "That word concerns me more than I can say. I had, and I certainly still have, a horror of incompetence." Although he rightly believes himself a competent moralist, he thinks himself an incompetent metaphysician. Like so many French moralists, Duhamel does without metaphysics. Not without regrets. "We," he said, "who must each day search for our East, take our bearings, restore all our values, invent for each problem not only a solution but even a whole method, we, who suffer without great hope, and even without any hope, we are sometimes tempted to look enviously at our old Christian brothers, comfortable in their certainty . . . It is at such moments," adds Duhamel, "that Mauriac intervenes: 'You can see very well,' he says, 'that I who have faith, am as unhappy, as miserable, as desperate as you . . .' And it is this that may be the voice of true charity." He doesn't renounce metaphysical certainties lightheartedly. There is none of the defiance of aggressive unbeliever. While recognizing that he doesn't know, he suffers from not knowing. "I lost the Catholic religion thirty-five years ago. Once past the age when pride consoles us while leading us astray, I have very often regretted—let's say a little more each day—that faith which satisfies everything— as it offers a metaphysics, an ethic, a system of the world and even a political philosophy. Sincere regrets. Vain regrets. Pascal's thought is too purely pragmatic to warm my heart . . ." Here is Duhamel courageously building an ethic on a disenchanted knowledge of men, of their weaknesses and of their ignorance. "It is," says André Rousseaux, "the language of souls who deny any comprehension of life but not a love of it. Who even find in the exercise of love a refuge from that despair which could germinate on the ruins of faith."

III. THE NOVELIST

For Duhamel, the novel has been the most satisfactory means of expressing and giving life to this philosophy. We have seen that he also employs the essay—and his first novels were, in effect, essays. Or, more precisely, philosophical novels built around an idea—like *Candide* or *La Peau de Chagrin*. *La Nuit d'Orage*, for example, shows us that even a scholar may, in spite of his experiences with scientific methodology, succumb to superstition under certain circumstances. That such morality tales can also be masterpieces is demonstrated in the famous examples I have quoted. The "thesis novel" is only a variation of this type, but one in which the author, instead of accepting (as Voltaire did in *Candide*) the unreal nature of the morality tale, attempts to embody ideas in men and no longer in the puppets employed by the authors of morality or philosophical novels. Duhamel began with philosophical novels and ultimately achieved the pure novel in the *Chronique des Pasquier*. The *Salavin* cycle, his first great work of fiction, is still a long morality tale in five volumes (*La Confession de Minuit, Deux Hommes, Journal de Salavin, Le Club des Lyonnais, Tel qu'en lui-meme* . . .) whose moral can be summarized as: "Seek perfection and you will find unhappiness." Nevertheless, this morality tale is an authentic novel because it presents characters whom we can almost all accept as human and real. The morality tale consists essentially of the discovery of the world by a hero who enters life with preconceived adolescent ideas and who sees little by little—in the course of his "years of apprentice-ship"—people and events transform his first ideal and false concept of the world. The discovery of the world by Fabrice is the subject of *The Charterhouse of Parma;* the discovery of the world by Salavin is the subject of the *Salavin* cycle.

One of the differences between a novel which is properly a morality tale (each as the *Chronique des Pasquier*) and the *Salavin* cycle is that, in the pure novel, the author does not judge his characters. At most he judges secondary characters through the eyes of the principal hero with whom the reader identifies. But Salavin is not a novelistic hero analogous to Julien Sorel or to Prince André. He belongs, rather, to Don Quixote's type, which is also Panurge's. The author dominates him and does not hesitate to ridicule him. Un-doubtedly, Cervantes admires certain traits in Don Quixote —he knows that Don Quixote sincerely and ardently desires to be a knight in order to defend the weak and destroy the wicked. But he is also aware that Don Quixote will always fail because he has formed, through reading the epics of chivalry, a radically false concept of the world. In the same way, Duhamel knows from the beginning that Salavin, though he seeks sainthood in good faith, is a badly adapted, badly adjusted human being who will never be able to re-solve his conflicts.

Who is Salavin? A French clerk—intelligent, liking good books, having a taste for ideas—but one who is tormented by an unhealthy sensitivity. He is unable to resist strange compulsions, such as touching his boss's ear (which costs him his job). He is proud: "After all, I am somebody, somebody. Someday they'll realize that I'm not like the others." But, at the same time, this proud man is humble and tortured by scruples. He has an admirable mother and accuses himself of having unfeelingly imagined her death. "That's the kind of man I am!" He has a wife, Marguerite —sweet, nice, devoted—and yet he one day finds himself desiring a friend's wife. In despair, he reproaches himself:

"Don't tell me—'Those thoughts are *in you* but they are not *you!* What! Aren't I the one who thinks them? Don't I nourish them? Above all, don't tell me: 'All that exists only in your mind.' The only thing that matters is what happens there. I am a bad son, a bad friend, a bad lover. In my secret heart I have killed Mother, defiled Marthe, and abandoned Marguerite."

We can see that Salavin believes in the truth of a dangerous doctrine, whose falseness I myself tried to point out in a philosophical short story (*La Machine à Lire les Pensées*)—namely that we are morally responsible for our subconscious. It appears to me that, on the contrary, we drive thoughts into our subconscious *because* we condemn them and that they would only become criminal if they determined our actions. But Salavin is ashamed of his fantasies. "I don't have a pure heart," he says remorsefully. In friendship as in love, he looks for perfection and thus destroys friendship, as well as love, because all men are imperfect. "As soon as I find myself face to face with living people—no longer with my fantasies—I quickly lose my courage. I feel my soul contract and my flesh become exposed. I just want to find my solitude again, in order to love men once more, as I love them when they are not there." We must clearly realize that, in order to attain sainthood, or even the wisdom of a Marcus Aurelius, he will indeed have to love men "when they are there."

Salavin's friend, Edouard, does not understand this morbid anxiety.

—But what's wrong with you?
Salavin sternly looked him straight in the eye:
—I have . . . I have . . . everything I don't have.
He shrugged his shoulders. Edouard ventured:
—But speak! . . . Tell me what's on your mind. What don't you have?
Salavin lowered his eyes:
—Things which you cannot give me, Edouard . . .

—And what things?

—Grace, joy, an eternal soul, God.

Edouard repeated in a troubled voice: "God!" Salavin
had a pitiful smile and said again:

—Yes, that, or something approximating it.

In the *Journal de Salavin,* Duhamel's hero struggles to
completely transform his life. "I am convinced—within myself—that I am worth more than I am. From today, the
seventh of January, on, I am determined to work for my
self-improvement . . . He who cannot achieve eminence
either in science, or in art, or through arms, or in words or
money, can at least, if he wants to, become a saint . . . Not
a saint according to the Church, an official saint . . . I
don't ask to be able to perform miracles, I am a reasonable
and humble man." What Salavin desires is to become a saint
in his own eyes. What must he acquire to achieve that? Not
renunciation, which is natural to him. "It may be that for
me the true renunciation is to renounce renunciation." What
about charity, tolerance, humility? After all, a saint must also
behave in a saintly way. What was he to do? He deprives
himself of many things, but he suffers from it. And his mother
and his wife, who must take care of him, suffer more than
he does. He takes a vow of chastity, but it is at the expense
of Marguerite's happiness. Little by little he discovers that
all his attempts to reach sainthood confound him. Doesn't
true humility consist in remaining what you are?

After this failure, and in a final effort to find brotherhood
among revolutionaries (Le Club des Lyonnais), he finally
decides to run away and begin his life again somewhere else.
He abandons his wife and hides himself in Tunisia. But no
one can begin life over again, for each man takes with him
a personality and a memory. Salavin becomes a hero. He
saves, at the risk of his own life, a little girl who is about to
be run over by a train. He knows that that intermittent
heroism could not be the way to salvation: "If you knew
how easy it was! Oh God! Too easy, I assure you." In vain

he donates blood for transfusions, and cares for contagious patients. Nothing gives him peace of heart. Finally a young native servant, whom he treated with too much kindness, kills him. The sweet Marguerite, who had finally discovered his retreat, brings him back to Paris, dying. He is convinced that everything is impossible, except "that, at last, eternity will change him." Isn't the fact that he has hoped for salvation with such ardor sufficient to save Salavin? "Isn't the desire for salvation the essence of salvation itself? Isn't it the only salvation?"

What is the deepest meaning of that discouraging adventure? Although Salavin has pathological traits—as can be seen in his idiosyncrasies, his tics, his irrational actions— Duhamel warns us that his story is not a description of a clinical case history. There is a little of Salavin in each one of us. Salavin's story is not the story of a madman. "It is the story of a man who, although deprived of metaphysical beliefs, still does not renounce a moral life and does not accept decadence." In other words, it is the story of a man who tries to practice Christian love without believing in Christianity.

Why does he fail? Perhaps because his behavior is based on a system and is not inspired by spontaneous love. "I have done the best I could, without love," he says himself. But no one can do anything without love. Salavin is not deeply attached to people, as are his wife and mother, nor to his profession, as is his friend Edouard. His only strong feeling is the mere desire to renounce. And that renunciation itself is pride. Hence the significance of the aphoristic, "Doesn't true renunciation consist of renouncing renunciation?"

In the final analysis, Salavin did great harm to all those close to him, to all those he attempted to help. "All that so Mr. Salavin's conscience could be at peace." But if Salavin had not been so concerned about his conscience, it might still be at peace. It is good to be scrupulous. It would be even better to be simple. "I have conceived great designs, imaginary duty, and I have neglected my own little duty, my true and wretched duty. No! It is much better for a man to stay in his own place." It would appear that the Salavin cycle turns its readers toward either the agnostic's calm despair, or the Christian moralist's saintly simplicity.

However, neither Duhamel's search for himself, nor his earthly pilgrimage, were ended. Salavin's failure did not resolve his conflicts. The *Chronique des Pasquier* is in a new cycle of novels which were dedicated to the same search for a philosophy and a system of ethics. "Since the completion of Salavin, I have attempted to tell another story. It is the story of a man who I know has triumphed over life and achieved most of his ambitions—and that is clear from the first page. I am sufficiently removed from my own work to understand that the story of a success closely resembles the story of a failure and that any victory leaves a bitter taste."

This quotation makes us aware that the *Chronique des Pasquier,* even though it is the story of a family, is essentially the story of one man—Laurent Pasquier. Like Salavin he wishes to purify and to redeem himself, but his nature is completely different from Salavin's, and it is as well adapted to the social life (after necessary trials) as Salavin's was badly adapted. Laurent Pasquier, when this chronicle begins, is about fifty. He is a professor of biology at the Collège de France and he has in the scholarly world a place similar to that which Georges Duhamel himself had made in the literary world. What Salavin understood only on the threshold of eternity, Laurent Pasquier reveals at the beginning of the book. It bears as an epigraph an essentially modest and humanistic thought of his: "A miracle is not an achievement." In other words: "You will earn your bread by the sweat of your brow and your salvation at the cost of your sufferings."

"The years of apprenticeship" of Laurent Pasquier are more fully told to us than were those of Salavin. In *Le Notaire du Havre,* we see him as a child and come to know the frightening and charming Monsieur Pasquier, his father, and the appealing Madame Pasquier. Around them are Laurent's brothers and sisters—Joseph, or the Cynic; Ferdinand, or the Egoist; Cécile, the saintly musician, and Suzanne, the actress-to-be. A small inheritance fires the expectations of the entire group. Each one finds in it the elements of a dream, but Monsieur Pasquier squanders the family fortune before they even receive it. When the lawyer from Le Havre finally pays out the money, it is hardly enough to meet the expenses.

That pattern, hope followed by disappointment, is the pattern for all the episodes of the novel. As the expectations of wealth proved to be a disappointment to Laurent Pasquier, so does the family: "Is this what a family is? Deceptions, betrayals, quarrels, blackmail, and lies? Is it really worth so much love, so much suffering, so much work and so many expectations?" Laurent suffers, like all young people: "I am an adolescent. So what? Pity me. Pity all the adolescents of the world. I'm not happy. Everything within me is in chaos and in conflict. My heart is a child's heart, but my deep voice is a man's voice. My beard is beginning to grow, and yet like a very small boy I'm sometimes hungry for a cookie, a candy . . . I'd gladly give up five years of my life, yes, five years, if I could be out of this odious adolescence . . ." (*Le Jardin des Bêtes Sauvages*).

In *Vue de la Terre Promise,* Laurent Pasquier glimpses liberation. In a symbolic gesture, he burns the first thousand-franc note he earned in his life—before the eyes of his money-loving brother Joseph. This is the way he proves to himself that he will not be enslaved by money. Laurent breaks with his family and chooses a brother: his friend Justin Weill, a high-strung and generous young Jew. He dreams of a distinguished scholarly career for himself, but in order to realize it he knows he must tear himself away from quarrelsomeness and triviality. "I want to live. I want to live for myself. I want to love. I want to enjoy the beauty of the world. I want to save myself all by myself." In *La Nuit de la Saint Jean,* he discovers that love, like the family, can be a failure. While listening to Cécile sublimely playing Mozart, several couples were freed from that carnal bondage which no longer allowed them the freedom to be themselves.

One temptation remains: friendship. Why could not men voluntarily accept a life of discipline and poverty similar to that of the religious, but without their metaphysical faith? One finds again in *Le Désert de Bièvres,* a very beautiful but unfailingly pessimistic book, a recalling of the attempt made by Duhamel and his friends during the period of the Abbaye de Créteil. At the urging of Justin Weill, Laurent Pasquier and several of their friends try to live together on the income from their printing jobs. But manual work was much more difficult than they had imagined. Dissensions arose and increased. In every group of men, there is necessarily a certain proportion of the worthless and the weak. Laurent Pasquier is discouraged: "What can I do?" he says to Justin Weill. "I ran away from my family because I was sick of all the pettiness, all the meanness, all the little jealousies. And then I find the same thing here all over again. I'm convinced that men don't know how to live any other way."

"There must," Justin said solemnly, "there must be a rule from above. There must be the Law."

"Even with a rule from above, even the Law, they don't know."

"Then it would be better to die."

Justin himself ends by admitting failure: "They are incorrigible. I am. We are all incorrigibles." But he refuses to believe that the experience is conclusive: "Basically, the concept of a human association which would not be endured, but sought, accepted with joy, is not absurd. We ourselves, we are intellectuals, that is to say, hot-heads. Our failure proves nothing about the mass of other men."

But Laurent's dreams cannot contain the hope of the

Jewish people in the millenium. "A miracle is not an achievement." Now he will devote himself to his work as a biologist. But that work itself is frustrated by the essential baseness of mankind. In *Les Maîtres,* Duhamel shows us that scholars are not above the lowest of human passions. In *Le Combat Contre les Ombres,* Laurent, whose professional reputation is beginning to grow, must deal with envy and deceit. Accused (like so many honorable men) of having done things he has never even thought of, he discovers that credulity and cowardice are omnipotent. "To work, to seriously attempt a great task, you should not know anyone, interest yourself in anyone, love anyone. But then what reason would you have to achieve anything? That is the insoluble problem. *There are only insoluble problems.*" Justin himself—noble and honorable Justin—surrenders to the collective hysteria and condemns Laurent for statements he never wrote. I quote the passage because it is important and because we have all, unfortunately, fought against elusive shadows:

> "Wait!" said Laurent, always very calm, raising his open hand.
> "Wait, Justin. I can see clearly that you are convinced I was capable of writing that pointless stupidity."
> "But, my dear friend, I read it, as did everyone."
> Laurent had just opened a drawer and taken out of it a newspaper clipping. He was smiling sadly.
> "You no longer know how to read, Justin. And it's apparent that no one in the world knows how to read any more. The author of that filthy article did what many other polemicists do: he attributes to me statements which I have never made, Look! Look! Justin! He writes: 'Monsieur Laurent Pasquier will not fail to reply . . .' And he puts between quotation marks that sentence which you condemn me for, and which you would be right to blame me for if I had written it. But I didn't write it. And this is the way public opinion is molded in France, and probably everywhere. Today, who takes the trouble to read anything at all correctly? Everyone has too many things to do. Most people I see form an opinion about

men and facts by listening to a neighbor speak, who himself knows what he knows because he had it from another who, perhaps, associated with the people and read the texts. All of this is not very sound. Ah! Justin! Dear Justin!"

Amid this universal hopelessness, only Cécile sheds a bright light. And yet she, too, has her sorrows. She is married to a man who does not love her and who courts her sister, Suzanne. And she loses her child, who meant everything to her (*Cécile parmi Nous*). But Cécile is saved by faith. She tries to persuade Laurent to go into a church: "Come in with me," she says. He shakes his head: "No, I cannot. From the beginning I drank potions which have poisoned me for the rest of my life. And now I must fight against that burdensome faith in reason which does not satisfy me, but which has given me tyrannical habits from which I know I can never free myself. But I envy you, sister, I envy you. It is as if I were watching the departure of a beautiful ship and were left alone on the shore waving a handkerchief."

What will Laurent Pasquier become? Undoubtedly what Duhamel is himself. But his years of apprenticeship have been hard. They are for every man—and end only when his life ends. Even Suzanne, the delightful actress who sought a refuge in art, and wanted to believe that love is "that enchanting song whispered on the stage, in the blaze of the footlights," even Suzanne comes up against the hypocrisy of directors, the vanity of actors, the greed of the backers, the desires of young men. Even Suzanne sees her dream shattered on the shoals of reality. Every life is a shipwreck which ends on a desert island. The castaways must have courage and each one must try to save whatever he can.

IV. THE ARTIST AND THE TECHNICIAN

Is Georges Duhamel a novelist? Any writer who knows how to give life to a world is a novelist, and the world of the

Pasquiers is alive. Salavin's story is less moving because it remains too close to a morality tale. Duhamel himself rightly thinks that the most beautiful novels are those which don't prove anything. "Postwar problems, or the conflicts between generations are poor subjects for novels." To see the world through the soul of Laurent Pasquier, reliving with a hero the apprenticeship of life, is an excellent subject for a novel —and perhaps the only one.

In a lecture, Duhamel once distinguished two kinds of novels: those which make us forget our lives—for example, *Treasure Island*—and those which make us understand our lives—such as *Dominique* or *Le Désert de l'Amour*. Those that he has attempted to write belong to the second category. The type of fiction to which he aspires is the one he identifies as the fiction of everyday life. He attempts to make us appreciate and understand the extraordinary in the everyday, the marvelous in the ordinary. And succeeds. His universe is undoubtedly less extensive than Balzac's, but it is much fuller than that of most contemporary novelists.

A great novelist must know diverse aspects of human life. Duhamel's range is wide. He has not only closely observed family life and the passions it gives rise to, but his practice of medicine has made him understand special techniques. Neither is he ignorant of anything in the scholarly world, nor in the literary world. His knowledge of the world of business is less directly acquired, but it is not negligible. *Suzanne et les Jeunes Hommes* is one of the best books on the life and ways of the theater. *Le Combat Contre les Ombres* is an excellent study of the effects of calumny. Duhamel never lacks for subject matter.

He possesses a sense of humor—a rare quality among French novelists. Virginia Woolf contended that it constitutes a dangerous virtue for novelists, and that it is humor which makes Dickens inferior to Tolstoy. She was right in cases where humor (and this often occurs with English writers) pervades the entire work and removes seriousness from passion. But in some areas humor is necessary. There are desperately serious aspects to the lives of all characters, which demand the sympathy of the author and the reader, as well as futile aspects which call, rather, for an ironic response. Duhamel combines humor with tenderness. His portrayals of the avante-garde theaters in *Suzanne et les Jeunes Hommes,* and the vanity of scholars in *Les Maîtres,* constitute excellent satire. But Cécile lies completely outside the areas illumined by humor, and Justin Weill is sometimes within the circle of humor, sometimes within that of tenderness.

In his style, as well as in his philosophy, Duhamel belongs to the classic French tradition. In his essays he is not afraid of oratorical effects. His sentences are harmonious, and studied, his syntax irreproachable. He has written a great deal on grammar and attaches a rightful importance to the choice, as well as to the sequence, of words. In dealing with all these technical questions, he has the conscientiousness of the good craftsman.

The first thing is to ask yourself if what you have just written exactly expresses your thoughts. Most authors either violate common sense or good taste. That is all there is to grammar. Let's see. You write: "Strangly chiseled in clay!" Well, you see, one chisels *wood,* but clay one *molds.* You write: "A model the reader knows much better than ourselves." Ourselves is both subject and object. If I understand correctly what you have in mind, it should be written this way: "A model which the reader knows much better than we know it ourselves." It's more pedantic, but it is more precise. This is not a matter of grammar, it's a matter of honesty! And now what do I see? "An opinion that we share completely." There is opposition between the words "completely" and "share." As soon as a thing is shared, it is no longer complete. At least to my way of thinking. Do you mean a division which involves the totality of the object? If that is so, it is very poorly expressed. And now another example: You mention a "wormy peach." It would be better to say an apple.

Not such a pretty word, but it is more accurate. Peaches are seldom wormy. And as for your image of ants, let's examine that for a minute. You write: "as ants dragging their eggs." I beg your pardon, but ants don't drag their eggs, they carry them. Carry them in front of themselves. It is not the same thing.

If political speeches and statements were written by writers as scrupulous, people would be less continually confused. A respect for grammar and a love of language are essential virtues. Clarity of writing is a sign of an honest mind. One can write more brilliantly than Duhamel—he has sometimes, for the same worthwhile reasons as Flaubert, a Flaubert-like heaviness—but one cannot write more honestly.

V

Duhamel began life, like his heroes, as a dreamer—optimistic and generous. When he discovered the harshness of reality he observed it sadly and escaped from it by describing it. The view, like that of Mauriac, is black, because the world is black, very black. But the sentiment is not one of despair. Far from it. "Great men bicker—thought goes on anyway . . . All the leaves are rotten, all the trees are sick, but the forest is magnificent . . . I will construct my philosophy from all my disillusionments." It is good that young men, on the threshold of life, read *Salavin* and the *Pasquier*. From these books they will learn of the frightening storms that await them, but also that man can, after stormy nights and struggles with chimera, enter the peaceful waters of stoic wisdom through the channel of work well done.

ANTOINE DE SAINT-EXUPÉRY

AVIATOR, CIVIL AND military pilot, essayist, and poet, Antoine de Saint-Exupéry is—after Vigny, Stendhal, Vauvenargues, and with Malraux, Jules Roy, and a few soldiers or sailors—one of the rare novelists and philosophers of action produced by our country. Unlike Kipling, he was not merely an admirer of men of action; like Conrad, he himself took part in the actions he described. For ten years he flew over the Río de Oro, over the Andes Cordillera; he was lost in the desert and rescued by the lords of the sands; he crashed into the Mediterranean and also in the mountains of Guatemala; he fought in the sky in 1940 and again in 1944. The conquerors of the South Atlantic, Mermoz and Guillaumet, were his friends. From this comes the ring of truth in every word—and from this also comes a practical stoicism, for action brings out the best in a man.

But Luc Estang, who wrote the beautiful *Saint-Exupéry par Lui-meme,* was right in saying that action was never an end in itself for Saint-Exupéry. "The plane is not an end, it is a means. It is not for the plane that one risks one's life. Nor is it for his plow that the peasant labors." And Luc Estang adds, "Nor is it a matter of digging the furrows, but of sowing them. Action is to the plane what plowing is to the plow. Action enables what seeds to be sown for what harvests?" I think the answer is that it enables one to sow rules of life and to harvest men. Why? Because man does not understand anything in which his body has not participated.

This explains Saint-Exupéry's anguish, which I witnessed in
Algiers in 1943, when he was not permitted to fly. He was
losing contact with the earth because he was denied the sky.

I. PORTS OF CALL

Many witnesses have told of this brief and full life. First
there was Antoine de Saint-Exupéry, a "strong, happy, forthright" child who, when twelve, invented a bicycle-airplane,
telling everyone that he would fly away, and the crowds
would cry out, "Long live Antoine de Saint-Exupéry!" An
indifferent student, who showed a kind of genius but seemed
poorly adapted to schoolwork. His family called him the
Sun King, because of his golden locks. His friends called
him *pique-la-lune* because his upturned nose pointed toward
the stars. Actually, he was already "the little prince,"
sovereign and absent-minded, "smiling but slightly be-
wildered." All his life he will remain bound to his childhood,
always amazed and curious, and successfully playing the
magician, so that everyone will cry out, "Long live Antoine
de Saint-Exupéry!" This is the way it will happen, except
that they will say instead, "Saint-Ex, Antoine or Tonio,"
for he will become part of the private life of all who know
him or read him.

Never was the vocation of aviator more clearly indicated,
never more difficult to realize. He was accepted into military
aviation only in the reserves. And it was not until he was
twenty-seven that civil aviation made him an airline pilot,
then a *chef de poste* in the middle of a Moroccan revolt.
"The little prince became a great Arab chief." He publishes
Courrier Sud and annexes the sky to literature, which does
not prevent him from remaining a brave and efficient pilot,
and an Aeropostale director in Buenos Aires, alongside of
Mermoz and Guillaumet. He has many serious accidents,
and it is a miracle that he survives. In 1931 he marries
Consuelo, the widow of the Spanish writer Gomez Carillo.

Consuelo was a South American whose capriciousness delighted "the little prince." The accidents continue—once Saint-Ex is badly cut in a terrible fall, once he is lost in the desert after a crash landing. Tortured by thirst in the desert, how great a need he feels to find again the *Terre des Hommes!*

Nineteen thirty-nine. War. Although the doctors stubbornly declare him unfit to fly (a result of so many broken bones and smashups) he finally succeeds in being assigned to the 2/33 reconnaissance group. At the time of the invasion, after the fighting is over, the gorup is sent to Algiers and demobilized. I saw Saint-Ex when he arrived in New York at the end of that year. There he wrote *Pilote de Guerre* which had an enormous success in the United States and even in France, then occupied. We became close friends and I can say, as did Léon-Paul Fargue, "I loved him greatly and will mourn him always." How was it possible not to love him? He had, at the same time, strength and tenderness, intelligence and intuition. It pleased him to surround himself with rituals and mysteries. His indisputable mathematical genius was combined with childish playfulness. Either he dominated the conversation, or he dreamed of some other planet.

I visited him on Long Island, in a big house he had rented with Consuelo while he was writing *The Little Prince.* He worked at night. After dinner he would talk, tell stories, sing, do card tricks. Then, around midnight, when the others were going to bed, he would sit down at his desk. I would go to sleep. Toward two o'clock in the morning, shouts on the stairs would wake me up. "Consuelo! Conseulo! . . . I'm hungry . . . Come fix me some scrambled eggs." Consuelo would go down. Awake, I would join them, and again Saint-Ex would talk brilliantly. His hunger appeased, he would go back to work. We would try to sleep. Not for long, for two hours later the house would echo with clarion cries—"Consuelo! I'm bored. Come and play chess." Then he would read what he had written, and Consuelo, herself a poet, would suggest clever episodes.

When General Bethouart came to the United States to obtain arms, Saint-Ex and I asked to re-enlist in the French army in Africa. He left New York a few days before I did, and when I got off the plane in Algiers I saw him waiting for me. He seemed unhappy. He who felt so strongly the ties that bind men together—he who always felt a little responsible for the destiny of France—had found the French divided. Two headquarters faced each other. Placed in a reserve status, he did not know if they would let him fly. At forty-four he demanded, with obstinate insistence, to pilot a P-38, a fast plane made for younger hearts. He finally got it, thanks to the intervention of one of President Roosevelt's sons. While waiting he had worked on the book (or poem) which was later called *Citadelle*.

Promoted to major, he succeeded in rejoining his beloved Group 2/33, the one of *Pilote de Guerre*. But his worried superiors wangled missions for him. He had been promised five. He managed to get three more. From the eighth mission, above occupied France, he did not return. He had taken off at 8:30. At 13:30 he had not come back. His comrades in the squadron, gathered in the mess, looked at their watches. He had only enough fuel to last an hour. At 14:30 no hope was left. Everyone remained silent a long time. Then the squadron leader said to an airman—"You will take over Major de Saint-Exupéry's mission." It had ended like one of Saint-Ex's novels and one could well imagine him, low on fuel and perhaps hope, climbing like one of his heroes toward some celestial landing field, floodlighted by stars.

II. THE LAWS OF ACTION

The laws of the heroic world are constant, and in Saint-Exupéry's work we should expect to find them almost identical with those we have known in Kipling's stories.

Discipline is the first law of action. How could a few thousand English soldiers in India govern several million men? Was it because they were better armed? That would not have been enough. Kipling explains to us that the Indian army had held that giant country for a long time because the people of India were divided, whereas, in the British army, the private obeys the corporal, the corporal the sergeant, the sergeant the sergeant-major, and so on up to the commander in chief, who obeys the Viceroy. What is true of an army is also true of any collective action. For an aviator entrusted with the mail, there is one thing in the world more important than his ideas, his loves, and his life—and that is the mail.

Discipline demands that the subordinate respect the chief. It also demands that the chief be worthy of that respect and that he himself respect the laws. How terrible is a chief's function. "Ah! Lord I have lived powerful and lonely," said Vigny's Moses. Rivière, head pilot in *Vol de Nuit*, encloses himself within a voluntary solitude. He loves his men with a brooding tenderness. How could he openly be their friend when he has the duty to be hard, demanding, pitiless? It is painful for him to punish, and he even knows that sometimes punishment is unjust, that the man could not have behaved differently. But only the strictness of discipline protects the lives of the other pilots and assures the regularity of the service. "Regulations," writes Saint-Exupéry, "are comparable to the rites of a religion, which seem absurd but which mold men."

Sometimes it is necessary for a human being to die in order to save the lives of many others. To the chief falls the terrible responsibility of choosing the victim, and if it is a friend who is sacrificed, he unfortunately does not have the right to hesitate, nor even to show his anguish. "Love those you command, but without telling them."

What does the chief give his men in exchange for their obedience? He gives them "directives"; he is for them like a beacon in the night of action. From his spirit come the unwavering beams of light whose rays guide the pilot. Life is a tempest, life is a jungle; if man does not fight against the waves, or the encroachment of the vines, he is lost. Unceasingly goaded on by the firm will of the chief, man triumphs over the jungle. The one who obeys finds the severity of the one who commands legitimate, if that harshness gives to life a lasting and solid armor. "The men love their work *because I am harsh,*" says Rivière.

What else does the chief give to those he commands? He gives them victory, grandeur, continuity. Looking at an Inca temple on a mountain, the only evidence of a vanished civilization, Rivière asks himself—"In the name of what ruthlessness and of what strange love did the leader of those ancient peoples compel multitudes to drag this temple onto the mountain and inspire them to raise up their own eternity?" To which, no doubt, some Man of Good Will would answer: "Wouldn't it have been better that that temple not be built and that no one have suffered building it?" But man is a noble animal and he loves greatness more than comfort, more than happiness. At the level of action—no longer of command—the laws of the heroic world require friendship between the participants. The ties created by a common danger, common sacrifice, common skills engender friendship and then nourish it.

"Such is the moral code which Mermoz and others have taught us. Before everything else, the greatness of a profession, may consist in its uniting men. There is only one true luxury and that is the luxury of human relations." To work for material things? What a deception! For that way man amasses only money that turns to ashes. It doesn't procure anything that is worth living for. "If I search my memories for those which left me lasting pleasure, if I make the balance sheet of the hours that have had meaning, I unfailingly discover those that no fortune could have obtained for me." The rich man has hangers-on and parasites, the man of power has courtiers, the man of action has comrades who are also friends.

We felt the same kind of lighthearted warmth that is felt at a carefully-organized party. And, nevertheless, we were desperately poor. Wind, sand, stars. A severe rule made for Trappists. But, around this badly lighted table, six or seven men who no longer owned anything in the world except their remembrances, divided invisible riches among themselves . . . We had finally met. We travel for a long time side by side, each of us enclosed in his own silence, or then we exchange words which don't mean anything. But now the hour of danger has come. Then we stand shoulder to shoulder. We discover that we belong to the same community. We extend ourselves through the discovery of other consciousnesses. We look at each other and smile broadly. We are like that released prisoner who is astonished at the immensity of the sea . . .

Joined to other men in a squadron, in an army, in a factory, or in a team, man finds himself in forgetting himself. "It is only when we are united with our brothers in a common goal, which is outside of ourselves, that we can breathe. And the experience shows us that to love is not to look at one another but to look together in the same direction. Comradeship can only exist when men are tied together by the same rope, climbing toward the same summit . . ." Because his comrades trust him and because he wants to be worthy of that trust, man in a team infinitely surpasses man.

And even far from the team, he carries in his heart that need for accord and approval. Lost in the snow, exhausted, Guillaumet would like to lie down and die: "But the men think I'm still on my feet; they all have faith in me. And I'm a bastard if I don't keep going . . ." Furthermore, that friendship, that comradeship, also have their harsh side. "When a comrade dies, even his death seems no more than an event which is part of the profession." And yet no new friend could take the place of the lost comrade. "You cannot make old comrades for yourself."

What is the woman's role in this heroic world? In Kipling's works, a woman appears either as a companion sharing in dangers and enterprises (*William the Conqueror*), or as a temptress who tears a man away from his vocation ("The Story of the Gadsbys"). In Saint-Exupéry's novels, one occasionally sees, in the background, the pilots' wives, sweet, loving, resigned to live always awaiting a man stalked by death. There have been times when the man of action idealized the woman from whom he was separated. Thus the Crusaders gave birth to the ["woman of beauty,"] the ["honorable woman"] of the *chansons de geste*. But, if one studies Saint-Exupéry's heroes, it appears that the aviator has much less time than the foot soldier or sailor to dream of a distant beloved. The danger of his calling is, for him, more immediate and more constant. An engine which fails means death. A clogged oxygen tube at high altitude means eternal sleep. For such a man, what are cities and women? Ports of call. For a moment he is deeply touched by the pensive beauty of a young girl he glimpses (*Pilote de Guerre*). So what? He must take off.

The aviator is also different from all other men of action in that his world is strangely abstract. Seen from such a height, the earth is empty. For nine out of ten hours, the plane flies over the oceans, or the desert, or the jungle. Between Marrakech and Dakar, man barely hangs on. Between Dakar and Brazil, nothing. And even in Brazil, how many lagoons, how many forests where man never ventures. For the air traveler, climates and seasons no longer have meaning. He goes from spring to winter, to return a few hours later to summer. Life is truly a dream for him. It has its madness and its abrupt changes. Saint-Exupéry tells how, the first time he landed on African soil, he was there for thirty seconds. As he landed he was signaled to park alongside another plane which was waiting for him. "You're leaving immediately for France with the mail," his chief told him. And he left again immediately. How could his Africa be that of the Spahee or the Algerian soldier? For the pilot many cities are no more than an aviation camp or a landing field. Whether he goes to Melbourne or to Chungking, to Calcutta or to New York, to Tunis or to Río, he sees runways, hangars, a gasoline truck, sand, packed earth, and, perhaps, in the distance, a few trees.

For him reality is elsewhere. Human reality is the squadron, the comrades of the airline; he knows the reality of nature through his plane. He knows it as does the peasant: "The earth teaches us much more about ourselves than all the books. Because it resists us. Man discovers himself when he pits himself against an obstacle. But to overcome the obstacle he must have a tool. He must have a scraper or a plow. Little by little, the peasant by his labor wrests a few secrets from nature, and the truth that he exposes is universal. In the same way the plane, the tool of the airlines, puts man among all the old problems." The sailor knows and understands the sea, the currents, the harbingers of storms, the clearings, because he must save his steel or wooden craft. The aviator learns to interrogate the clouds, the bumps of the air routes, and the obstacles on the ground. See, in *Terre des Hommes,* how the old pilot describes Spain to his comrade who is going to fly over it for the first time. There is no question of towns, nor of people, but of such and such a brook, which treacherously softens a pasture, of three trees which are a landing hazard, of the danger of a panicky flock of sheep. And read again what the retreat of 1940 becomes, when seen from such a height: "And so I fly over roads black with an endless syrup which cannot stop flowing." For the aviator to speak of a river of humanity is not a poetic image; it is the simple and truthful description of what he sees. No spectacle has meaning unless it is seen in terms of a calling. The pilot lives on the scale of constellations and continents. But what can the bureaucrat know of the world?

> Old bureaucrat, my comrade, no one has helped you escape, and you are not responsible for it. You have constructed your peace by piling up cement, as the termites do in closing all lighted openings. You are all wrapped up in a ball of your bourgeois security, your routines, the suffocating rituals of your provincial life; you have raised up a modest rampart against the winds and the tides and the stars. You do not want to concern yourself with great problems, you have had enough trouble in forgetting your human condition. You are not the inhabitant of a wandering planet, you do not ask yourself unanswerable questions: you are a *petit bourgeois* from Toulouse. While there was yet time, no one grabbed you by the shoulders. Now, the clay of which you are made has dried, and has hardened, and no one will ever know how to awaken in you the sleeping musician, or poet, or astronomer, who perhaps still live within you . . . I no longer complain about the rainstorms. The magic of my calling unfolds before me a world where I will encounter, in two short hours, black dragons and blue-streaked clouds, and at nightfall—liberated—the night having come, I will navigate by the stars. . . .

The man of action is a poet in the best sense of the word —because he is "the one who does, the one who creates." I love to hear Saint-Ex (I am speaking of the man and no longer of the writer) describe an event. Sometimes—even when among friends—he would remain silent for a long time. Then, suddenly, because one of the subjects that was close to his heart had been touched upon, he would take off on it and soar up, straight as an arrow. Discussing a problem of strategy, or even of politics, he would make it simple because he saw it from such a height. He talked as a man of science, with extreme precision of both vocabulary and reasoning. But, at the same time, he spoke as a poet. His voice restored life to people and objects. The short free-flowing sentence, never rhetorical, was like a gesture modifying an idea. The images were fresh and spontaneous, often coming out of his profession itself. The whole group, spellbound, would listen until the time when, having finished his poem or his demonstration, Saint-Ex fell back again into his taciturnity, did a card trick, or sang a song—for it is still another of the laws of heroic action that it creates human beings who have difficulty in accepting worldly and social conventions.

III. THE WORK

Novels? They can hardly be called that. The fictional element is reduced from book to book. They are rather essays on action, on men, on the world, on life. The backdrop nearly always represents an airfield. Not from a desire on the author's part to become an authority on the sky, but from sincerity. That is the way Saint-Ex thinks and lives. Why shouldn't he describe the world to us in terms of his profession as a pilot, as long as that is the way he makes contact with the world.

Of Saint-Exupéry's stories, *Courrier Sud* is the most fictional. The aviator, Jacques Bernis, Aeropostale pilot, comes back to Paris where he rediscovers a childhood friend, Geneviève Harpin. She has an ordinary husband; her child dies; she loves Bernis; she agrees to go away with him. But Bernis knows immediately that they are not suited to each other. What is he looking for? A "treasure," which is truth, the "key word." At first he thought he could find it in a woman. That failed. Later, he hoped to find it, like Claudel, at Notre Dame, which he had gone into because he was so unhappy. That hope was also in vain. Perhaps the answer is in his profession and doggedly, courageously, Bernis carries the Dakar mail over the Río de Oro. One day, the author finds Bernis' body, slain by Arab bullets. But the mail has been saved. It will arrive at Dakar in due time.

Vol de Nuit belongs to the South American period of Saint-Exupéry's life. In order that the mail from Patagonia, Chile, and Paraguay reach Buenos Aires on time, Aeropostale's pilots must fly at night, over immense mountain ranges. If a storm surprises them, if they lose their way, they are finished. But Rivière, their chief, knows that that risk must be accepted. With him, with one of his inspectors, with the wife of the pilot Fabien, we follow the flight of three planes through a thunderstorm. One of them, Fabien's, is lost in the storm. The whole cordillera seems to close in front of him. The aviator, with only half an hour's fuel left, knows there is no hope for him. Then he climbs among the stars where there is no life other than his own. Discovering fabulous treasures, Fabien is going to die. That young woman, that lighted lamp, that dinner prepared with so much love, will wait for him in vain. Meanwhile Rivière, who also, in his way, loved Fabien, proceeds coldly, despairingly, to dispatch the mail for Europe. Rivière listens for the transatlantic plane to "rise up, roar and fade away," like the awesome tread of an army marching among the stars. Looking out of the window, he thinks:

> Victory . . . Defeat . . . Those words are meaningless . . .
> A victory weakens one people, a defeat arouses another
> . . . Only what is happening now matters. Within five
> minutes, the radio stations will have alerted the posts
> along the line. Over an area of fifteen kilometers, the
> vibrant force of life will have resolved all problems. Already an organ sound is rising: the plane. And Rivière
> slowly goes back to his work among the clerks who shrink
> under his stern gaze. Rivière-the-Great, Rivière-the-Conqueror, bearing his heavy victory.

Terre des Hommes is a beautiful collection of essays, some of which take the form of novellas. The story of the first flight over the Pyrénées, of the initiation by the older fliers, of the trip and of the fight with "three elemental divinities—the mountain, the sea, and the storm." The portraits of comrades—of Mermoz, lost in the ocean, of Guillaumet, saved from the Andes by his own endurance. The essay on "the airplane and the planet," celestial landscapes, oases, descent in the desert among the Moors, and the story of the day when, lost in the gluelike sands of Libya, the author almost died of thirst. But subjects have little importance. What counts is that the one who sees the world of men from such a height knows that "only the Spirit, if he breathes over the clay, can create man." For the last twenty years, too many writers have told us of man's weaknesses. Here, at last, is one who speaks of his grandeur. "Don't you see that what I have gone through," says Guillaumet, "no animal could have gone through."

Finally, *Pilote de Guerre* is the book written by Saint-Exupéry after the short campaign—and the defeat—of 1940. . . . During the German offensive in France, Captain Saint-Exupéry and his crew receive from Major Alias, their Major, the order to make a reconnaissance flight over Arras. There is every likelihood that they will find death there, and a useless death, for they are asked to gather information which they will never be able to pass on. The roads will be bottled up, the telephones will be out of order, the headquarters will have moved. Major Alias, who gives the order, knows himself that the order is absurd. But what is there to say? Who thinks of complaining? They answer, "Yes, sir . . . Very good, sir . . ." and they leave on that futile mission.

The book is the meditation of a pilot while he flies toward Arras, then returns amid the enemy shells and fighter planes. It is a very beautiful meditation. "Very good, sir . . ." Why does Major Alias send men who are his friends to a useless death? Why do thousands of young men accept to die in a battle which even then appears lost? Because they feel that by that hopeless fight they maintain the discipline of the army and the unity of France. They know that they are not going to transform the conquered into conquerors in a few moments, by a few gestures, by the sacrifice of a few lives. But they also know that defeat can prove to be the way to resurrection. Why do they fight? Out of despair? Not at all:

> There is a higher truth than the pronouncements of intelligence. Something which passes through us and rules us, which I submit to without yet sensing. A tree has no language. We are part of a tree. There are verities that are evident although they cannot be formulated. I do not die to oppose invasion, for there is no shelter to which I can repair with those I love. I do not die to save an honor that I refuse to believe is involved: I impugn the judges. Nor do I die out of despair. However, Dutertre, who is consulting the map, having calculated that Arras is over there, somewhere within 175°, will, I feel it, tell me within thirty seconds:
> —Aim at 175°, Captain . . .
> And I'll accept.

These were the reflections of a French aviator while he was awaiting death over burning Arras. And as long as such men will have such thoughts and will express them in a language as beautiful, French civilization will not perish. "Very good, sir . . ." Saint-Ex and his comrades will say nothing else. "Tomorrow we won't say anything either. Tomorrow, to the witnesses, we shall be the vanquished. The vanquished must be silent. Like seeds."

One is amazed that there were some critics who thought that beautiful book "defeatist." I don't know of any other single book which imparts greater confidence in the future of France:

> "Defeat . . . Victory . . . ," he answers quoting Rivière, "I don't know how to make good use of those formulas. There are victories which exhalt, others which degrade. Defeats which murder, others which awaken. Life is not definable by states, but by actions. The only victory which I cannot doubt is the one which resides in the power of

seeds. The seed planted in the midst of the black earth is already victorious there. But time must be unfolded to witness its triumph in the wheat . . ."

French seeds will germinate. They have sprouted since the season when *Pilote de Guerre* was written, and the new harvest is already growing. But the France who suffered and waited patiently for the new spring, is grateful to Saint-Exupéry for never having renounced her:

As long as I am one of them, I will never deny my own, whatever they may do. I'll never preach against them in front of others. If possible, I'll take their defense, I'll defend them. If they cover me with shame, I'll enclose that shame within my heart, and keep silent. Whatever I then think about them, I'll never serve as witness for the prosecution . . . Thus I will not disassociate myself from a defeat that will often humiliate me. I am of France. A France which molded a Renoir, a Pascal, a Pasteur, a Guillaumet, a Hoche. It also molded incompetents, petty politicians and cheats. But it seems to me too easy to claim kinship with some and to deny all kinship with others. Defeat divides. Defeat unmakes what was made. There is a danger of death: I will not contribute to those divisions, by throwing the responsibility for the disaster on those of mine who think differently than I do. There is nothing to gain from that trial without a judge. We have all been vanquished . . .

To accept for oneself, as well for others, the responsibilities of defeat is not defeatism; it is fairness. To counsel to the French that unity which will make possible future greatness, is not defeatism—it is patriotism. *Pilote de Guerre* will probably remain, in the literary history of France, a book as important as *Servitude et Grandeur Militaires*.

I shall certainly not try to "explain" *Le Petit Prince*. That children's book for grownups is alive with symbols which are beautiful because they seem, at the same time, both lucid and obscure. The essential virtue of a work of art is that it has its own significance, without reference to abstract concepts. A cathedral does not require commentaries, the starry vault does not require footnotes. I believe that *Le Petit Prince* may be an incarnation of Tonio as a child. But as *Alice in Wonderland* was at the same time a tale for little girls and a satire on the Victorian world, *Le Petit Prince*, in its poetic melancholy, contains a whole philosophy. The king is obeyed only when he orders what would, in any case, occur. The lamplighter is respected because he is occupied with other things besides himself; the businessman is scoffed at because he thinks that stars or flowers can be "possessed"; the fox lets himself be tamed in order to recognize a footstep that will be different from all others. "One only knows the things that one tames, says the fox. Men buy things already made in the stores. But as there are no stores where friends can be bought, men no longer have friends." *Le Petit Prince* is the work of a wise and tender hero who did have friends.

At this point, mention must be made of *Citadelle*, a posthumous book for which Saint-Ex had left numerous notes, but which he didn't have time to compose or to edit. For these reasons, any judgment is difficult. Of course, the author attached great importance to *Citadelle*. It was a summing up, a message, a testament. George Pélissier, who was Saint-Ex's confidant in Algiers, asserts that the essence of his thought is to be found in that work. He tells us that a first draft bore the title *Seigneur Berbère*, and that Saint-Ex wanted, for a moment, to call this prose poem, *Le Caïd*, then returned to *Citadelle*, his first idea. Another friend, Léon Werth, writes: "The text of *Citadelle* is a matrix. And of the most surface kind. It is made up of notes tossed into a dictaphone, spoken notes, haphazard notes . . . *Citadelle* is an improvisation."

Others proved to be more reticent. Luc Estang, who so greatly admires the Saint-Ex of *Vol de Nuit*, of *Terre des Hommes*, confesses that he cannot accept that "monotonous chant of an oriental prince-patriarch." And that chant continues for many hundreds of pages. Inexorable running out of sand. "One picks up a handful of it. There are beautiful spangles, but they are immediately buried by a monotony into which the reader also sinks. Attention is diluted; boredom submerges admiration." That is true. The very nature of the work is dangerous. There is always something artificial in a contemporary Westerner taking the tone of the Book of Job. The parables from the Gospels are sublime, but brief and mysterious, while *Citadelle* is long and didactic. Granted there is *Zarathustra,* and Lamennais' *Paroles d'un Croyant;* of course, the philosophy remains that of *Pilote de Guerre,* but its concrete support is lacking here.

However the spangles, which remain in the strainer after reading the book, are pure gold. The theme is highly Saint-Exupérian. The old prince of the desert who communicates his wisdom and his experience to us has been a nomad. Then he came to understand that man only finds peace if he builds his citadel. Man needs a dwelling, a domain, a country to love. A pile of bricks and stones is nothing; it lacks the soul of the architect. The citadel is, first of all, within the heart of man. It is made of memories and of rituals. It is important that one be faithful to it, "for I will not beautify a temple if I begin it anew every moment." If a man tears down the walls to assure himself freedom, he is nothing more than a "dismantled fortress." Then begins the anguish of not being. "My domain is much more than these sheep, these fields, these dwellings, and these mountains, but rather that which dominates them and *binds* them together."

The citadel and the dwelling rest upon a tangle of relationships. "And rituals are in time what the dwelling is in space." It is good that time is also a construction, and that man go from feast to feast, from anniversary to anniversary, from grape harvest to grape harvest. Already Auguste Comte and Alain plead for ceremonies and commemorations, without which there is no society. "I re-establish hierarchies," says the Lord of the Desert. "From today's injustice, I create tomorrow's justice. And in this way I exalt my empire." Saint-Ex, like Valéry, praises restraints. For if restraints are denied, if they are forgotten, man becomes a savage again. "The prattling imbecile" reproaches the cedar for not being a palm-tree; he would like to unify everything and tends to create chaos. "But life resists disorder and natural declines."

There is the same inflexibility in love. "I confine a woman in matrimony and order the adulterous wife stoned." He clearly understands that a woman may be so excited, so tormented by her need for tenderness, that she will make her appeal to the immense darkness. But vainly would she pass from bed to bed, for there would be no man capable of giving her fulfillment. What would be the use of allowing the changing of a spouse?

"I spare only the one who discovers her fulfillment within her own nature. I spare the one who doesn't love love, but the particular face that love assumes." A woman must also have the citadel in her heart.

Who issues these orders? The Lord of the Desert. And who orders the Lord of the Desert? Who dictates to him that respect for restraint and for ties? "Obstinately, I climbed towards God to ask Him the meaning of things. But on the mountaintop I discovered only a massive block of black granite, which was God." And he implores God to instruct him. But the block of granite remains impenetrable. He must remain so. A god that can feel is no longer a god. "Neither is he if he answers prayer. And, for the first time, I divined that the beauty of prayer resides primarily in the fact that it is not answered and that in such an exchange there is none of the ugliness of a business transaction. And that the apprenticeship of prayer is the apprenticeship of silence. And that love begins only when there is no longer any gift to expect. Love is first of all the exercise of prayer and prayer is the exercise of silence."

And this is, perhaps, the last word of mystic heroism.

IV. THE PHILOSOPHY

Some would have liked Saint-Exupéry to have been satisfied to be a novelist, a celestial traveler, and said; "Why is he so determined to philosophize when he is not a philosopher?" As far as I am concerned, I am pleased that Saint-Exupéry philophizes.

"One must think with one's hands," once wrote Denis de Rougement. The aviator thinks with his body, and with his machine. The most magnificent portrait painted by Saint-Exupéry, even more magnificent than Rivière's, is that of a man so unaffectedly courageous that it would be ridiculous to retell his acts of courage:

Hochedé is an old non-commissioned officer, recently promoted to second lieutenant. Undoubtedly he had had a mediocre education. He wouldn't have had any insight into himself. But he was a complete, an integrated person. The word *duty,* where Hochedé was concerned, lost all redundancy. We would like to submit to duty the way Hochedé did. Seeing Hochedé, I reproached myself for all my little evasions, my negligence and my laziness, and above all, when it appeared, my skepticism. That is not a sign of virtue, but of well-understood jealousy. I would like to exist as much as Hochedé existed. The tree is beautiful, firmly rooted. Hochedé's permanence is beautiful. Hochedé could not disappoint.

Courage cannot come out of a carefully written speech, but only out of intuition translated into action. Courage is a fact. A tree is a fact. A countryside is a fact. We could break down these concepts through analysis, but that would serve no purpose and it would weaken them. Hochedé is not determined *because* . . . He is determined naturally.

Saint-Exupéry has not much more than contempt for discursive intelligence. He has no faith in ideologies. He would be ready to say, as does Alain: "All proofs are, for me, clearly discredited." How can abstract words contain the truth about man? "Truth is not what can be demonstrated. If, in such a soil and not in another, orange trees push down strong roots and are loaded with fruit, then that particular soil is the orange trees' truth. If that religion, that culture, that scale of values, that form of activity—and not the others—facilitate man's enrichment and enable him to discover in himself a great nobility that he ignored, it is because that scale of values, that culture, that form of activity are man's truth. Logic? Let it find a way to give an explanation of life."

Who is right? The Right or the Left? This party or that party? Don't expect answers from Saint-Exupéry to such futile questions. Those controversies seem contemptible to him. What matters is that man rises above himself. But what elevates one lowers the other. Every movement, as Péguy said, has its mystics and its politicians.

The man who, not suspecting the unknown asleep in him, but having felt it awakening once, in Barcelona, in a cave filled with anarchists, in the name of sacrifice, of mutual help, of an inflexible image of justice, that man would no longer know but one truth: the truth of the anarchist. The man who once stood guard to protect a terrified multitude of kneeling little nuns, in the monasteries of Spain, he— he will die for the Church . . .

What is truth? Truth is neither a doctrine nor a dogma. It is not acquired by adhering to a sect, to a school, or to a party. "Truth, for man, is what makes a Man of him . . ."

To understand man and his needs, to know what is essential in him you must not put the evidence of your truths in opposition to each other. Yes, you are right. All of you are right. Everything is demonstrable through logic. The man who blames the ills of the world on hunchbacks is right. If we declare war against hunchbacks, we would quickly learn to glorify ourselves. We shall avenge the crimes of the hunchbacks. And certainly hunchbacks also commit crimes . . . What is the use of discussing ideologies? If everything can be proved, everything can also be contradicted, and such discussions make one despair of the salvation of man. While man, everywhere, all around us, shows the same needs . . . We want to be saved. The one who wields a pickax wants to give his work meaning. And the strokes of the pickax, which humiliate the convict, are not the same as the strokes of the pickax used by the prospector, which magnify him. Penal servitude is created where the pickax is used. There is no material horror. Penal servitude is created where the pickax is used without meaning. When its strokes do not join the one who wields it to the community of men . . .

He who has formed that relative concept of truth cannot reproach other men for having beliefs different from his own. If the truth for each man is what makes him more, we can, you and I who do not share the same discipline, feel close to each other through our common love of greatness, through our common love of love. Intelligence has value only in the service of love.

We have been mistaken for too long on the role of intelligence. We have neglected the substance of man. We have believed that the virtuosity of ignoble souls could help achieve the triumph of noble causes, that clever egotism could exhalt the spirit of sacrifice, that dryness of heart could, through long-winded discourse, establish fraternity or love. We have neglected the Human Being. The seed of the cedar, come what may, will become a cedar. The seed of the bramble will become a bramble. From now on I'll refuse to judge man according to formulas which justify his decisions . . .

What is important to ask about any man is not—"What are his beliefs? How is he labeled? To which party does he belong?" What must be asked is: "What kind of man is he?" What *man*, and not what individual. What counts is a man integrated into a group, into a country, into a civilization. The French have written on the face of their monuments: Liberty, Equality, Fraternity. They were right; it is a beautiful motto. On the condition, adds Saint-Exupéry, that it is understood that men can be free, equal, and fraternal only in someone or in something.

> What does deliverance mean? If, in a desert, I free a man who feels nothing, what does his freedom mean? There is no freedom except for someone who is going somewhere. To free that man would mean to teach him thirst and to trace a road toward a well for him. Only then would he be faced with steps no longer lacking significance. To free a stone means nothing if there is no gravity. For the stone, once free, will go nowhere . . .

In the same way, "the soldier and the captain are equal in the nation." The believers were equal in God.

> Expressing God, they were equal in their rights. Serving God, they were equal in their duties. I understand why an equality established in God does not entail either contradiction or confusion. Demagoguery is introduced when, lacking a common measure, the principal of equality degenerates into the principal of identity. Then the soldier refuses to salute the captain, for the soldier, in saluting the captain, would be honoring an individual and not the Nation . . .

And, finally, fraternity:

> I understand the origin of the fraternity of men. Men were brothers in God. One can only be a brother *in* something. If there is no bond which unites them, men are juxtaposed and not joined. One cannot be just a brother: My comrades and I are brothers *in* the Group 2/33; the French *in* France.

To summarize: A life of action is dangerous; death is always very near; absolute truth does not exist; but sacrifice molds men who will be masters of the world because they are masters of themselves. Such is the aviator's stern philosophy. The strange thing is that he extracts from it a form of optimism. Sedentary writers who stew in their own passions are pessimists because they are isolated. The man of action does not experience egoism because he only knows himself as a member of a group. The fighter disregards the pettiness of men because he sees the goal. Those who work together, those who share responsibility together, fly above hate.

Saint-Exupéry's message remains alive. "I will appear to be dead and it won't be true," says le Petit Prince, and he says also: "And when you are consoled (we always console ourselves), you will be happy to have known me. You will always be my friend." We are happy to have known him; we will always be his friends.

JACQUES DE LACRETELLE

HERE IS a writer who differs somewhat from those we have
studied until now. He belongs to an old aristocratic family,
with liberal and Protestant traditions, and although he quickly
acquired the techniques and assurance of a professional
writer, he has always sought to preserve in his writing the
attitude and the tone of an amateur. "I'm sure none of my
colleagues will be surprised when I say that very early in
our careers we face two dangers: the exploitation of our
profession and what is called its craft . . . The amateur is a
man whose personal characteristics will never be concealed
by his craftmanship. He will have a manner, a style, mannerisms—but they will derive directly from his nature." And
he cites as bright stars among the constellation of amateurs:
Benjamin Constant, Stendhal, Mérimée, Delacroix, and even
Turgenev. The amateur will often be considered a minor
writer by his contemporaries. "But, later, his very independence and detachment will be the qualities which will
increase his fame." Lacretelle is related to Constant and
Mérimée by more than one trait.

I. YOUTH

We learn from Larousse that Pierre-Louis de Lacretelle,
French journalist and political writer, was born in Metz in
1751 and died in Paris in 1824. He was elected to the

Estates General, and later to the Assembly. His brother, Jean-Charles-Dominique de Lacretelle, surnamed the Younger, was elected to the French Academy in 1811. The latter's son, Pierre-Henri de Lacretelle, writer and politican—who published poetry, novels, and a play—lived in the chateau of Cormatin, in Burgundy. He was for thirty years the Lamartinian deputy from Tournus. Finally, Larousse tells us that Pierre-Henri's grandson, Jacques de Lacretelle, was born at Cormatin (Saône-et-Loire) in 1888.

So it was that *our* Lacretelle came into the world at the foot of the "rolling hills" of Maconnais. And if, during his adolescence, he grew to disdain those tranquil landscapes, and to dream of romantic crags or tempests, it would still be to the classic and eloquent company of Racine, Sainte-Beuve, and Renan that he would return in his maturity. His neighbor in the country, the critic Albert Thibaudet, divided French writers into two lines—Chateaubriand's and Stendhal's. Or, as he said, the Viscount's and the Lieutenant's. It might also be necessary to consider a third—the Voltaire-Anatole France line, represented by the iconoclastic Eliacin, who toward the end of his life becomes a philosopher in a dressing gown. Lacretelle clearly belongs to Stendhal's line, which itself descends from the Rousseau of the *Reveries*. And, in his youth, with his taste for self-critical introspection, with his indefinite and poetic enthusiasms, and with a purity of style at once both classic and informal, he fitted into Gide's sphere of influence.

In his father's family he found two well-established traditions—love of letters and freedom of thought. He was essentially French and, during a period when it was fashionable to deplore the fact that our country's writers were not crazy enough, he unfashionably praised French literature for its ability to clarify and "refine" ideas. "Consider," he wrote, "our most daring and the most unconventional writer. No matter what Gide says or does, he remains bound to logic . . . Although we may sometimes be impatient with our own wisdom and our unfailing sense of proportion, we may be sure that those attributes do not make the same impression outside our borders." To illustrate, he points out how Anatole France, whom young French writers condemned for his pedantic irony and cloistered paganism, was for many foreigners the symbol of freedom of thought and of the most outspoken criticism.

Lacretelle went to school in Paris, at the Lycée Janson-de-Sailly, which he later described in *Silbermann*. The newest of the great Parisian lycées, Janson did not cater to the same social groups as Henri IV, Louis-le-Grand or the Condorcet of Proust, Martin du Gard, and Romains.

> Janson was a crossroads. The extension of Paris towards the Bois de Boulogne, the influx of a large number of foreign families into the capital, the closing of the parochial schools, the survival of the small provincial islands of Passy and d'Auteuil, had furnished it for years with a diverse and shifting clientele, which certainly did not resemble that of Condorcet or of Louis-le-Grand. Because of this, there was very little *esprit de corps* at Janson, no collective soul, at least in my time. Beyond the unchanging face of youth and its ordinary pastimes, each student spread out in front of him his little personal possessions, working according to his abilities, but perhaps also without any strong ambitions. The whole was harmonious, although I have an idea that, because the most brilliant students were not those who listened to the lessons the most attentively, the teachers' tasks were a little thankless . . .

Unanimisme would have had small chance of being born in the Lycée Janson-de-Sailly. But a classical writer, independent and solitary, could develop there. One of Lacretelle's professors was Andrew Bellessort, a fiery and bombastic teacher, who used paradoxes to stimulate his students. Bellessort would roar, "Shakespeare? A villain!" But he also read Verlaine to his students at a time when his colleague Jules

Lemaitre still made fun of Verlaine. Bellessort taught his class the love of the great works of French literature, as well as the love of common sense and clarity. In the margins of one of Lacretelle's essays he wrote, "A certain sense of style, but be more simple and restrained." This was a period in which such phrases as "blond haloed foreheads" and "purplish lips" would slip even into the essays of rhetoric students. Bellessort's vigorous irony, and his admiration for the true masters, helped form Lacretelle's taste.

During this time, the student at Janson had no thought of becoming a writer. At the most, while studying philosophy, psychology, and ethics, he told himself that these clinical lessons on man and his passions would one day be valuable in helping him give direction to his life: "I imagine that if each one of us made his confession—and all were gathered together, studied and compared, and generalizations drawn from them—that not only would false vice and false virtue be unmasked, but also that it would help each of us to strive more freely toward reason and sanctity . . ." This was already the thought of a moralist and of a novelist.

Today, in these reveries of an eighteen-year-old, we may be able to sense Lacretelle's promise. But this contemplative adolescent, who finished college around 1905, did not feel himself attracted to literature. A dreamer, indolent and apparently rather selfish, he was—with some anxiety—searching for himself. A handsome mask of aloofness and calm gave him an unusual appearance. In one of his books, to which I have remained unfailingly partial, *Dixjours à Ermenonville,* he describes what he calls, referring to Rousseau's stay on the Lake of Beienne, "les îles de Saint-Pierre." For the artist, an island of Saint-Pierre is one of those lonely and beautiful places where, the spirit being at rest, the creative imagination can function: "We have all had islands of Saint-Pierre in our lives. It is there that we have found forming within ourselves a sensation like the desire to love

. . . as well as the curiosity to understand the universe . . ."

For Lacretelle, Cambridge University was the first of those islands of Saint-Pierre.

> I had had, for some time, all the freedom that a boy just out of college can have, and wasted no time in enjoying it. Having read all that had been forbidden to me, I wasn't reading anything any more; I had a passion for gambling, and the pleasures of the flesh were too easy and seemed to me too insignificant for me to be tempted to pursue them with any artistry. It came about that I lost a sum which I was not able to repay immediately. That embarrassment made me stop and think. Finally I managed to settle my debt. That wasn't accomplished without family scenes. They reproached me for my idleness, they urged me to take up a career, they wanted to impose one on me. Unable to answer, saying only "No!" to everything, I had anguished thoughts: "Everything would change if they told me what I am. I don't feel anything; therefore I'm not worth anything." They decided to send me away from Paris. I left for Cambridge . . .

It was vacation time. The colleges were empty and the young Frenchman spent his days on his boat, under the willows of the river bank, reading *The Red and the Black* and then *War and Peace*. Madame de Rénal and Natasha became for him "the Nymphs of the Cam," and it was while looking into their faces that he glimpsed the writer's secret—that mysterious alchemy which can make of a complex, elusive human being the hero of a novel. Then he began to observe his surroundings, to evoke certain memories of his childhood, and to ask himself whether he would be capable, and by what means, to translate them within some fictional form, similar to those he so much admired. Like Marcel Proust standing before the three trees of Tansonville, Jacques de Lacretelle, tying his boat to the river bank between King's and Trinity, asked himself with trembling

emotion, "Could I, as well, one day . . . ?" And so, on the
transparent waters of Cam, where Byron so often swam, a
French writer was born.

> To those solitary reveries at Cambridge I also owed certain
> convictions of my heart to which I have never ceased to be
> faithful and for which I am thankful; certain principles by
> which to govern myself, which were later strengthened and
> which, although unable to make me live in wisdom, far
> from it, have brought me nearer to it than any human
> exhortation could have done. More precisely, I submitted
> myself, without knowing it, to that thought of Jean-Jacques
> which I was to read later: that it depended on me, not to
> make myself another temperament, nor another nature, but
> to take advantage of that which was mine in order to be
> good to myself, and not unkind to others . . .

For a long time to come he doubted his own powers. But
he wanted to write and he lived among writers. He had
become a friend of Marcel Proust and owns a copy of
Swann's Way which has a priceless dedication of which,
unfortunately, we can only here give a fragment: "Dear
friend, there are no keys to the characters of this book; or
then there are eight or ten for each one. It is the same with
the Church of Combray—where my memory lent me many
churches as models. I could no longer tell you which ones . . .
The "brief musical phrase" is, in succession, a mediocre
theme of Saint-Saens', *The Good Friday Spell,* Franck's
Sonata . . ." The writer, the recipient, the confidence . . .
What an extraordinary combination! But what is important
to our study is that Marcel Proust showed so much respect
for the taste and intelligence of this young writer just then
starting out.

Lacretelle's first book, *La Vie inquiète de Jean Hermelin,*
dates from 1920. And though its simplicity and restraint can
be appreciated, it would be difficult to discover a creative
novelist in it. "The umbilical cord was not yet severed."
On the contrary, *Silbermann* (1922) and *La Bonifas* (1925)

are objective novels. The second recalls Flaubert without the extreme tension of the Flaubertian style. *Amour Nuptial* and *Le Retour de Silbermann* were originally planned as one book (1929) and both of them suffered (especially the former) from that surgery which was unnecessarily performed on them. But *Les Hauts-Ponts* (1932–36)—the story in four volumes of a family estate which was lost, then regained, then lost again—pleases us with the poetry of its portraits and landscapes, with the simplicity of its tone, and with a penetrating and honest sense of nature.

A true classicist is always a self-controlled romantic. In his adolescence Lacretelle had found within himself the elements of romantic anxiety. A superficial observer might have been deceived by his impenetrable mask, but that lack of expression hid a real violence and a strong self-control, revealed to us in the *Journal de Colère*. Later, Lacretelle learned how to turn his very anxiety and violence into a personal philosophy. He has been called an "Apollonian" romantic. That is, in fact, one of the secrets of his works, and he undoubtedly owes that fortunate development to the wise organization of his life. "The soul that I have made for myself," he says somewhere . . . It is apparent that he learned to shape that soul through meditation and solitude. Married, and happily so, he is the father of three children who, through their mother, Yolande de Naurois, are direct descendants of Jean Racine. In Montfort-l'Amaury a little old town at the edge of the forest of Rambouillet, he owns— as a refuge from the multitude—a comfortable house, a garden filled with lilies, fruit trees, and a wisteria vine.

Today it is a countryside whose every shadow and line I know, because I have seen it shriveled in winter and bounding in the spring. There are brooks and ordinary wild flowers which initiated me into mythology and into the great religious celebrations. I know of a place where a resonant tranquility reigns, for if useless thoughts are smothered there, the echo of the others will return again and again until I hear it. A chosen place, I mean to say, a place where choices are made. A retreat, a protection against excess, against speed and the multitudes which confuse the game of life. A bath which washes away the stains of hypocrisy and soothes the itching of ambition. There are there the balances that one always rediscovers, and it is to them that one brings the most beautiful books, the most beautiful enterprises. Of course, I will never renounce Paris, but that is because it pleases me to be devoured . . . for a moment. Very quickly I take back to my island, in order to better enjoy it, the remembrance of that quick and agreeable sensation . . .

No novelist could live away from the world without revisiting it on occasion. In order to describe other men, he must sometimes observe them. And so Lacretelle would stay at small hotels in Provins and Fontenay-le-Comte, studying worlds unknown to him, but from which he wanted to create the background for his next book. But if elements of poetry can only be gathered by contact with the external world, poetry itself can only be distilled in the alembics of monotony. "O solitude!" Barrès wrote, "only you have not corrupted me!" Out of the other tradition, so close to his own, Lacretelle replies, "If I ever amount to anything, it will be thanks to my islands of Saint-Pierre." That ambivalence is entirely legitimate. Stendhal also wrote: "How can passions be described if one does not know them? And where will one find the time to develop talent if one remains always aware of those passions agitating the heart?" Every poet knows that poetry is born from "emotion recollected in tranquility."

By that time, Lacretelle's personality and political attitude were formed. To a conscious and deliberate frivolity (from time to time he enjoys the races, gambling, society), and to the nonchalance of the amateur, he adds a deep seriousness, a taste for analysis, and a distrust of false virtue. He is not at all indifferent to national affairs and, in politics, he is faithful to his family's liberal traditions. He praises this letter from Victor Hugo: "We cannot tolerate that the rabble smear our flag red . . . Those people have held back a political ideology which would have advanced without them . . . They make a straw man of the Republic . . . Let's talk a little less about Robespierre and a little more about Washington." For a young romantic, Lacretelle adds, this showed a commendable impartiality.

At a time when France was torn apart—divided by the *Front Populaire* and the *Front National*—Lacretelle, as a liberal Frenchman, attempted to awaken good will and restore harmony: "On both sides, men's minds have taken intransigent positions, but on issues that don't matter very much . . . Civil Servants must be reminded that in attacking the authority of the State, which provides them with a livelihood, they fire on their own family . . . And those that curse the taxes of a republican regime and try to evade them must also be reminded that neighboring dictatorial governments are even less scrupulous, whether it has to do with land, investments, or professional income . . ."

Lacretelle's "unfailing objectivity," which refuses to permit intelligence to surrender to political passions, has been held against him. It was said of him that he had withdrawn into "the desert of the intellect," that he had exiled himself from life, that he had refused to accept a necessary compromise between the perfection of the Greek temple and original chaos. I do not find these criticisms justified. He loves perfection, but he knows that it is acquired, not given. And any analysis of his novels will show that he does not ignore "the fatalism of nature." In his writing, as in his thought, what strikes me the most is his essential honesty. A respect for form, for the exactness and precision of words, for ideas that don't try to clothe themselves in clouds or darkness—those are Lacretelle's characteristics, as they are those of the best classical writers. "To know the true value of words," he says, "is the great secret of good writing. The most unadorned word, put in its proper place, is much more effective than the uncommon term."

Toward thirty, he had finished sharpening his instrument. Now the good craftsman needed subjects worthy of him. To the passionate amateur, those subjects had to be close to his heart.

II. THE NOVELS

We have already spoken of *La Vie inquiète de Jean Hermelin*. The book is pleasing, moving in places, but all told it resembles many adolescents' novels. It is with *Silbermann*, when he was thirty-four, that Lacretelle became an original novelist. The boon dealt with—one many centuries old—was the Jewish problem, or, more exactly, the problem of a Jew living in a Christian society, and it described his eager efforts to assimilate himself and his painful failure.

The narrator is a young Protestant, brought up at the Lycée Janson-de-Sailly in Paris, and resembling the author in more than one way. In class he sits next to David Silbermann, who seems strange and brilliant to him. As soon as the professor gives him the chance, Silbermann talks a great deal and with surprising ease. At first he is timid, almost fearful, in his relations with his schoolmates—then, when he seems to have some success with the more impressionable boys, he becomes domineering. When he recites Racine's poetry, he not only reveals a remarkable memory but also acting abilities: "His eyes sparkled; his lips were slightly moist, as if he were tasting something delicious." More than the other students at Janson, this "young rabbi" seemed susceptible to the beauty of the great French texts.

Fascinated by this precocious intelligence, the narrator becomes friends with Silbermann, who reveals to him the beauty of unknown books. But their friendship is neither easy nor happy. The young Protestant suspects, in Silbermann, the existence of secret and painful areas, a raw wound, a "private, continuing, incurable agony such as that felt by a cripple." At the lycée, his companions dislike him. They criticize his orations, and his need to always have the last word. They persecute him. Nevertheless, underneath Silbermann's awkwardness, the narrator senses a touching desire to be a complete Frenchman. Silbermann's ancestors had come from Poland:

> But I know that I was born in France, and that I want to remain. I want to break with that nomad life, to free myself from that hereditary destiny which makes vagabonds of most of us. Oh, I don't deny my origin—he said, with that small quivering of the nostrils which revealed in him a swelling of pride—on the contrary: To be Jewish and French, I don't believe there is a more favorable condition for the accomplishment of great things!
> I saw, [says the narrator] a little lake in Judea, similar to this one, from whose shores some Jews had once departed. I envisioned these Jews through the ages, wandering around the world, encamped in the country on barren lands, or tolerated in the cities within certain boundaries and under an infamous habit. Everywhere oppressed, escaping torture only by accepting humiliation, they consoled themselves for the terrible treatment inflicted on them by men by worshiping a God even more terrible. And at the end of those generations burdened with miseries, I saw, seeking refuge at my side, Silbermann. Sickly, glancing about anxiously, often prey to curious twitchings, as if, feeling the pain of those exiles and of all the suffering endured by his ancestors, he wished to find rest at last among us. Through contact with us he wanted to lose those faults which persecutions and a life lived among themselves had imprinted on his race. He offered us his life and his energy. But we rejected his alliance. He threw himself against a universal execration. Ah! before those fateful images, in the presence of such an awful inequity, a feeling of pity exhalted me . . .

Inspired by the sympathy which always unites minorities, Jacques' Protestant parents welcomed David Silbermann to their home. But almost immediately he disturbs then irritates them with his dogmatic statements. "He is very intelligent," they say with icy courtesy. At school the violence and brutality of the persecution increase. (It is the time of the Dreyfus Affair.) The narrator defends Silbermann, although he is disturbed to find in him not only a feeling of injustice, but also a desire for revenge. Now Silbermann says, "The French act this way," as if he himself was no longer part of the country. The narrator counsels reflection and serenity, and assures him that this hostility will not last.

"It will last," retorted Silbermann. "Ah! You cannot know what it is to have always felt the whole world marshaled against you!" What answer could I make to that? I shuddered when I heard such poignant confidences, as if, having thrust my head into a hideous dungeon cell, I had seen a man dwelling there. . . . At the same time, through a sort of bravado, or perhaps to lessen his feeling of personal shame, he had gotten into the habit of telling me stories in which members of his race were made objects of ridicule. He told them artfully, imitating the Jewish accents and borrowing their most common names. In his case, those buffooneries had something sinister about them. Far from making me laugh, they froze me, as when one hears someone who knows himself fatally stricken make jokes about his illness . . .

At that moment, a charge of fraud is brought against Silbermann's father, an antiquarian. The narrator, at David Silbermann's request, appeals to his father, a prosecutor. After the scandal, young Silbermann believes there is no future for him in France. He decides to go to America. But leaving France tears him apart.

To be Jewish and French! How fruitful that combination could be! What hope I held for it. I did not want to ignore anything of what you had thought and written.

What emotion I felt when I became acquainted with a great work born of your genius! . . . Now I have left my dream behind. In America I'm going to make money. With my name, I was predestined for it, wasn't I? . . . David Silbermann, that looks better on the brass plate of a diamond merchant than on the cover of a book! I had hardly prepared myself until now for that profession, but I'm not concerned about my future; I know I'll make out. Over there I'll marry according to the unchanging traditions of my fathers. What nationality will my children have? I don't know and I don't care. For us, fatherlands don't matter much. Wherever we settle throughout the world, isn't it always on foreign soil? But what I'm sure of is that they will be Jews; and I'll even make good Jews out of them, and instruct them in the greatness of our race and to respect our beliefs . . .

David Silbermann then leaves France and the narrator is slow to forget him. Silbermann, so quick to criticize and to contradict, has heightened the young Protestant's ability to see flaws in everything. He has overthrown the household gods. He has sounded, in the world of an adolescent nourished on the Gospels, the cry from Ecclesiates: "Vanity of vanities!" But, little by little, his influence fades and the narrator forgets him.

Or, rather, believes he has forgotten him, because seven years later, in 1929, the same narrator is going to publish a new story: *Le Retour de Silbermann*. In it David Silbermann returns to Paris beaten, despairing, mortally wounded. In America he tried to make himself believe all he had said before leaving Paris—about the existence of Jewish patriotism, about feeling of racial unity. He didn't succeed. " 'I could only think of all I had learned and loved in France, and that stood between me and my life as a Jew. How many times, at my uncle's, have I cried with rage! Everything that I afterwards undertook I did without real love, and in a manner I constantly criticized myself for . . .' "

And so the unhappy young man is no longer a Jew at

heart, nor French in nationality. He becomes disheartened
and enjoys, with a bizarre perversity, his awful misery. He
dies gazing at the rooftops of Paris and a corner of Notre
Dame from the windows of the shabby house where he lives:
"The little rabbi," he murmurs, "was wrong to listen to the
stories of the Christians . . . He was wrong to lift up his
eyes to their churches . . . He should have stayed among
his own people . . . for the *goyim* have poisoned him."

The two *Silbermanns* (especially the first) are painfully
beautiful books. On finishing them we ask ourselves what the
author has tried to prove? Has he attempted to depict the
Jewish "race"? Knowing the intellectual honesty of Lacretelle,
we know that he would never have set out to achieve such
an objective. He himself tells us that all the laws "that one
attempts to apply to such a collectivity" are conventional
and false. "And this is to be particularly feared when applied
to the type of Jew around whom has been created a legend
as coarse as a cheap lithograph." Silbermann would be an
unjust portrait, very unjust, if it was of a race, but it is only
the portrait of an individual. And, in dealing with him,
Lacretelle would like to be completely fair. But that would
require so much retouching and so many changes! How
many writers—some half-Jews themselves, such as Marcel
Proust, others calling themselves friends of the Jews, such as
Romain Rolland—have, in spite of themselves, been led to
copy the old cheap lithographs when they created Jewish
characters! Can portraits less subtle, less human than Proust's
Bloch, than Romain Rolland's Sylvain Kohn and Lucien
Lévy-Coeur be imagined? The only carefully delineated portraits of non-conventional Jews are Proust's Swann and
Duhamel's Justin Weill.

Lacretelle clearly saw the danger. He understood—and he
wrote—that the position of the Jew in the modern world
deserves a very particular sympathy because, no matter what
he does, he remains the scapegoat. When he is proud he is
thought arrogant. When he is humble he is thought servile.

When he is passionately loyal to his own country—and to it alone—there are those who say he is a bad Jew. When he puts Jewish interests before national feelings, others accuse him of being a bad citizen. Truthfully, as Figaro could have said, considering the virtues demanded from men with Hebrew blood, how many Christians would be worthy to be Jews? The problem is infinitely complex. For some, the honorable solution is Zionism, the affirmation of a Jewish nationality—and this is perfectly legitimate for those who believe in it. For others (and I am among them) it is the total assimilation of each Jew rooted in the country in which he was born, which is his, which was his ancestors, and from which he has inherited traditions and a culture. For yet others, a compromise solution—which remains always painful and imperfect. It is this last, the most dangerous, which creates Silbermanns. Pity them, help them to choose —do not blame them or hate them. This is the message—if there is one—of *Silbermann*.

The subject of *Silbermann* is not easy to deal with. But then nothing that is true is easy, because truth is always complex. *La Bonifas* is the meticulous, almost clinical, study of a character's development. It portrays a woman who, from childhood, is disgusted by men and who, without knowing it, and without ceasing to be chaste, is attracted by women, acquiring little by little a man's mannerisms and way of thinking. Finally, during the war of 1914, during the German occupation, she reveals a degree of courage equal to that of the bravest of men.

Like *Silbermann*, this is an original subject and its treatment is no less so. "Many novelists," says Lacretelle, "have a tendency to move their characters from one compartment to another, as if the successive periods of human life—infancy, adolescence, maturity—were analogous to the altogether different stages through which an insect passes. In fact, these methods of establishing continuity are false. There is nothing which is not implied in us from the beginning. The transformations of our nature are more specious than real. And when, in a work of fiction, the life span of a character is studied, it is not the skill of the author, but psychological truth, that will show the essential fabric of that personality and, in large measure, develop its potential."

A work of fiction is necessarily controlled by exterior events and chance, that is to say accidents and hazard. Marie Bonifas had been interested in certain novels which revealed a woman's life. But none, to be honest, had satisfied her. The authors of those novels told that story as if it concerned a stone which had been kicked into a ravine, been carried away by the water, and then become lodged in a crevice, until such time as another circumstance moved it elsewhere, and so on . . . From time to time, there was a quick glance at the stone, a word about the color and the form that it had taken, but, in the final analysis, the novel retraced the path followed by the stone, more than the story of the stone itself. And Marie Bonifas, who did not distinguish any steps in her past, and who had the feeling that the distinctive quality of her life was formed and continued to be formed around a kernel that no exterior influence affected, would have liked to better know the essential nature of the stone.

—Why don't they show us how, following what events, at what time, we were formed?—she said to herself over and over—And why don't they also tell us that never, yes never, no matter at what age, no matter what happens in our lives, do we have the impression that our being changes? . . .

All those things that *they* do not say, concerning Marie Bonifas, Lacretelle has tried to say. He shows how, since childhood, the sight of her father, Major Bonifas, created in her a feeling of revulsion for all men. She would see this old and lecherous widower courting the serving maids—and it was through her closeness with one of these servants, Reine, a beautiful and gentle country girl, that she came to know love:

Reine sat down and, straightening her dress, would make room for the little girl beside her. And the lesson began, a lesson in Natural History, or Sacred History, naïvely explained by Reine. Marie, with uplifted face, tried hard to understand. Reine, while speaking, took her hands and caressed them. And often, then, the child felt a sort of numbness. It seemed to her that an extraordinary sweetness, emanating from Reine and filling the air, sapped all her strength. Vague sounds would buzz in her ears; a shiver ran up and down her spine, and for a rather long moment she was incapable of movement and only semi-conciousness of her surrounding. In her childish language, she called that *melting*. That sensation was pleasant and she surrendered to it willingly, but she had never spoken of it to Reine.

Little by little, we see converging the elements which are going to form this personality. A horror of man, of his presence, of his smell. A liking for those masculine sports— fencing, horseback riding—that Major Bonifas, lacking a son, had wanted to teach his daughter. A desire to command deriving at the same time from heredity and from temperament. Then we observe the carefully described consequences of those characteristics. Marie Bonifas is not depraved. She is attracted to women without knowing it, without wanting it. Finally, she offers the hospitality of her house, in all good faith, to Claire Allandier, a sick, tubercular girl to whom she was attracted. Marie loves Claire. She believes she loves her as a sister, but she is jealous of her. She drives Claire's fiancé away. The little town, less pure than she is, is suspicious of her, ostracizes her, and watches in horror as "La Bonifas" walks through the streets in too masculine an attire. However, the day will come when those very traits, which make an outcast of "La Bonifas," will make her a heroine.

Often, lofty sentiments (or those that society holds to be such) are directly descended from sentiments said to be evil. "Our virtues," La Rochefoucauld has already written "are most often no more than vices in disguise." Lacretelle, in this little town of Vermont, gives us another example:

Madame de Fombert was a benevolent despot. Knowing all the people and all the doings of the town, she would not allow a decision to be made without her opinion being asked. She was praised for her kindness, and she was, in fact, capable of generosity, but it may have been a desire to meddle in the lives of others which was the strongest element in her love of neighbor. And when, at the end of a visit in a poor household, she left a little money on the table, deliberately rattling the coins, and then hurrying out with the feigned confusion of a mischievous child, she had paid very little for the pleasure she felt in inspecting, questioning, ordering. Nevertheless, as it offends common sense that a virtue be born from a vice, or vice versa, no one noticed that and Madame de Fombert was loved by all.

The day in 1914 when the Germans bombard Vermont, Marie Bonifas, suddenly reveals herself to be heroic. Unexpectedly, her ridiculed masculinity becomes a virtue. With the Major's heavy field glasses slung over her shoulder, she climbs a tower, observes the enemy, comes down, and goes on horseback as an emissary to meet the Germans. She wears a little tricorne of black felt, and her tailored suit of alpaca shines like an armor. Her firmness saves the town, and when she returns the townspeople hail her. " 'You must stand up to them,' " she orders. " 'Your duty commands you not to be victimized . . . For us, the war is beginning!' "

Everyone approves of La Bonifas: " 'You are in command. The whole town is behind you . . . We will obey you.' " It is then that she experiences an emotion she had never felt before in any moment of her life:

Several times she would repeat to herself: "Our war begins . . ." She went back home. Some of the troops had not gone to the barracks and were camping under the linden trees of the Place d'Armes, in front of her house.

She made out shapes lying on the ground, one against the other. She discovered sleeping faces among the folds of their greatcoats. Sometimes, guttural calls, half-understood words would reach her ears. And rising above that disordered crowd, she inhaled an odor which, since her childhood, she could not smell without a feeling of nausea: the smell of man.

La Bonifas is, in my opinion, Lacretelle's most perfectly realized book. *Silbermann* has a moving and tragic beauty; *Les Hauts-Ponts* the charm of a French engraving, but *La Bonifas* remains the most successful work of art because of the complete objectivity of the novelist, the perfect balance of its proportions, the unity of its subject, and the controlled intensity of its passions.

It is neither possible nor useful to summarize here the whole complicated story of *Les Hauts-Ponts,* which fills four volumes. The central subject is the desperate attachment of the book's heroine, Lise Darembert, to the Hauts-Ponts property. You would have to have lived in the French countryside to be able to understand what the family home and the lands that surround it can mean to a certain kind of Frenchwoman. Their property really becomes their flesh and blood. Lacretelle, who doubtless suffered in his youth to see the ancestral château of Cormatin "pass out of the family," had himself felt the sensation of being uprooted. He has always been attached to the physical surroundings of his life and he has written beautiful pages about his home of Montfort-l'Amaury: "They will say it is the love of possessions, a rather petty sentiment. Not at all . . . I love Montfort-l'Amaury only because of the soul I created there for myself . . . What I would wish is to make people understand that each of us possesses a Montfort in his inner self, and that he loses his life if he neglects it too much . . ."

It is apparent that, for a long time, Lacretelle had this subject in mind for a novel: the story of a woman passionately attached to a family property and its many memories

—a love of the land which had become an obsession. But he searched in vain for a suitable background in Berry, in Poitou. Then, one day, traveling from Poitiers to La Rochelle through the Vendee, he had the impression of crossing "an island—fields with perfect boundaries, something peaceful, remote, unchanging. One imagined an elderly peasant woman, plain and silent, still working with her hands in the old-fashioned way . . ." He went through the forest which had been the cradle of the fairy Melusine and where she had built castles. "A dream rooted in the earth—that was the whole subject of my novel."

Between the chosen surroundings—trees shrouded in fog, calm rivers—and the author's talent, there existed a pre-established harmony. Lacretelle's sentences are so simple, so unembellished, that they recall at times the dreamlike landscapes so delicately drawn by some "limpid and subtle Chinese artist," or those luminous and gray landscapes, relieved here and there with a dash of color, painted by Eugène Boudin.

The first volume, *Sabine*, takes place in 1880; in it we come to know the Hauts-Ponts property and the heroine's mother, Sabine Darembert. Although married to a fool, Alexandre Darembert, she is naturally happy. She could love one of their neighbors—Jean de La Fontange—and she is delighted to please him. But "her desire to charm springs essentially from her kindheartedness. When she finds herself alone, after having been courted by a man, she naïvely says to herself, with the sweet satisfaction of having done a good deed, 'I believe he likes me.'" Sabine gently enchants the reader with her blend of coquetry and purity, the grace of her actions, her sense of good taste in dealing with life around her.

André Rousseaux thinks that she has "a reflected charm," that she is a lady of 1880 displayed in a "showcase," an object d'art from the "collection of a tasteful amateur." But doesn't any character from a vanished epoch give us that impression of desuetude? We also experience it in reading the novels of the period, those of Maupassant, for example. How could a novelist who re-creates an epoch avoid it?

Sabine dies young and her daughter, Lise, is a more primitive human being. Left a poor orphan, having lost Hauts-Ponts, she has but one desire—to own it again. She finds lodging very near the property. Watches it, covets it. How can she get the money? A rich marriage? She hopes for it, but nothing works out. She then becomes the mistress of middle-aged Jean de La Fontange, a married country neighbor, who was in love with her mother. She enters into this affair with the preconceived notion of having a child by him, and of getting from her timid lover, terrified by scandal, the means of buying back Hauts-Ponts. Does she love him? Not at all. She is aware, lying beside Jean on the grass of the forest, in the shelter of a thicket, of fulfilling her destiny:

> She surrendered to that idea as another woman would have yielded to the flesh. Her hopes, her dreams of greatness, the visionary part of her being took root in those sensations. It seemed to her that she affirmed herself in giving herself to that man and, finally, overcome by so many visions, she slipped into a vague dizziness. Then, lying on the ground, chewing a piece of grass between her pointed teeth, she would begin to talk with an unaccustomed volubility. . . . She had never felt anything that resembled desire, or a physical yearning for another human being. The impulses of her heart were always born out of a will to achieve, out of a haste to discover the future.

She has the son she wanted so badly, Alexis Darembert, but not the help from Jean de La Fontange, who deserts her. Despite this, she loses none of that persistent hope which alone enables her to go on living.

> —Have you sometimes thought, she asked her son, that we might one day buy back Hauts-Ponts? . . . Who knows? Often, when there are no children, an estate is put up for sale, the distant heirs no longer wanting it. Do you see yourself going back there—as master—with me? . . . You would

have trees to look at and thickets to explore . . . There is
also the river which flows at the bottom of the park, and
the whole beautiful house . . . It's a real castle. You remember it, don't you?
Several times, when they had been out walking, she had
shown him the estate from a distance. Alexis slowly turned
his head, but didn't say anything. Ah! How the child's
failure to pay attention irritated her sometimes! She repeated her question and squeezed his shoulder a little.
—Yes, Yes! Alexis said quickly and, after an effort of memory, he saw again the soaring rooftops of the dwelling.
—Yes, I remember well . . . Is there an attic?
—What? said the mother, a little disconcerted. —But, of
course . . . A very high attic, with an immense beam ex-
tending from one end to the other. It looks like a mast lying on its side. When I was a child and would climb up
there, I always thought of a ship. And there are also underground passages that lead from the kitchens. But they were
blocked up. Once they believed that a treasure had been
sealed up behind them. My father's grandmother searched,
but found nothing . . . Nevertheless . . . Do you think
that one day, if we live there again, we might discover
that treasure?
   Alexis lifted his head: his eyes shone piercingly as if he
were trying to see into the underground passages. Then
his mother, aware of that curiosity, drew her son close.
—Come sit beside me a little while, she said soberly.
—Listen . . . If I tell you these stories, it is because I would
so much like you to think about that house which belonged to your grandfather . . . where I was born . . .
where I was happy, when I was your age . . .
Her voice, which faltered, seemed to be entreating. She
pointed to the little picture on the wall and continued:
—A moment ago, just by looking at that landscape I felt
an emotion so strong that I wanted to have you near me.
Look up . . . It is a photograph that Maman once had
colored, for my father's birthday. Look . . . See the entrance and the stairs? To the left is the terrace where we

would go after meals. How real those things still are in
my mind, in spite of twenty years! When I close my eyes,
I see again even the little clumps of moss on the bench
placed against the wall. And there are nights when I dream
that I'm still in my room, over there . . .

The son, like the lover, betrays the dream. Alexis begins
as a gambler, a libertine, a romantic in the style of Rolla.
He tries everything, tires of everything, and finally repents
and enters a seminary. We find Lise again as a lonely old
woman who has managed to be employed by the new owners of Hauts-Ponts as a seamstress. But she terrified everyone by her almost insane attachment to that property. The
mistress of the house does not like to see that old woman
prowling through the halls searching for lost memories. The
child is frightened when she takes him deep into the park and
there suddenly loses all sense of time. He runs away and his
father comes to say to Lise: "There is no point in coming
back. We will not need your services any more and I have
given orders that you are not to enter Hauts-Ponts."

Driven from the house which has been her only reason for
living, Lise gradually fails. One day, when the owners are
away, she slips through the bars of the iron fence and sees
Hauts-Ponts again: "The slate of the roof, smooth and slop-
ing, seemed to her as beautiful as angels' wings." (This image
brings to mind a Vermeer and Bergotte's little piece of a
wall.) At that very moment, dazzled, shattered by emotion,
she has a heart attack and dies. "When the moon rose over
Hauts-Ponts it shone on the body thrown there. It lay along
the path, both arms stretched in front. The mouth was wide
open and seemed to be eating the earth, but the face had
assumed a look of serenity.

There is grandeur in that final taking possession—by a
corpse—of the land so beloved. Possession? Nothing is ever
possessed, no one is ever possessed, unless it be in death.
The slow rise and the increasing scope of the catastrophes
which finally crush Lise Darembert recall the effects achieved

in certain of Balzac's novels (the final impoverishment of *Père Goriot*, the deterioration of Baron Hulot). Every person drains the final measure of his capacity to produce tragedy. This was already the case with Silbermann. It is also the case with the hero of *Amour Nuptial*—the intellectual in whom the love of intelligence ultimately destroys all true feeling.

(1948) Since this study was written, Jacques de Lacretelle has published a long novel, *Le Pour et Le Contre*, which deserved a large audience but did not find it, perhaps because it described literary circles little known to the public. And yet there it swarms with people who are very real, and among whom the initiated recognize—or think they recognize —writers, editors, and famous women of our time. It is a book which was not given its chance, but which may have it one day.

III. THE TECHNICIAN

A preoccupation with means is one of the characteristics of our age. The modern writer thinks and writes a great deal about the technique of his craft. Probably all the great writers of all periods have asked themselves such questions, but in the past they were at least less conscious of them. And yet we have from Montaigne more than one essay on the *Essays*, and from Racine, in his prefaces, the partial history of his tragedies. But it was not until our time that the *Journal de Faux-Monnayeurs* could be published at the same time as *Les Faux-Monnayeurs*. In this, Lacretelle resembles Gide. He likes to observe in himself the birth of a new work. At the same time that he was writing a novella, *Colère*, he wrote the *Journal de Colère*, and the *Journal* is more interesting than the fiction.

We already know how Lacretelle conceived of the writer's work. First of all, he believed that a novelist's writing must be in constant touch with his life. "That's how inspiration can still retain some freshness." There is always, in the composition of a novel by an experienced professional, one part technique. The writer who does not unceasingly renew himself through contact with his own passions, runs the risk of turning out assembly-line work. Kipling, in a poem about the artists of the prehistoric caves, cautioned novelists against "the yearly buffalo." Lacretelle believes a good way to meet this danger is to write, from time to time, stories about oneself and to publish them as if they were fictional. "The writer will gain from this the ability to put more life into his art and, perhaps, more art into his life." Balzac, in *Le Lys dans la Vallée*, and Dickens, in *David Copperfield*, substantiate him. He also believes, like Goethe, that "fear and trembling are the best part of man." It is after bad times that good books are written.

"I believe the hand that holds the brush or the pen must be steady, but what seems impossible to me is that the brain which directs that hand should not be wildly agitated by curiosity, doubts, and uncertainty. It is this indiscernible tremor which creates a presentment of the true nature of the object, which makes revelations and permits the representation of something beyond the ordinary vision. Suppress that, and the artist will have left only his gift for reproducing, with more or less clarity, scenes more or less well ordered. An artist without anxiety would not be much more than a photographer. Torment of mind and constancy of execution make the most beautiful marriage."

In his analysis of the passions, Lacretelle is heir to the seventeenth century classicists' particularly La Rochefoucauld. We have already shown that, like the latter, he excels in the discovery of vices that have succeeded in masquerading as virtues. "How well I understand a Jean-Jacques—his brain full of ideals and eager for sorrow—who, after thirty years of dealings with the world, can only consider any good deed suggested to him as a trap put in his path and concealing some evil . . ." Nevertheless, it pleases him to think that if La Rochefoucauld had written a novel, "He would have written parts of it with more serenity and with that kind of gentle light which the course of a whole life throws on our base actions. I do not know any biography so evil that it does not inspire pity in the end."

He often concerns himself with the question of how a novelist can create enduring characters. He thinks it is done with a complex formula. It is not enough to appear true to life, it is necessary to both copy life and to reshape it. It must seem true, but be larger than life, be "precise and disproportionate, trivial and poetic." It is obvious that the characters of the most famous novels and plays would have been impossible in life. "Harpagon screams too loudly about his strongbox; Vautrin and Nucingen are mythic figures; Monsieur Verdurin and Cottard are foolish automatons." Balzac achieves his greatest effects by pushing a character beyond the limits of reality—and Lacretelle used the same method, although with more restraint, to create his two most enduring characters: Silbermann and La Bonifas.

To be merely alive, Lacretelle says that the character of a novel "must have three dimensions—that is to say, the reader must know his religion, his sensory pleasures, his political opinions. Stendhal, Balzac, Proust (in the latter the cult of the unconscious takes the place of faith) were well aware of this and understood thoroughly the wide range of political colorations." Nevertheless, Lacretelle does not believe that an artist should exhibit his own political opinions in his work. His innermost beliefs act upon the choice of subject and style. "I will not go so far as to say," Lacretelle states, "as did one of my old professors, that Racine was a royalist and Corneille a republican (today, undoubtedly, he would identify Michaelangelo as a Communist and Raphael as a Fascist), but you don't need very much perspicacity to determine, behind the draperies of fiction, the political ideas of a man."

"And don't let those who refuse to define their political

positions more clearly be accused of cowardice. For—outside of a concern about nuances—their reserve reveals a scrupulousness for tomorrow's truth and a respect for contrary convictions, in brief, those are sentiments worthy of the enthusiasm of partisan writers. If they stand aloof, it is in order to judge more sanely."

Finally, there is a fourth dimension which seems necessary to him to insure the lasting qualities of a work—and there he makes, I believe, a most significant contribution to criticism.

> The secret of a great work, what stirs up men's emotions around it, and what assures it a place in eternity, is the miracle of an author who succeeds in uniting an ordinary subject, a true subject, to the theme of Fate. There is the fourth dimension. To show all the strengths of a human being, and to show him, at the same time, crushed under a superior law which he ignores, is to make him a beneficiary of the continuing tragedy that began with the first man and will probably end only with the end of the race. Such a character will reflect in the depths of his astonished eyes the marvel of having seen the first waters and the terror of having seen the last ray of the sun. I admit this perspective disheartening, and the echo of that perpetual defeat painful to hear, but if Phèdre, Hamlet, Anna Karenina haunt us, it is because they wear the fatal garment.

IV

If we now try to identify Lacretelle's essential characteristics, this is what we find: A writer in the line of Rousseau-Gide, but with more self-control than Rousseau in the expression of sentiments, and more skill than Gide in the technique of fiction. A *French writer* in the most complete and best sense of the word. French in the great tradition, capable of discipline in his style and moderation in his ideas, not because his emotions lack strength, but because he has the strength to control them. In sum, a self-mastered Romantic who chose to describe romantic heroes—introspective, obsessed by a curse or by a passion—with a sureness of touch that belongs to the classical writer.

JULES ROMAINS

Of all the French writers of our time, Jules Romains is the one who has dared undertake the most monumental project. What *Les Misérables* and certainly *La Comédie Humaine* are to the French society of the first half of the nineteenth century, *Les Hommes de Bonne Volonté* aspired to be to the first half of the twentieth century. That this comparison is not shocking proves that the attempt is worthy of respect.

I. THE FORMATION TAKING FORM

Born in a village of the Cévennes, St. Julien-Chapteuil, Romains retains the roughness of his region's mountaineers, who in the course of history have been both religious and revolutionary. In *Cromedeyre-le-Viel,* he has portrayed those solid, rocklike men. "Yes," say the inhabitants of Cromedeyre, "we are worth more than all the others." Those Cévennes peasants are proud to have always been heretics—that is to say, original in matters of religion. Jules Romains, who is one of them, has written a *Manuel de Déification* and entitles one of his books *Retrouver la Foi.* He has an affinity for secret societies and intellectual conspiracies, which sooner or later become real conspiracies. In his mind, *Les Hommes de Bonne Volonté* is not only the title of a *roman-fleuve,* but also the rallying cry of an "outright conspiracy."

When Romains began his education, his father was teaching in a Paris elementary school. But, during his vacations, the child played in the mountains with the little peasants, helped them watch their cows and talked with them around wood fires. This explains his knowledge, well entrenched in childhood memories, of the Paris streets and the French countryside. In order to understand the political life of the Third Republic, a writer must thoroughly know Paris and the provinces. Jules Romains found both within his heritage.

Politics since 1880, in the eyes of many Frenchmen, seemed to be a struggle between primary and secondary education, between the teacher and the professor, between the public school and the lycée—occasionally between the lycée and the religious boarding schools, either Dominican or Jesuit. But Romains went from the public elementary school in Montmartre to the Lycée Condorcet—that is to say, from the essentially working-class school to the essentially bourgeois lycée, "a milieu where one came in contact with the thinking, the traditions, even the prejudices, most characteristic of the middle and upper Parisian bourgeoisie of that time, sprinkled with a little of the old aristocracy." Albert Thibaudet said of Romains that he pitted men of good will against the scions of good families. I don't think that's correct. Jules Romains is a republican, he loves the French people; I don't believe he is a sectarian. He respects the teacher, and he is right. But he does not respect him, that I know of, at the expense of other Frenchmen. In fact, although he has, like any man, his preferences and prejudices, I consider him a fair man, capable of conceiving and desiring that essential unity of France, without which there would no longer be a France.

The Lycée Condorcet was a good school, where Romains acquired a sound education. Among the writers studied, he sought out the masters and aimed high. The young Victor

Hugo used to say, "Chateaubriand or nothing." Romains fed
on giants: Homer, Lucretius, Goethe, Hugo. Excellent fare.
Giants, confirmed by the centuries, stimulate the mind more
than fashionable midgets. Cusenier tells us that one night,
on leaving the Condorcet and walking along the rue d'Amsterdam, Romains had the revelation which was to form the
basis of his work: "The concept of a vast and elemental being, of whom the streets, the cars, the passers-by formed the
body, and of whom he, at this privileged moment, could
call himself the consciousness." Doubtless, the process must
have been more complex, and this sudden "Encounter with
Unanimism the way to the *gare St. Lazare*" partakes of myth.
However, it is true that often great works are born from such
a brief illumination, and Romains, like all Frenchmen, is fond
of memorable "days."

He entered the Ecole Normale Supérieure in the liberal
arts section to get a teaching degree in philosophy, but he
studied the sciences as well, particularly biology. That dual
culture, literary and scientific, was later to stand him in
good stead. In *Les Hommes de Bonne Volonté*, through the
characters of Jallez and Jerphanion, which are among his
best, he has described the intellectual exaltation that the
Ecole Normale could create. I don't believe that such a spiritual climate, such a respect for ideas, such a love of literature, such a faith in the primacy of the spirit, can be found
in any other country of Europe. Oxford and Cambridge em-
phasize social and aesthetic values; German universities have
had their time of greatness; but the Ecole Normale has produced an Edouard Herriot, as well as a Jean Giraudoux and
a Jules Romains. For more than forty years, it has been the
bond between the Republic of the Professors and the Republic
of the Poets. It has produced the "canular"—a somewhat pedantic but nevertheless very amusing type of humor. Some of
Jean Giraudoux's comedies and some of Jules Romains' novels
are "canulars" of genius.

In 1906 (he was twenty-one), Romains joined, not in the

founding, but in the life of L'Abbaye, Duhamel's and Vildrac's phalanstery. It was there, one day in 1909, that "a muscular, blue-eyed cyclist" still attending the Ecole Normale brought the manuscript of a collection of poems: *La Vie Unanime*. Its originality was admired by the Abbaye group. In that lyricism of the collective, there was a "system," as well as beauty. A city, a boulevard, a barracks, a theater, a church, a café—such were the subjects and the "heroes" of these poems:

The shopkeepers are seated in the doorways of their shops;
They look about. The roofs join the street to the sky.
And the cobblestones seem fruitful, under the sun,
    Like a cornfield.
The shopkeepers have left the desire for profit,
Which has been at work since dawn, asleep near the counter.
It seems that, in defiance of their usual soul,
Another soul advances and comes to the threshold of themselves,
As they come to the threshold of the dark shops.
They would simply like to have a breath of air and sit down.
One sees them, near houses, here and there.
They are people taking a breadth of air. Nothing more.
However, among themselves, all along the sidewalk,
Something has suddenly come into existence.

II. UNANIMISM

What was "Unanimism?" It was not at all, in young Romains' eyes, a literary school, like romanticism or naturalism. It was not even a novelty. Some of the most ancient writers of the world, for example the Greeks in the choruses of their tragedies, had unknowingly been Unanimists. Reduced to its essentials, Unanimism consists in thinking that 1) human groups can feel collective sentiments; 2) the individuals forming these groups can participate in collective thought and enter into instinctual communion with the

Unanime; 3) the poet can express that intuition of the Unanime and thus help the individual become integrated into the collectivity.

The matter, then, is to reveal a pre-existing sensibility, rather than to create a form of new sensibility. Participation in the Unanime, and the existence of a group consciousness, are very easily observable facts. Take a certain number of individuals, each with his own personality, ideas, dislikes, and idiosyncrasies; put those individuals together, by incorporation or mobilization into an infantry battalion; rapidly they are going to acquire collective traits: an esprit de corps, a comradeship, a respect (or in certain cases, a contempt) for their superiors, new prejudices, a common desire to triumph over an enemy group by force, or over other battalions of the same army by courage and technical excellence.

Take a theater audience. It represents an emotional sum far greater than the sum of the individual emotions of the spectators if each had read the play in private. Here the whole is greater than the sum of the parts. As far as crowds are concerned, two and two make ten. Those comic or tragic effects which do not at all affect a man alone, enchant an assembly. That's why we are often disappointed on reading a speech which has had a rousing success. Another, even more elementary example: Take a railway compartment. The people occupying it do not know each other; before meeting there they had nothing in common; they come from different towns and backgrounds. However, if the journey is long enough, they will develop "unanimous" sentiments and will present a curiously united front to intruders—railroad employees, customs men, new passengers.

What interest is there in noting these "unanimous" sentiments of Unanime? First the interest that there always is in describing true sentiments. Then, in our day, it is necessary to create obstacles to the unhealthy emphasis on the individual which tends to throw him into self-analysis and divert him from the more general—and more generous—aspects of life. Jules Romains warns against the dangerous temptation of spiritual isolation. Under the influence of Freud and Proust, contemporary writers have encouraged that tendency to have thought withdraw within itself, which in its ultimate form, as Pirandello has shown, is no more than madness. From the moment that a man refuses to think within society and says, "To each his own truth," he is, literally, mad.

That choice between the individual who is closed and the individual who is open to social influences is, according to Romains, one of the serious problems of our time. Each period in history, he says, has its questions it must answer. In the seventeenth century, it was the theme which concerned Jansenius and Pascal: "Is grace sufficient to achieve salvation?" In the eighteenth century, it was the question which opposed Rousseau to Voltaire: "Is man naturally good and perfectible?" In the nineteenth century it was the question posed by Darwin to Taine: "Is determinism true, and is the evolution of the species subject to physical laws?" In the twentieth century, the two major questions are: 1) Is individualism compatible with the security and survival of the State? 2) Can individuals demand the right to develop themselves independently of the societies of which they are a part? In fact, those two questions can be reduced to a single one: What must be, in each one of us, the role of Unanime?

Romains thinks that that role must be very large, that the individual is not made to live alone or to meditate on himself, and that in renouncing the delights of solitary reverie, he finds his recompense in an increase of life. As the Christian accepted to renounce his temporal happiness in order to do the will of God, and, in losing his life, saved it, so the members of a clan who accept to participate in Unanime enrich rather than impoverish themselves. Arbitrarily, Romains calls *gods* those collective souls who, through self-knowledge, enter into a spiritual life. The *couple* is a god

distinct from the lovers that make it; the *sect* is a *god*
distinct from the members; the nation is a *god,* the most
powerful, the most jealous of the gods of our time; Europe
could become a *god,* if Europeans learned to think of, and
especially to feel, Europe.

At the time when Romains was formulating his faith, there
was yet no question of totalitarian dictatorships. When au-
thoritarian doctrines became aggressively dangerous, some
reproached Jules Romains for justifying the surrender of the
mind's freedom in the face of totalitarianism. He forcefully
defended himself:

> Even in the early days, I always insisted on the idea that
> the hold of groups on the individual was justified only
> to the extent that it was expressed in, and for, the spon-
> taneity of the individual. I have condemned constraints ex-
> ercised on the person from the outside by society and in-
> stitutions. I have underlined, as strongly as I could, the
> contrast between society, in the sense of its being a system
> of constraints and institutions, and the "unanimous" life in
> the sense where it is the unrestricted living of human
> groups, and where it implies the surrender of man to its
> influences and its attractions. I have shown what was
> essentially dangerous in the very notion of the State, with
> all the germs of legalistic formalism and oppression which
> it contains. I have even declared that a certain amount of
> anarchy is indispensable in order to avoid the demonical
> mechanism of society and to preserve the "unanimous" life.

In summing up, two types of unanimities can be imagined:
One, imposed by force, violates spirits and hearts and is the
artificial unanimity of countries subjected to dictators. It is
unnatural; it encounters resistance, at least among the best
minds and hearts. The unanimity advocated by Romains
would be entirely different. It would have to be spontaneous;
it would consist of the natural harmony of men who sing
the same song because they share the same emotion. In fact,

"tidal waves of emotions, collective thoughts" are sweeping the planet in our century and a "unanimism of fact" dominates our time.

What would be gained [asked Romains] by ignoring it or misinterpreting it because of an attitude of disgust, or of fear? Can anyone believe that such manifestations of hysteria would be exorcised by qualifying them as gregariousness? One does not escape reality by refusing to recognize it, or by giving it a pejorative label. No more than one can possibly repulse the immense drive of the species towards the collective by cultivating nostalgia for the individualism of the past, whose very conditions will never be found again. The whole question is to know if we accept to be carried and broken by the waves of an unconscious *unanimism*—blind, fanatical, as inevitable as instinct, in a word, barbaric (the very one whose actual destructiveness makes us tremble)—or if we prefer to it a conscious *unanimism,* made susceptible to light and to reason, enlightened as to its own motivations and its own dangers, capable of criticism and of liberty—in sum, an *unanimism* which is spiritually oriented. There is no other choice.

III. UNANIMISM IN ACTION

What is the importance of this theory? Does being a Unanimist transform a man's life, as does being a Christian or a communist? Evidently not. In order to be efficacious, communion with Unanimism must be unconscious. The disciplined citizen, the good soldier, the activist, participate in that communion without belonging to a "school." But if the political and social influence of Unanimism is difficult to perceive, its esthetic and literary influence is apparent. That method of thought has furnished Jules Romains with most of the themes for his work. It has lead him to make not individuals but groups the heroes of a poem or of a novel. *L'armée dans la Ville, La ville Apprend une Chanson,* are subjects for an Unanimist writer. *The Moon Is Down,* by John Steinbeck, could be called: The Invader against the Invaded. The individual characters: the mayor, the colonel, the women, exist only as parts of a whole which extends beyond themselves and directs their actions. Undoubtedly, the tenacity with which the author endeavors to describe the "unconscious solidarity" of human groups is in part loyalty to a "system." But what does that matter? In every style there is a "system" and preconceived ideas. The Greek architect, the Gothic architect, the Jesuit architect have, throughout their entire lives, reconstructed the same monuments with an obviously preconceived idea. From this derives their place in the history of styles. No originality without monotony.

But the very diverse groups selected by Romains insure the variety of his work, within that monotony. *Le Bourg Régénéré* is the story of the transformation of a group through the influence of an inscription on peoples' minds. *Mort de Quelqu'un* is a novel or a poem which expresses what is actually, when society considers the phenomenon from the outside, the death of an obscure individual: Jacques Godard.

Romains describes not the descent of a stone which disappears and is swallowed up, but the concentric circles, progressively getting fainter and fainter, produced on the water's surface by the descent of the stone. The father, arriving for the burial, thinks: "Jacques is dead," and he feels himself strongly drawn to his son by a rapid and rhythmic wave of emotion. In the house where the body is laid out, pending the ceremonies, people are thinking, and the dead man's presence beside, above, and below them modifies their thoughts. The butcher imagines that he is talking with Jacques Godard; a woman imagines that Jacques Godard walks around his own coffin and blows out all the candles. Thus the dead man still lives in their thoughts.

Then he is buried and his flesh begins to rot. However, even then, he survives in the mind of his father, of his mother, of a few friends. At last, these die in turn, or forget him, and no one thinks of Jacques Godard any more. People, in moving a familiar object, no longer see him as the last in a list of memories; he no longer appears in dreams. He has almost reached the bottom of nothingness. But, one day, a young man, passing on a boulevard, remembers that one day, the year before, he found himself in this same place, in a procession. It was a funeral. But who was it for? He tries to remember the name. Wasn't it something like Bonnard, Boulard? . . . "Then the young man thought: Someone died last year. Yes, for a year that very man has been among the dead. A dead man! . . ." And he proceeds to meditate on death, on life. From now on that someone's death is part of him. "Turning his eyes toward the city, he was surprised to be within himself. He felt, with a kind of clarity, that his soul was not only in the place where he said: 'I.'"

The theme is beautiful (it is that of the death of Ivan Ilyitch) and the idea of selecting an event rather than an individual as the axis of a novel is a fruitful one. A novel once published in America, *Storm,* is the story of a hurricane— of its birth, of its effects on people, of its death. Alongside of the vertical novel, which digs always more deeply into a soul, the horizontal novel, which explores the concentric circles created by an act, certainly holds its place and has its beauty. Even in the theater, the horizontal development is very effective. Romains' most famous play: *Knock, ou le Triomphe de la médecine,* is the study of the influence over a village's whole population of a new and daring physician who succeeds in creating a "unanimous" malady and in putting an entire population to bed.

Every human group is a possible "hero." *Les Copains* is a group of friends, "one god in seven persons." Erudite hoaxters, *Les Copains* throw two small French towns, Ambert and Illoire, into an uproar with their outrageous practical jokes; but the emotion created by the hoaxes brings about a new and strange solidarity among the people. The *Psyche* trilogy is the story of the human couple, "god of bodies," possessing a unanimity so close and so strong that it attains a mystical level of existence in which love becomes strong enough to unite, through space, the bodies of separated lovers. *Le Vin Blanc de la Villette* evokes the great proletarian "days" of Paris, and there again, a hoax is practiced on the bourgeoisie by mocking workers.

All these books show talent, but they are uneven, sometimes devoid of humanity, and they do not yet achieve greatness. One senses a latent power in them. The architect who built these houses would be better qualified to build a city. The war of 1914 inspires in Romains an ill-defined desire that men of good will be born who will calm a Europe "intoxicated with history."

> I was born of little people
> Earning little for much labor.
> My ancestors have taken out of the soil
> More wheat than they have had bread.
>
> We are that small race
> Which the State gathers up by handfuls.
> A thousand of our days piled up
> Would pay for a whore's night.
>
> Others own the factories,
> The docks, the banks, the newspapers.
> At least its good that they think about us
> When Panama is lying in labor.
>
> Because for peace and for war,
> For stitching and unstitching life,
> The mighty of this world have
> Never needed our advice.
>
> Nevertheless, I speak in the name
> Of those men without importance.
> I have the audacity to act as if
> They deserve to be heard.

They say, mighty of this world,
That they are very tired of you;
That they have seen you playing for five years
With flesh and cannons.

But that is time, it is high time,
To sponge up our smoking blood
And finally to leave in peace
Those men without importance.

Beautiful murderers, famous bandits,
Forgive us our nature.
We are so many on earth, so many
Who have no need of war
In order to be intoxicated with virtue . . .

Do not take so much trouble
To forge sublime miseries.
I assure you that peace
Is much easier to achieve than it's said to be.

It takes ten years of your talking
To get us angry,
Thirty newspapers, a thousand drums
And great parades in the sun.

With a pity that our too proud hearts
Don't want to change the game!
We would listen to you much better
If you told us the opposite.

IV. MEN OF GOOD WILL

It was natural—and even necessary—that a writer whose
doctrine demanded from him an interest in groups and in
nations, who was a poet of modern life, and who, besides,
showed a curiosity about all forms of professionalism and
all milieux, be tempted to write a monumental narrative
work. From adolescence, Romains had selected Hugo and
Homer as his masters. Very early in life, he had imagined

"that one day he would undertake a vast prose work of fiction, which would express, in its movement and its multiplicity, in its detail and its dynamism, his vision of the modern world."

We have seen him until then successfully try diverse genres: poetry, the novel, the theater. To him, however, about 1932, nothing he had done until then was his work as he conceived of it. And so, at forty, vigorous, still young, and infinitely better equipped for this vast enterprise than he would have been as a thirty-year-old, he began the work on which he staked his career as a writer. Naturally, he had been preparing it for a long time. To put in motion an army of characters there is Balzac's technique: to write a series of novels, each one forming a complete whole, but in which the reader rediscovers the same characters, and which together ends by creating *La Comédie Humaine*. There is also Zola's technique: to write a series of novels whose characters are united by blood ties and to so demonstrate the truth of the laws of heredity. There is Proust's, which is also Romain Rolland's: to parade a central character moving among different people of many backgrounds. There are those of Galsworthy, Martin du Gard, Duhamel, who use Zola's method in that their characters belong to the same family, but Proust's also, as the work is continuous.

Jules Romains studied, tried, eliminated all those formulae. He thought Balzac's was rather artificial. Many of the novels are excellent, but the novels of *La Comédie Humaine* taken together do not impress the reader as a single work. (This is Romains' view, it isn't mine.) Zola's pretension seems puerile to him. How could a series of novels in which the writer includes only what he wants represent a scientific experience? Besides, it is artificial to devote each novel of the series to a particular background. In life, sportsmen and financiers, actors and politicians are mixed together. Reality is arbitrarily divided up when one groups all the men involved with finance in one novel, all the men involved with railroads in another, and all the military in a third.

The form selected by Proust is perfect if we are talking about a "novel of apprenticeship," where the reader must see the image of a world, limited by the dimensions of an individual existence, as reflected in the mind of the hero during his different periods. But if the author pretends to portray a whole society, or a whole era, in that way he would be led to credit his only hero with an unbelievable richness of adventures and he would fall into the artificiality of the picaresque novel, which Jules Romains rightly believes even *Wilhelm Meister* does not escape. When we read *Gil Blas* or *Wilhelm Meister,* we cannot help thinking: How kindly fate has been in offering so many contacts, so many experiences to one man, and exactly in the order in which our curiosity would wish them!

What is the common fault in these varied conceptions of the *roman-fleuve?* In the eyes of the Unanimist Romains, the fault rests in the idea of a society in which an individual, or a family, would be the center. The whole organic structure of society runs counter to such a notion. No individual destiny, be it that of the greatest man (Napoleon's for example), permits us to penetrate into all the nooks and crannies of a society. Napoleon knew only rather small groups of his time: the court, the headquarters of the army, the Council of State. What surprised him at Saint Helena is both touching and naïve. It is apparent that he saw only a very limited aspect of the Europe he dominated. No giant can carry the world of the Comedie Humaine. "In fact, in society, individual destinies travel their own paths, while ignoring each other, most of the time."

What is the solution to the problem? Jules Romains finds his in turning the basic question around. Instead of asking himself: "How should individuals be brought together to create an image of the world?" He asks himself: "How, in portrait of the world, can individuals be given their rightful place?" The hero of his magnum opus is a quarter of a century of French life, or even of European life. Here and there, great historical or geographical canvasses plunge the reader into that vastness which is the real subject of the book. At the proper time, social landscapes, pictures of Paris, of Rome, of Verdun, of Odessa, prose poems about crowds or about armies, restore to the work its proper epic scale. As for individual destinies (for there must be some in a novel) they emerge from the crowds as a shooting star is separated from the slow movement of the constellations.

Because "in life, individual destinies often ignore each other" we meet in *Les Hommes de Bonne Volonté* many characters who don't know each other, many also who appear for an instant and won't be seen again. Some of these destinies follow parallel paths because they are unknowingly subject to the same attractions, to the same pressures, because they are carried away by the same currents, which are those of our time. In fact, the group which gives its name to the book, the men of good will, "is not necessarily made up of men who know that they belong to it."

Who are the men of good will? They are all those who, during the years when the western world was heading towards the most absurd and the most horrible of catastrophes, were attempting to understand and to check that tendency. They are those who didn't share in a "dilettantism of chaos," those who believed in human solidarity. Those men existed. We have known a few of them; we have tried to take our place among them. Romains, who is not contemptuous of human nature, forcefully states that, in this difficult period, if the majority of men let themselves be led by the evil, the foolish and the proud, good will nevertheless existed and a real effort was made towards improvement. "Everything happens as if all had wanted to move forward by means of hard jolts. In the swarm of wills, there must surely be some that are good wills . . . It remains to be seen how many times they fooled themselves, how

many times they let themselves be tied to the enemy's chariot
or, like the blind horse of the chain-pump, to the windlass
of a well in which there was no longer any water." Who are
the men of good will? And where were they? They were
everywhere. Some could have been found in all countries, in
all classes, in all occupations. Péguy would have said that
there are mystics and politicians in all parties, and he would
have contended that only the mystics can be of good will.
But Romains would recognize a few of his own, even among
the politicians. For him, the distinction is between those who
actively or passively accept evil and those who work towards
the good, even if it be clumsily.

The existence of such a group and the history of its
efforts, constitute Romains' guidewire through the labyrinth
of facts. But an "epoch" represents an infinite multiplicity.
How to portray it? And besides, what rightly is an epoch?
When does it begin? When does it end? Romains selected
the sixth of October, 1908, as the point of departure for
his work. Why? Because, on that day, Austria by the an-
nexation of Bosnia and Herzegovina, broke the treaty of
Berlin and began the era of world wars. What will be the
final date? "Provisionally," Romains once wrote, "I expect
to continue this story up to a certain day in the year 1933, a
day to which I will dedicate a final volume as the counterpart of the *Six Octobre*. But it may be that events will suggest to me or impose on me another final date, or another
ending."

Nineteen hundred eight to nineteen thirty-three . . .
Once again, how to portray twenty-five years? How to dis-
engage from an infinite swarming of men and events the
basic and clear-cut lines required to form that totality,
"intelligible without reflection," which must constitute a
work of art? It seems that the cinema helped Romains discover his "technique." In the course of history different
art forms have influenced each other; toward 1920 the
influence of music on the novel was undeniable. The cinema

gave Romains a means of expressing the multiplicity of modern life through instantaneous shifting from one scene to another, through constant changes of country, background and mood.

As the techniques of the theater, in the seventeenth century, imposed on the author the unity of place, so the techniques of the screen, in the twentieth century, bring simultaneity and ubiquity. Besides, that simultaneity is legitimate even in the novel, because it well describes what goes on in the mind of modern man. For a woman living in the time of the Crusades, what was war, once the warriors were gone? A long reverie. For the woman of 1944, who saw newsreels each week at the movies, war was a succession of living, animated tableaux. For the woman of the 1960s, public life is a televised newspaper. It is valid and natural that the novel borrow that technique. However, it is necessary to select and to maintain the unity of the novel's world, in spite of the multiplicity of images and the variety of the angles from which they are seen. Romains succeeds in this, thanks to a certain number of techniques he uses with intelligence and skill.

A) Vast historic and geographic tableaux are not a novelty. Victor Hugo, in *Les Misérables,* introduced a picture of the battle of Waterloo, another of French society at the time of the Restoration. Balzac begins many of his novels with a long and admirable study of urban geography. From Romains must be read, for example: the *Présentation de Paris à Cinq Heures du Soir,* which is in Volume 1 of *Les Hommes de Bonne Volonté,* and the *Présentation de la France en Juillet 1914.* Neither Hugo nor Balzac wrote anything better.

B) Another way to insure the unity of a work is to have heroes representing the author move through it from beginning to end. *Les Hommes de Bonne Volonté* is not an autobiographical novel, of which Jallez or Jerphanion would be the hero. But Jallez and Jerphanion are two intelligent men in whose minds essential events are reflected. They

represent two aspects of the author—one his poetic side,
the other his realistic side. It may not be accidental that
their two names begin with *J* of *Je*. A conversation between
Jallez and Jerphanion is a dialogue between Jules Romains
and Jules Romains.

Toward ten o'clock, Jallez observed that Jerphanion had
raised his head from his books and, hands in his pockets
and legs outstretched, was leaning back in his chair. He
took advantage of it to say:

"I was thinking again about Baudelaire. There is a whole
area of his poetry that the banal baudelairian does not
frequent and which escapes your criticism."

"Mystic heights?"

"Not exactly. It is too easy to show that they derive from
his eroticism. 'In the dozing beast, an angel awakens.' No.
I think rather of the poet of Paris, of the streets, of the
ports, of the poet of a great modern city which he is always, even in the erotic pieces. Consider this astonishing
sentence to explain the birth of his prose poems: 'Visiting
the great cities and intercepting their innumerable cross-
currents.' Granted that he swoons over a woman's tresses;
but it is still Marseille or Alexandria which he inhales.
And then there are other kinds of freshness. A way of
remembering . . . You recall those lines of his, for example:

'But the green paradise of childish loves,
The running, the songs . . . the kisses, the bouquets . . .
With the jugs of wine, at night, in the groves.'

Read them again, old man. Eh! What do you think of
them?"

"Obviously, the whole passage has a very great charm."

"You say that without conviction."

"But no."

"Look, in dealing with such a theme, it is in the range
and depth of its accent that it touches us. Alongside of it
put some Murger, or even the *Chansons des rues et des
bois*. Oh! I don't scorn the *Chansons,* Oh! nor Murger.

Murger, when he uses the right word, which sometimes happens, succeeds in gripping the heart. But, nevertheless, it's true that you can hardly feel any of that."

"By why?"

"Because you lack a Parisian childhood. Where did you spend your early childhood?"

"In a village called Boussoulet, on the road from Puy to Valence."

"In the mountains?"

"Yes, between a thousand and eleven hundred meters. On a pass. Or, rather, at the entrance to an immense plateau."

"Your parents come from there?"

"My father was a teacher there."

C) Every epoch has its framework, a hierarchy, an administration, social classes. When Romains studies an event, he leads us through all the steps of the hierarchy by a series of "flashes." For example, in order to paint the battle of Verdun, he takes us into headquarters, into command posts, among fighting men, among civilians and, among the latter, politicians, purveyors to the armies, women who conduct salons, working people. Illustrating it with a series of snapshots, he gives us a national and "unanimous" idea of the event. (It is the plan of *Mort de Quelqu'un,* applied to a much more important theme.)

D) For a novelist who thus competes with history, a difficult problem is created by actual and historically important people—by which I mean monarchs, Presidents of the Republic, Prime Ministers, Commanders-in-Chief, famous artists. Credibility is one of the requirements of a novel. What credibility could a novelist hope to achieve if he described an imaginary king of England, at a time when we *know* George V was reigning, or, in 1915, a generalissimo other than Joffre? Balzac, in *La Comédie Humaine,* ventured to the edge of creative extremes when he brought into the world a great writer (Canalis) or a great minister (De Marsay). Jules Romains resolved this dilemma—ingeniously, and with a certain amount of success—by accepting a few protagonists from history and by combining them with his own imaginary characters. And so, Briand, Joffre, Clemenceau, Gallieni, Jaures, become characters in *Les Hommes de Bonne Volonté* and speak as they would in a historical novel, but with a commendable verisimilitude. Romains even gives Briand a whole interior monologue. It is at the moment when, in 1910, he has just ended a railroad strike through a mobilization.

Although Briand may surrender to all the excesses of his imagination, dismiss all restraints, even interior ones, he doesn't see himself moving along that kind of frozen path, on that small, terrible mountain or cliff-side path which is the power of one man. A man who, without being forced to it by his birth, like kings, separates himself little by little from other men, draws away, walks, battered by the wind, on a ledge which gets narrower and narrower . . . How pitiable! not to mention dangerous. Or, then, it would be a matter of being a little crazy. And Briand does not feel at all crazy. And even though he has no illusions about his friends, he does not conceive of a future without friendship. To attack popular liberties. To put the law in his pocket, for more than twenty-four hours. To order the police and the cavalry to convince the recalcitrants. To dispatch to Lambessa or to La Nouvelle those who insist upon not thinking straight . . . Never—even with the applause of the loiterers and the benedictions of the reactionary right. Granted; one doesn't always remain as intransigent as at twenty. But do those idiots imagine that I would want to rule if I felt the Republic against me? . . .

. . . Briand even doubts that it is ever otherwise. He doesn't believe that a man can succeed in finding, even in the flush of a delirious ambition, the courage to violate the law of a people, if he has not at least secretly received from certain people he holds as his brothers a mandate or *carte blanche* . . . Even Louis-Napoleon . . . You can't change opinion that he would not have undertaken the

2nd of December if the Carbonari, or others, had not said
to him: "You can march . . ." The attendant comes to
tell him, without special emphasis:

"Monsieur Gurau is here."

But Briand wants to dream a little longer. He answers
softly:

"Ask him to wait five minutes."

E) Finally, a balance had to be maintained between the
"unanimous" novel, which is that of France, the novel of
the group, and individual destinies; for these are, after all,
the stuff of which life is made. In this, it can be said that
Romains succeeded in great part. In his book, many individual destinies are at once absorbing and moving. The
reader takes a genuine interest in Jallez' loves, in Gurau's
humiliations, in the childish joys and sorrows of little Louis
Bastide. Read the entire chapter on the yellow shoes in *Les
Humbles*. It is a model of simple and true emotion. The
Bastides are poor, the father earns 210 francs a month.
But little Louis has gotten good marks in school and his
mother has promised him yellow shoes. At first he seems
proud and happy.

But while they were walking in the rue Ordener, she became aware that the child seemed preoccupied. He fixed his
eyes before him. He gave the impression of trying to follow
an idea a little difficult for him, a little far off.

"What are you thinking about, sweetheart?"

"Nothing."

"Aren't you happy?"

"Oh, yes!"

"Then what is it?"

"How much did my shoes cost?"

"Nine and a half francs. Didn't you listen when I was
bargaining?" (He had heard, but he was afraid he had
misunderstood.) "He was only willing to take off eight
sous. Oh! They're expensive. But they are really of first
quality. The leather is very fine. And although they have
a pointed toe, they hardly pinch you."

"But, Mommy."

"What?"

"How much money does Papa make a day?"

"What are you worrying about? It has nothing to do with you." She almost blushed. In front of her child she was overcome with a kind of modesty. She had found his question out of place, and she would have answered him even more sharply, but, in his wide open eyes, still staring ahead, his pupils shone with seriousness. She did not even have the courage to lie.

"How much does Papa make . . . ? Well. He makes a very good wage. First of all he is paid for the whole month, Sundays and holidays included. Whether he works or whether he rests . . . It isn't like other jobs . . . It's a great advantage he has over laborers . . ."

"Yes, but how much does that amount to per day?"

"For each day of actual work?"

"I don't know . . . No . . . By day, that means by day of living."

She blushed again.

"I've never figured it out . . . Of course, not ten francs. Only the most important employees earn ten francs."

"Ah! . . . Not even nine francs, either?"

"In any case, that's not very far from the right amount. But what are you trying to figure out?"

She leaned forward a little to look at him more closely. His radiant look of a moment ago was completely gone. He had a small frown and his lips quivered. His eyes continued to look ahead; but around their light there was now a moist veil. He squeezed his mother's hand more tightly. Suddenly her heart was struck by the thought which tormented her child. She made a great effort to prevent her own tears from coming. Leaning over him, caressing his hair, his beret, she said to him, in a muffled tone:

"My little boy. My poor little boy. My darling little Louis . . ."

F) The role given to eroticism by Romains is much larger than that granted to it by Balzac or Stendhal. Alain in his

Système des Beaux-Arts maintains that true fiction is chaste
and that the description of physical love is not a subject for
the artist. He argues that the sensual emotions thus aroused
in the reader or the spectator are too strong to allow for
aesthetic emotion. The painting of a nude woman only becomes aesthetic through a certain stylization. It is Apollo
and not Priapus who inspired masterpieces from sculptors.
I believe that it is a question of time and mores. Petronius,
Rabelais, Laclos, Proust, or Hemingway describe scenes that
neither Racine, nor even Retz, would have dared evoke. Is
that to say that Racine and Retz were less sensual than
Laclos, Proust, and Romains? The truth is that the freedom
with which a writer speaks of love is a function both of
the artist's temperament and of the mores of his time.
Romains, himself, attaches great importance to these descriptions and uses them often. He says, "The manner in
which a man makes love is one of his most characteristic
traits." Alain—and Stendhal—would reply: "Most characteristic traits of a living man . . . Yes . . . But not of the
hero of a novel."

Did the author of *Les Hommes de Bonne Volonté*
achieve his design? Did he give us a complete and moving
picture of our time? Let us say immediately that no fictional
picture could be complete. *La Comédie Humaine* is a gigantic
work, but it is not a comprehensive picture of France in the
nineteenth century. Workers are almost entirely absent from
Balzac's work; so are big businessmen and the Court; the
novels about the Army were not written; and relations with
foreign countries are hardly mentioned. No matter. There is
no reason for us to try to find, in a single work, a picture of
the whole known world. We have only the right to expect
that the author know well what he describes.

Is this true of Romains? It has been said that he has a good
knowledge of normal students, of professors, of writers, but
a poor knowledge of society people and princes of the Church,
both of whom he describes inexactly. It seems to me that the

[10] *Jacques de Lacretelle*

[11] *Jules Romains*

[12] *André Malraux*

[13] *Simone de Beauvoir and Jean-Paul Sartre*

[14] *Albert Camus*

answer ought to be: 1. No one can know everything. Romains' area of observation is one of the most extensive in literary history. He has carefully observed France, he has traveled much abroad. Not only his professors and his writers, but his politicians, his military and businessmen are completely believable. That's a great deal. 2. That his society people and his ecclesiastics are, if not true, at least as true as those of his rivals. Balzac's duchesses sometimes make surprising statements. Victor Hugo's Bishop Myriel is no more a living person than the Abbé Jeanne. De Marsay is less successfully done than Gurau. In the whole immense work there are jarring chapters. But only great writers have the courage to take great risks. 3. That the painstaking and intelligent study of many occupations gives the work a singular solidity. I have already spoken of the descriptions of the military at Verdun and of politicians in relation to Briand, but here is a tiny example which I admire for the truthfulness of detail. It is a description of the thought processes as understood by little Louis Bastide:

When one has been playing with a hoop for a long time, like Louis Bastide, and when one has had the luck to find a hoop that one likes well, one begins to see that it is very different from ordinary running. Try to run by yourself; you will be tired at the end of a few minutes. With a hoop, fatigue is delayed indefinitely. You have the impression that you are supported, almost carried. When you feel a moment of lassitude, it seems that the hoop, in a friendly gesture, lends you strength.

Besides, one doesn't always need to be running very fast. With a little skill, one can almost walk. The trick is to be sure the hoop doesn't go to the right or to the left; or get tangled in the legs of a passerby, who struggles like a rat caught in a trap; or fall on the ground after extraordinary contortions. You must know how to use the stick, to give very light strokes, hardly touching, which accompany the hoop. Above all it is necessary, between the strokes, to remain the master of the slightest swerving of the hoop, thanks to the stick which never ceases, from one side or the other, to caress its edge, which sustains and corrects its progress, and whose tip intervenes quickly at any place where there is a danger of swerving . . .

Sometimes the hoop lurches, and escapes. The tip of the stick pursues it, without being able to touch it. And it tilts, it veers. It behaves in exactly the same way as animals whose flight is not reasonable for long. You must know how to catch it without too much impatience. If not, one risks sending it against a wall, or flattening it on the ground.

When the times comes to get down from the sidewalk, it is a pleasure to wait, to watch the hoop's little leap. One tells oneself that one is dealing with an animal, sensitive and nervous. And then, all the way to the sidewalk across the street, it doesn't stop leaping over the cobblestones, rolling in the cracks, with all sorts of irregularities and capricious changes of direction.

It has also been said: "Why does he give so much space in his work to bizarre and criminal characters, such as Quinette, or to such extravagant conspiracies which verge on hoaxes?" Partly, probably, because Romains himself, as we have indicated, shows a strange affinity for conspiracies— the "secrets of the King," mysterious emissaries, secret societies—but also because he *believes* in their importance in history and, perforce, in the structure of society: "The Church itself is a secret society . . . One cannot understand any of the histories of monarchies in Europe without placing in the center that formidable spider's web which was the Society of Jesus . . . As for the Revolution—it is only explained by the long preparatory work of secret societies . . . Have you ever asked yourself how, in an unprepared France, not undermined in advance, the fourteenth of July explosion could have occurred with such lightning speed? . . . If history is studied from the angle, everything in it becomes surprising, changeable, thrilling, enchanting. And the childishness that could develop from such a storybook notion is tempered by the sense of a profound burst of idealism. Those dark machinations, which might occasion a smile, appear to be the tortured gestation of the modern world, and also the secular determination of man to discover a way out of his prison . . ."

Men of good will are engaged in a secret crusade against tyranny, against disorder, against war, against the power of money, against cruelty. There is nothing in this which is not laudable. That they were very often mistaken about the merit of the leaders they supported, about the nature of their objectives, and about the immediate effects of their actions, is likely. It is even inevitable. One cannot act without committing errors. But one cannot doubt that their goal was noble and their intentions pure. And in writing this, I am also thinking of their creator, who is himself one of his heroes and whom I do not hesitate to place among the men of good will. It is not only because of its dimensions, its intelligence, but also because of the love it expresses that *Les Hommes de Bonne Volonté* is a great book.

Finally, it has been said: "The scale of the work is too vast. A work of art must be limited; it must be grasped at a glance; it must leave in the mind the impression of a coherent and intelligible whole. The reproduction of the multiplicity and the disorder of the world is not a work of art. A collection of newspapers published between 1908 and 1933 would be even more Unanimist than *Les Hommes de Bonne Volonté*. It would not be a creation. Where is the plan for this one?"

To which I answer that this plan, already glimpsed by the reader, will only be made completely clear once the work is finished. Remember Proust's great novel. While it was being published, we admired its fragments without grasping its unity. But when the *Temps Retrouvé* was opposed to the *Temps Perdu,* when the images of the beginning, the little cake, reappeared at the end, then we realized that that great arch rested on two strong and symmetrical pillars. It will probably be the same with *Les Hommes de Bonne Volonté* when the final day will balance the initial day.[1]

V

A poet of modern life, intrigued with its manifestations, its octopuslike cities, its secret springs. A powerful novelist, who has known how to animate a world, and in Verdun how to resurrect an army. A man of good will, who believed, who still believes, in the power of intelligence and in human solidarity. All that makes of Jules Romains one of the great writers of our time. Others have better understood and described diverse aspects of mankind. Balzac and Proust have more completely studied the passions of the soul. But, in his field, which is the poetry of human groups, Romains is without peer. His intelligence and his culture have permitted him to do, for the life of our time, what a Retz or a Saint-Simon did for the life of the seventeenth century. In order that the Human Comedy of one of the most confused and unhappy periods of history be written, it was necessary that there coexist in one mind, a poet, a philosopher, a chronicler, and a novelist.

[1] That final day, the *Sept Octobre*, was, in fact, the subject of the last volume of *Les Hommes de Bonne Volonté*. (1948 note)

ANDRÉ MALRAUX

"ONE DAY the world began to resemble my books," Malraux has written. In his novels he had depicted danger, warfare, revolution; and the whole world became rebellion and war. All his life he had sought a virile literature in which sentimental values would be replaced by courage and pleasure. The spirit of the time proved him right. Sentimental values had been supreme during epochs of stability and leisure. A youth brought up amid the sound of spitting machine guns sought sterner masters. It has less interest in the analysis of the individual than the communion of the masses. Malraux's work which, like Hemingway's, threw youth into a bath of bloodshed and heroism, was bound to please it, and did.

But the basic reason for his prestige was that his life was the touchstone of his work. Somewhere he said that memoirs are the only books that deserve to be written. His novels are the transposed memoirs of a brave and intelligent man. Malraux has known and "lived" the China of *Les Conquérants* and of *La Condition Humaine;* he has fought in Spain with the volunteers of *L'Espoir;* he was in the tanks of 1940 like the hero of *Les Noyers de l'Altenburg;* he commanded a brigade during the campaign of liberation. Veterans know these things and respect him. "For many of us," wrote Gaëtan Picon, "Malraux has been what Péguy, Barrès, and, before them, Chateaubriand were for other men's youth." Even more than Chateaubriand, he made his life his masterpiece.

Not that it didn't have difficult moments. An adventurer takes risks. For fifteen years, Malraux clung to the world revolution, without, however, joining the Communist Party. We will see how, later, he veered toward the national war, Gaullism and power. "A man—eager to act out his biography as an actor plays a role," at once author and interpreter of his life's drama, he gave himself a beautiful script. Whatever happens in the future, the game seems to have been won.

I. THE FORERUNNER OF THE ABSURD

Much has been made in our time about the absurdity of the world. The major part of Camus' work is devoted to the "absurd man," he who has measured the abyss between the hopes of man and the indifference of the universe. Actually, it is not a new idea. Malraux, like so many others, cites Pascal: "Let us imagine a great many men in chains, and all condemned to death; some of them being strangled in front of the others, and those who remain see their own condition in that of their companions . . . that is the picture of men's condition." Yes, there lies the essence of the absurd. Death "is the irrefutable proof of the absurdity of life."

For believers, the problem of the absurd contains an evident solution. Their universe is not indifferent; it obeys an all-powerful God, who watches over the destiny of all creatures and who can be moved to mercy through prayer. Death is *not* for them the end of everything, but the beginning of true existence. "Death, where is thy victory?" The soul survives and rejoices in the presence of God. But, for Malraux's heroes, for Garine and Perken, for Gisors and Magnin, God is dead. What can be done with a soul if there is no God? Garine *needs* to believe in the absurdity of the world. "There is no power, nor even real life, without the certainty of, without the obsession with, the vanity of the world."

Nowhere does Malraux say that he agrees with Garine, and I don't believe that he does entirely. But he himself states: "The absence of life's finality has become a requirement for action." That absence liberates action. If there is nothing, anything can be attempted. It is, says Pierre de Boisdeffre, "the temptation of Lucifer, from which Malraux will barely escape, but to which conquerors, from Caligula to Hitler, generally succumb." A man whose soul possesses nothing can engage in the most daring gambles. What is there to lose? Chinese terrorists and aviators in Spain cast their lives like dice on the green felt. Their stake, in their eyes, has little value.

But why? Wouldn't it be more natural, in an indifferent universe, to live for the happy moment rather than to look for brawls, torture, and death? For it is not for "the cause" that Garine is fighting. With scornful irony, he speaks of men who pretend to work for the happiness of humanity. "Those damn fools want to have the right reason. In fact, there is only one reason that is not a mockery: the most efficacious use of one's own strength." Ambitious? Garine (who is in part, but only in part, like the young Malraux) does not feel the ambition which evaluates the future and prepares successive conquests, Rastignac's planned ambition, "but he does feel within himself the stubborn, constant need for power." From power he expects neither money, nor consideration, nor respect; only power itself. "He came to think of the exercise of power as a solace, as a deliverance. He wanted to play *himself*. Brave, he knew that every loss is limited by death."

Such thoughts stumble at every step against death, which sometimes appears as a solution. Grandfather Berger, of *Les Noyers de l'Altenburg,* commits suicide, as Malraux's grandfather had done. However, two days before his death, the same Dietrich Berger had asked his brother: "If you could choose a life, which one would you choose?—And you?—Well, *whatever happens,* if I had another life to live

over, I would want no other then Dietrich Berger's." Suicide
was already present in "whatever happens"; and that man
had loved his life and fanatically loved himself. It may be for
that reason that he killed himself.

For other of Malraux's characters, the idea of death becomes an obsession to kill. That harshness appears mostly
in men who have been humiliated. "Intense humiliation calls
for the negation of the world. Only ceaselessly spilled blood,
drugs, and neuroses can feed such solitudes." The German,
Klein, in *Les Conquérants*, "quivers with hate."

"It's not always the same one's turn to suffer. I remember
a party once where I was looking . . . Ah! A few bullets
to smash that . . . I don't know how to say, that . . . smile,
that's what. The sight of the mugs of all those people who
have never been without grub! Yes, make those people
realize that one thing, called human life, exists." And again:
"The revolution, what is it? I'll tell you: one doesn't know.
But it is first that there is too much poverty, not only
lack of money but . . . always there are those rich people
who are living and the others who are not living."

It is not pity, a feeling to which Malraux's heroes are
hardly susceptible, and which many among them would
scorn. It is the need to recover, for themselves and for others,
human dignity. "What do you call dignity?" Kyo is asked
(*La Condition Humaine*). He answers: "The opposite of
humiliation," which is not a bad answer. Dignity is the respect
which a man owes to himself and which he can demand
from others. Dignity which is not respected is changed into
humiliation, which in turn incites terrorism.

Hong (*Les Conquérants*) has freed himself from poverty,
but he has not forgotten its lesson, nor the picture of the
world it creates, colored by impotent hate. "There are
only two races," he says: "the poor and the others." He has
discovered that he does not hate the happiness of the rich
so much as he envies their self-respect. "A poor man," he
also says, "cannot have self-esteem." He wouldn't have that

feeling if he believed, as did his ancestors, that his existence was not limited to his own life. But he has ceased to believe that. Then the human condition appears to him in all its absurdity and he clings to what is left to him—his hate. He hates idealists because they pretend to arrange things. Hong doesn't want things to be arranged. He is an anarchist. It is the ultimate attitude of the man who knows he is absurd. There are more constructive attitudes. From which come recourse to action.

II. ADVENTURE AND ACTION

"A life is nothing but a stone thrown into the ocean, but when a man knows this, he risks everything on its trajectory." However, there are a thousand ways of risking everything and a thousand kinds of adventures. The young Malraux had chosen revolutionary war. Not because he believed in the Communist revolution. At no time does he reason as a Marxist. Some of his heroes are Communists: Borodine, Kyo. Gisors, Kyo's father, says: "I don't want to go to Moscow. Marxism has ceased to live in me. In Kyo's eyes it is will; in mine it is fatality." (This is not to deny Marxism, but in present-day jargon, "to demystify it.") Garine has not wanted to join the party, knowing that he could not take its discipline. "If he was attracted by the Bolsheviks' technique of insurrection and their liking for it, he was exasperated by their doctrinal vocabulary, and especially by their dogmatism." Garine does not like the people. Naturally he prefers the poor to the rich because they have more humanity, but he senses that it is in them the virtue of the defeated. "I know very well that they would become abject, as soon as we triumph together."

Malraux's heroes are more interested in action than in doctrine. Naturally, they are different, one from the other, in their ideas. Much more than has been recognized. A critic (André Rousseaux) has written: "Malraux's characters are so little alive that they die immediately in the reader's memory. From Garine to Vincent Berger, I only remember silhouettes expounding, with a bomb or a revolver in hand, and a metaphysical brain." I don't share that feeling. Garine is unforgettable; the terrorist Hong terrifying; the idealist Tchen-Dai surprisingly human and varied; the Kyo-May couple tragically lives out a strange love; the great businessman, Ferral, is a vigorous portrait. But all those men don't like their will to be transformed into intelligence. They need to be projected outside of themselves, outside of their consciousness of the absurd. Adventure is their excuse. Risk is their element. "As with all intense sensations, danger, in leaving him, left him empty; he wanted to find it again." That sentence applies to Tchen, a character of *La Condition Humaine*, but see how it suits Malraux himself who, hardly out of one danger, voluntarily throws himself into another, and only leaves the International Brigade to join the French Resistance.

Until then, many of his heroes, and some of the best, had been strangers to the country for which they were fighting. Garine was not Chinese; Kyo is a half-breed; Borodine couldn't care less for China; by definition, the International Brigade is not Spanish. The modern adventurer—be he the English Lawrence who fights at the side of the Arabs, or the American Hemingway who fights alongside the Spanish republicans—has most often been a stranger to the country for which he offered his life. More paradoxical yet, Malraux's hero (until 1940) hardly fights for an idea; he is ill-at-ease in a political party. He fights against the rich, the powerful, officialdom; he takes issue with universal hypocrisy as Van Gogh does with academicism; he fights to fight. All that without illusions, with the certainty that hypocrisy will be reborn under another form. It is pure action.

I imagine that on the day that Malraux discovered in De Gaulle a hero after his own heart, without many more illusions than he had about men, and not a stranger to his cause but, on the contrary, tightly bound to it, he found great peace. To put adventure in the service of order clarified the problem. To fight for France, even to fight for the West, for culture, at last coincided with Malraux's deepest feelings. François Mauriac, a man of penetrating intuitions, had foreseen that evolution from the day *La Condition Humaine* won the Prix Goncourt and a bourgeois, capitalistic society, in a sort of frenzy, lionized a young man who had threatened it with revolt, with general strikes, and who had worked with those who were going to drive Europe out of Asia.

"We are living in a strange society," then wrote Mauriac; "it is old, it is bored, it forgives any one who knows how to entertain it, even while frightening it . . . Talent disarms it. Here is a young man who, since his adolescence, has come toward it with a dagger in his hand . . . So what? He has talent; he has more talent than any young man his age . . . In the year of grace, 1933, a beautiful book covers up everything." It is astonishing that the Prix Goncourt and that success, led Mauriac to foresee "the intrusion of success into a destiny oriented toward despair." He concluded: "After all, ambition is a possible way out." In 1945 Mauriac had won that wager with himself and Malraux was a Minister of State.

As for me, I had been struck, in all his books, by the technical competence he showed in very diverse areas. There are manual workers, like Tchen, who exist for direct and brutal action. But action demands commanders also, and commanders, in order to command, must know what they are talking about. Malraux had amazingly understood the mechanics of subversion, of terrorism and of revolution. He was also going to understand the mechanics of government. He knew that, in the last analysis, only technicians can bring about the triumph of revolution. "At the beginning, the revolution is only a vast abuse of authority," says Garcia

(*L'Espoir*); Hernandez answers: "Those militia there could
be crushed by two thousand soldiers who knew their job."
And Ximenes: "Courage is a thing which is organized, which
lives and dies, that must be cared for, like a rifle . . ."

Malraux speaks of war as a professional soldier: "To kill
is a problem of economy: to expend the largest possible
amount of hardware and explosives, in order to expend the
least possible amount of living flesh." The American generals
I knew in 1943–45 applied that principle. It must not be
forgotten that Malraux was an active aviator, a squadron
chief in command of republican planes in the battle of
Medelin. That competence gives his descriptions of war an
uncontestable veracity.

> The three planes from Teruel flew over the landing field,
> each searching for the position lights of the others in order
> to take the flight formation. Below, the trapezoidal landing
> field, very small now, was lost in the nocturnal immensity
> of the countryside which, for Magnin, converged entirely
> towards those wretched fires. . . . One after the other,
> one, two, three, four, five, six, seven enemy planes came
> out of the clouds. The republican fighter planes were the
> single-seaters, with low wings, and they couldn't be mis-
> taken for the Heinkels; alertly Magnin put down his bin-
> oculars and had the three planes maneuver close to each
> other. "If we had decent machine guns, we could still stand
> up to them," he thought. But he had the old uncoupled
> Lewis—"800 rounds per minute $\times$ three machine guns $=$
> 2400. Each Heinkel has 1,800 rounds $\times$ four machine
> guns $=$ 7200." He knew it, but repeating it to himself always
> gave him pleasure.

Revealing a more astonishing competence, one worthy of
Balzac, Malraux fully understands Ferral, a business entre-
preneur. I like the scene when Ferral finds himself face to
face with "the directors of the great financial establishments"
. . . "Since the war, he thought, that bunch sitting on the
sofa has cost the French economy, in state funds alone,

eighteen billion. Very well; as he said ten years ago: *Any man who asks advice on investing his fortune from a person he doesn't intimately know deserves to be ruined.*" This sentence could be Gobseck's. I mean it as a compliment. Gobseck was a great businessman, and Malraux is not duped.

The pattern of his life of action is clearly indicated in the titles of the three parts of *L'Espoir:* 1. *The lyrical illusion.* It didn't last long and gave way to a despairing clarity. 2. *Lesson from the Apocalypse.* It is war for war's sake, terrorism for terrorism's sake. 3. *Hope.* Beyond adventure the will to hope is coming like the dawn. "There are not fifty ways to fight; there is only one way and that is to win." Man is the sum of his actions. In acting he becomes history. Let history be as big as possible. There is an objective and one gets out of the absurd.

III. THE MAN AND HISTORY

Malraux has a naturally universal mind. What he sees always evokes for him what has been. A prisoner in 1940, he looks at his companions and discovers in them (as Proust had recognized in the soldiers of 1914 the Frenchmen of St. André-des-Champs), Gothic faces and the secular memory of the plague. "Under that secular familiarity with misfortune, lies that no-less-secular craftiness of man, his clandestine faith in a patience however much filled with disasters, which was perhaps the same that, long ago, faced famines in the caves . . . In our lair, numbed under the great sun of always, a prehistoric voice is whispering." Arriving with his tanks in an evacuated village, amid the changing of caterpillar treads, he finds in it again the barns of always, the harvests, the eternal mongrels.

Beneath that picturesque profusion, I hear the muffled sound of centuries, which extend as far as the darkness of this night: these barns bursting with wheat and grains and straw, these barns with beams hidden among the husks, filled with harrows, with ramrods, with beams, with wooden carts, barns where everything is grain, wood, straw, or leather (the metals had been requisitioned), all surrounded with the extinguished fires of the refugees and the soldiers, they are barns of the Gothic age; our tanks at the end of the street are filling up with water, kneeling monsters before the wells of the Bible . . . O life, so old!

He likes to evoke the millennia and to hear the whispering of the centuries. But because he is very intelligent, he also asks himself whether it is logical to look for eternal man beneath contemporary man. That is one of the subjects of the colloquy which fills a large part of *Les Noyers de l'Altenburg*. That beautiful book, one of Malraux's best, reminds us of the conversations at Pontigny, Charles du Bos, André Gide, Paul Desjardins. And, if I am not mistaken, Malraux, while depicting the colloquy of l'Altenburg, thought of the Cistercian abbey. It seems to me that I recognized Charles du Bos's characteristics in a Count Ravaud. But Malraux has, most of the time, given the floor to a German scholar: Mollberg, who expounds ideas similar to those of Frobenius.

According to Mollberg, a specialist on Africa and on ancient civilizations, when the scholar goes back to the beginning of time, he finds there, before the kingdom of Ur, before the Sumerian world, once again cities, once again a State, and a society which resembles that of ants; before the priests, the King whose power increases with the moon, and who is strangled when an eclipse occurs. That king is, at the same time, himself and the moon. We are in a cosmic domain anterior to any religion. "They kill within the eternal. The gods have not been born." Later, be it Buddhism, Judaism, Christianity, Islam, the entire known world will think religiously. "But the mental structure implied by cosmic civilization is as exclusive of that implied by religion, as Christian faith is exclusive of Voltairian rationalism." Where is eternal man there?

Other populations haven't discovered the connection between the sexual act and birth. How then to make them understand Christianity and the Annunciation? Others again ignore barter. How to explain to them our economy, our social structures? Where is the tie between them and us? "It is history, says Mollberg, which has to give meaning to the human adventure—like the gods. To bind man to the infinite . . . We are men only through thought; we only think what history lets us think, and it probably has no meaning." But we cannot bear that it have no meaning. Be it called history or otherwise, we must have an intelligible world.

> Whether we know it or not, he, he alone, satisfies our rage to survive. If the structures of the mind disappear forever like the plesiosaur, if succeeding civilizations are good only to hurl man into the bottomless barrel of nothingness, if the human adventure maintains itself only at the price of an inexorable metamorphosis, what does it matter that men transmit to each other, for a few centuries, their concepts and their techniques: for man is an accident and, essentially, the world is made of oblivion.

Mollberg personifies a part of Malraux, the negative part. When another member of the colloquy states that all that is a paradox, that there is in man something eternal, and that we fully understand an Egyptian or Gothic work of art, the answer is that the artist (and those who understand him) are exceptions; that Christendom was filled with people who were not Christian; that Egypt was filled with laborers who were not Egyptian. Are eternal barns and harvests found again? Of course.

> The less men participate in their civilization, the more they resemble each other: agreed! But the less they participate, the more they vanish . . . One can conceive a permanence of man, but it is a permanence in nothingness . . . Outside of thought, you have now a dog, now

a tiger, a lion if you insist; always a beast. All men eat, drink, sleep, fornicate, of course; but they don't eat the same things, they don't drink the same things, don't dream of the same things. They have scarcely anything in common except sleeping when they sleep without dreams—and to be dead.

It must be remembered here that this is only a colloquy. Mollberg's thesis is exaggerated and Malraux knows it very well. Another speaker doesn't see at all why the human adventure should not become history. "The greatest mystery, says Walter Berger, is not that we are cast haphazardly between the profusion of matter and the profusion of stars; it is that, in that prison, we extract from ourselves images powerful enough to deny our nothingness." We will find that idea again when we examine Malraux's ideas on art. But history is another form of creation. It imposes an intelligible order on the apparently incoherent mass of facts, which is also the role of science. Malraux does not accept the Hegelian or Marxist view of an all-powerful history, an inevitable current which carries humanity along. History is made up of the human will exercised at each moment in every part of the earth. "Man is not what he hides . . . a wretched little heap of secrets . . . Man is what he does."

And if what he does is now understood in millennia to come, as the lunar king and the panther men are no longer understood, what does it matter? Péguy has earlier shown that those who are concerned with posterity have never reflected on what posterity is: "Posterity is like them. Posterity is them later on. They want to make a judge of posterity. But posterity will have other fish to fry, that is to say, its own fish." Péguy is right. Of course, posterity has been concerned with Caesar, but less than with some minor official (in his time), less than with some "stars" (in their time). Posterity still thinks a little about Caesar, about Louis XIV, but not very much at any one time. Or, if it thinks of Louis XIV, it is because of Versailles or of Saint-Simon, that is to say because of works of art. Which brings us back to the essential idea: Man is what he does or what he causes to be done.

Malraux and his heroes are not uninterested in winning a place in history. "To exist among a great number of men and perhaps for a long time. I want to leave a scar on that map. If I must gamble against my death, I'd rather gamble with twenty tribes than with one child." With twenty tribes? Better still with a nation, with an old nation which makes to the hero the enormous contribution of its past and its glory. For a people are also what they do.

> Leaning against the cosmos like a stone, there is the French peasant . . . Doors half-open, linens, barns, signs of men, biblical dawn where centuries crowd against each other, how the dazzling mystery of the morning is deepened into the one which rises to those worn lips! That in an uncertain smile reappears the mystery of man, and the earth's resurrection is no more than quivering scenery.
>
> I know now the significance of the ancient myths of beings dragged away from the dead. I hardly remember the terror; what I carry in me is the discovery of a simple and sacred secret.
>
> It is perhaps thus that God looked at the first man . . .

A cosmic sense of the sacred and a historical sense of France are perhaps what is most vital in the mature Malraux.

IV. EROTICISM AND LOVE

Many human beings believe they can find an absolute in love, a communion both carnal and mystical. These are not Malraux's heroes. They seek refuge not in love, but in eroticism. "There is eroticism in a book as soon as the idea of constraint is added to the physical love that is described," writes Malraux in his preface to *Les Liaisons Dangereuses*.

Almost all the men he portrays dream of situations where they will impose embraces or pain on a woman. For them a woman is a thing of pleasure, her body one object among many.

"What did you feel afterward, with the first woman you slept with," asked Gisors.

Tchen clenched his fist.

"Pride."

"At being a man?"

"At not being a woman." His voice no longer expressed bitterness, but a complex contempt.

To impose their will, to scorn, and in so doing to demonstrate their power, this is what Ferral (*La Condition Humaine*) and Perken (*La Voie Royale*) seek in eroticism. It pleases them that their victim (one cannot say their partner) be unwilling. And they want her to be anonymous, and simply "the opposite sex." Perken believes in the basic misogyny of almost all men. "He possessed a body as if he were striking it." As for Ferral, "it was clear that his pleasure sprang from his putting himself in the place of the other; constraint from the other, constraint from him. In effect, he never slept with anyone except himself, but he could only do this on the condition that he was not alone."

This was an attitude that would justify a woman's fury and hatred. Here is the letter that Valérie, a courageous woman, sends Ferral: "I am not, my dear, a woman to be had, a mindless body besides which you find your pleasure while telling lies as you would to children and to the sick. You know many things, my dear, but you may die without having noticed that a woman is *also* a human being . . . I refuse to be a body just as you refuse to be a checkbook." Claude Mauriac has shown that some of Colette's intimate thoughts echo those of Malraux's Valérie. What does a man know of the sensuality in a woman? Almost nothing. What she is willing to express—or to pretend.

But, in Malraux's men, that ignorance becomes acutely painful. Claude Mauriac has noted that D. H. Lawrence "fascinates Malraux" in the way in which he attempts to study the erotic experience from women's point of view. "No man can speak about women," says Valérie, "because no man understands that any new make-up, any new dress, any new lover, suggests a new soul." And that is true. Ferral does not understand. Then he tries to crush.

It is easy to conceive of this eroticism, which needs resistance, turning into sadism, into the need to cause suffering. Ferral imagines his mistress "tied to the bed, crying with sobs which seemed so much like the sounds of pleasure, bound up, thrashing in the throes of suffering, since she did not do it in the throes of sex." A step further is the obsession to kill. The terrorist begins by having a horror of his actions. He ends by enjoying them. Tchen, and so many others, are obsessed by blood. "An almost erotic feeling for death," writes Gaëtan Picon, and Marcel Thiébaut: "A novel oozing blood." For a Tchen, the memory of murder is much less remorse than desire. Like the man-eating tiger, the terrorist who has killed once sees a barrier being raised; he feels the need to do it again. Or to risk his own life. Defying death is a form of eroticism, the exercise of an ultimate power.

That sadism also works on the reader who is left, for pages, in suspense and growing terror. The ending of *La Condition Humaine,* where the prisoners are waiting to be tortured, then burned alive by being thrown into the firebox of a locomotive, is hardly bearable.

Is there a place for romantic love in this inferno of eroticism and sadism? It has long been maintained that romantic love is an admirable Christian invention, related to the respect for human life, to the cult of the virgin, and finally to the Crusades which endowed women with virtues intensified by absence. But other forms of love are more ancient, that of Hector for Andromache, of Ulysses for Penelope, of Jacob for Rachel. An attachment in which an enduring affection strengthens desire is not only conceivable but prevalent in all advanced civilizations.

Malraux has sometimes portrayed a love where an elemental sexual need is allied to an intuitive knowledge of the other person. As for example, Kyo and May:

> That love, so often hurt, which united them like a sick child, that shared sense of their life and their death, that carnal understanding between them . . . To May alone, he was not what he had done; to him alone, she was much more than her biography. The embrace, by which love glues human beings together against solitude, did not help the man; it helped the madman, the incomparable monster, preferable to everything, that each human being is to himself and which he pampers in his heart. Since his mother died, May was the only person for whom he was not Kyo Gisors, but the closest accomplice. "A complicity consented, conquered, chosen," he thought in extraordinary agreement with the night, as if his thoughts were no longer made for the light . . . "With her alone I have this love in common, torn or not, as others have sick children who can die . . ." It was certainly not happiness, it was something primitive which was attuned to the darkness and which caused a warmth to rise in him, ending in a motionless embrace, as of check against check—the only thing in him that was as strong as death.

Yes, it is truly love, as is also the feeling which unites Anna and Kassner (*Le Temps du Mépris*). But for Kassner, as for Kyo, the absolute is elsewhere.

V. THE COIN OF THE ABSOLUTE

Under various guises, Malraux's heroes have always been in search of this Grail: the Absolute. Some thing or idea, complete in itself, unshakable, to which the drifting and transitory individual can cling. God being dead, the only thing left to them was revolution, hope. But they would still have to believe in it, and they hardly do. The opium of pure action, of war for war's sake, had for a time replaced Marxist faith, which had died in its turn. The war for France, the reconciliation with history, offered a more beautiful path, and that is the one Malraux has chosen. He sees another chance for salvation in culture, which is allied to history; another method to free oneself from the world, art, which is the re-creation of the world. "History attempts to transform fate into consciousness, and art attempts to transform it into freedom." And elsewhere: "Art, through the trembling of a senile hand, will revenge itself against a crushing and derisive world by forcing it into immortality."

All great art is an act of creation. It brings forth an intense emotion, but not necessarily by representing what incites it in life. "In a painting a magnificent sunset is not a beautiful sunset, but the sunset of a great painter." To reinforce Malraux's thesis with a musical example, the *Forest Murmurs* in *Siegfried* contains not birds' song but Wagner's song. Malraux cites a garage owner from Cassis who had watched Renoir paint: "He had a large canvas. I said to myself, 'Let's go see' . . . it was naked women bathing in *some other place*. He was looking at I don't know what and he changed only a small portion of it.' His vision was less a way of looking at the sea (from which he made the stream of *Les Lavandières*) than the creation of a world to which belonged that blue he reclaimed from infinity."

In brief, "the great artists do not transcribe the world, they compete with it." Balzac said: "Competition with vital statistics," but it is much more—it is competition with the universe, and on that rests the possibility of salvation through art. In a beautiful work of art, the discord between man and the cosmos disappears. The artist ceases to be the absurd man. The world of art is "a portion of the world controlled by man." The artist loses the feeling of his dependency, as the astronaut loses the sensation of gravity. He escapes from the pull of society. It is more than an image. Ballet liberates us from the force of gravity through the lightness of the dancers; an animated Walt Disney cartoon is a victory over Newton. An inspired portrait is a painting with value in and by itself, before being considered as the representation of a face. Titian's *Venus* does not make one want to make love; it makes one want to admire. A performance of *Oedipus Rex* does not make the spectator want to gouge out his eyes; it makes him want to return to the theater. The liberated artist brings to his admirers the echo of their liberation. "Posterity is the gratitude of men for victories which seem to promise them their own."

I explained elsewhere why I believe the artist, like the scholar, can only control nature by obeying it, or, more precisely, by borrowing from it the material for his work. It is important that the forces of nature, and not the tractable fantasies of the mind, be dominated through art. The sublime is born when the great upheavals of the world (passions, storms, tempests, wars) are molded into a form by the artist. Through Shakespeare's genius, the most frightful dramas become the inspiration for the greatest poetry. Dostoievski wrote: "It is essential to make a work of art out of the Karamozov." Malraux agrees that the artist should minimize his borrowings from the world, that he should simplify the forms, and even that he invent them. Great modern painting refuses to pander to the sentimentality or the sensuality of the public, in order to exist in its own universe where it meets again the greatest artists of the past, and even of a prehistoric past which they illuminate. Manet, Braque, Rouault enable us to understand the great Buddhist art, Sumerian art, pre-Colombian art. Before the advent of modern art, one did not see a Khmer head, much less a Polynesian sculpture, because one didn't look at them.

A culture is a heritage; a great culture brings to us the heritage of all humanity. "All culture attempts to maintain, to enrich, or transform, without weakening, the ideal image of man received by those who labor over it. And if we see the most future-minded countries, like Russia and the Americas, more and more interested in the past, it is because culture is the heritage of the best of the world." Through the Museum Without Walls, now open to all, the art of all times becomes accessible. And one discovers in it man's unchanging and, in one sense, eternal values.

That communion creates bonds "which permit man to no longer be an accident in the universe." I myself remember my feelings when, this summer, I received a visit in the country from fifty students who had come from all corners of the globe: black and yellow, American and Russian, and I realized that it was easy to communicate with all of them in Stendhal and Chekhov, in Melville and Dostoievski, in Hokusai and Cézanne. "Art is anti-Fate." It juxtaposes to the antique and fearsome Fate another fate, made by the hand of man.

It is a kind of Temps Retrouvé (in the sense of Proust), on the scale of humanity. "The victory of each artist over his servitude is joined to that of art over the destiny of humanity." According to Malraux, humanism is not to say (as Guillaumet did, according to Saint-Exupéry) "What I have done, no animal would have done," but rather: "We have denied what the beast in us wanted, and we want to find man again wherever we have found what crushes him." A believer would find very precarious that survival of man through so many metamorphoses; a thermonuclear bomb could annihilate tomorrow not only Chagall's windows and Picasso's blues but the statues of the Memphite dynasties as well. Frankly, what does it matter, as anguish would disappear with the anguished, and the need to survive disappear for lack of survivors. But "it is beautiful that an animal who, knowing that he must die, extracts the song of the stars from the irony of the nebulae, and that he hurls it at random at centuries on which he will be imposing unknown words."

This is Proust's theme when he describes the death of

Bergotte. "They buried him, but throughout the funeral night, in the lighted shop windows, his books, arranged three by three, watched, like angels with outspread wings, and seemed, for the one who was no more, the symbol of his resurrection." To which Malraux echoes: "During the night when Rembrandt continues to draw, all the illustrious Shades, and those of the cave-dweller artists follow with their eyes the hesitant hand which sketches their new survival or their new sleep . . . And that hand, whose trembling in the twilight is watched over by the millennia, trembles with one of the most secret and most exalted expressions of the power and honor of being Man." Malraux shows, in his philosophy of art, the same cosmic sense, the same affinity for panoramic vision which surmount the centuries, as in his philosophy of history. In art he has found the coin of the absolute.

But only the coin. Flaubert put the artist above the saint and the hero, and he demanded from the writer the denial of the world and of passion. "You will portray drunkenness, war, and love, my good man, provided you are neither a drunkard, nor a lover, nor a soldier . . ." "Such a thought," writes Malraux, "would have been inconceivable for Aeschylus as for Corneille, for Hugo as for Chateaubriand, and even for Dostoievski." Malraux the aesthetician rightly decides that it is not passion which destroys a work of art (as Flaubert thought) but the desire to prove something. A masterpiece may be "committed"; it is never didactic. It must not bear witness for a party, but it can very well expound values of sensibility—for example, courageous fraternity (Saint-Exupéry), instead of personal individualism (Stendhal). And that is, in fact, what Malraux has done in his novels—and in his life.

If I had to write a biography of André Malraux, which will never happen because he is too young and I am too old, I would give it this Balzacian title: *André Malraux, or the Search for the Absolute.*

JEAN-PAUL SARTRE

THE SUDDEN RISE of Sartre was, from roughly 1942–46, *the* event of the literary scene. Prior to the war Sartre was known in informed circles for a collection of short stories, *Le Mur* (*The Wall*) and for a novel, *La Nausée* (*Nausea*). By the end of the war, however, he had acquired—through his works for the stage and through his philosophy, *L'Etre et le Néant* (*Being and Nothingness*), an immense public. He was considered the head of the whole school of existentialism, which provided an entire generation with a stance toward the world as well as rules of conduct. In actuality, however, most of the people who talked about existentialism knew next to nothing about it. They were not, for instance, aware of how much Sartre's doctrine owed to Kierkegaard, Heidegger, and Husserl. But these philosophers had never reached as broad an audience as Sartre. Sartre embodied difficult ideas —ideas the public would have had considerable trouble grasping in abstract form—in dramatic characters. It happened that these ideas answered the needs of a generation of young intellectuals left shattered by the war, acutely aware of the absurdity of the world, and sickened by hypocrisy. A legend was born, a legend which rather superficially equated existentialism with Latin Quarter café life. The image of the free life presented by this legend helped boost the popularity of existential works. But since Sartre had a remarkable intellect, real dramatic talent, and rare reasoning powers, his success has not

faded. Indeed, it has just recently been enhanced by the publication of a brilliant autobiography, *Les Mots* (*The Words*),
his best written and most human book.

I. THE LIFE

As Sartre has himself often reminded us, he belongs by
birth to the French petite bourgeoisie. His paternal grandfather was a country doctor practicing in the town of Thiviers
in the Dordogne. His father, a graduate of the Ecole Polytechnique and a naval officer, died in 1907, wasted by a
fever contracted in Cochin-China. His mother, Anne-Marie
Schweitzer, the widowed mother of a two-year-old son, went
first to live with her parents in Meudon, and subsequently
to Paris. The Schweitzers were Alsatian Protestants. The
renowned Dr. Albert Schweitzer also belongs to this branch
of the family. Sartre's maternal grandfather, under whose
roof he spent his entire childhood, was a bearded patriarch
who "so resembled God the Father that he was often taken
for Him." He was a nineteenth-century man who "slightly
overdid the sublime." Forever looking to bring off one or
another stage effect, he was the victim of two recently invented techniques: the art of photography and the art of
being a grandfather. He "struck poses" for the camera and
played at the role of grandfather. He had crushed his own
sons, but he adored his grandson and praised his prattlings
and antics and steered him toward the teaching profession.
For although he had no degrees, Grandfather Schweitzer
was himself a teacher. He had founded an Institute of
Modern Languages where he taught French to transient foreigners, mostly Germans.

"I began my life as I shall no doubt end it: amidst books."
This is a revealing remark. Sartre's knowledge of men came
to him mostly through books. What he lacked in experience,
the unabridged Larousse supplied. He found more reality

in words than in things. "It was in books that I encountered the universe . . . and I confused the disorder of my bookish experiences with the random course of real events. From that came the idealism which it took me thirty years to shake off." His atheism, which developed at a very early age, is at least partially explained by the Catholic and Protestant schism in his immediate family. The philosophy of the grown man would later but confirm the feelings of the adolescent. Sartre seems on the whole to have hated his childhood (which was, to all appearances, happy), but it undoubtedly made him what he is today. "I wouldn't listen to my grandfather's voice, that recorded voice which wakes me with a start and drives me to my table, if it were not my own, if, between the ages of eight and ten, I had not arrogantly assumed responsibility for the supposedly imperative mandate that I had received in all humility."

This mandate, issued by his grandfather, his family, was first that he should become a teacher. Charles Schweitzer had no college degrees. His grandson was to make up for that. Little "Poulou," however, had even more ambitious ideas; he felt he was destined for some great mission. Around 1912 his favorite book was Jules Verne's *Michael Strogoff*. "I worshiped in him the disguised Christian that I had been prevented from being. . . . For me, that book was poison: Was it true that certain individuals were chosen? Was their path laid out for them by the highest necessities? Saintliness repelled me; but in Michael Strogoff it fascinated me because it had donned the trappings of heroism." But was he cut out for the life of the hero? Encounters with his playmates, his judges, made him aware that he was short, a "shrimp." He couldn't get over it and avenged his disappointment by massacring a hundred henchmen in his book-fed dreamings. "In any case, things weren't going right."— "I was saved by my grandfather: he drove me, without meaning to, into a new imposture that changed my life."

This imposture, or rather evasion, was writing. The child

Jean-Paul began to write adventure novels, borrowing elements for these from magazine and newspaper serials and from movies. Under different *noms de plume* he singlehandedly put whole armies to flight. "By writing I was existing, I was escaping from the grownups." He had dreamed of becoming a swordsman, a swashbuckler. But he found himself obliged to sheath his sword, to take pen in hand and join the common herd of the great writers, nearly all of whom were puny adults, rheumy old men. "I palmed off on the writer the sacred powers of the hero. . . . I, the imaginary child, was becoming a true paladin whose exploits would be real books." As an eight-year-old novelist whose unpolished efforts were read aloud in the family, he affected the role of heroic martyr. He felt himself to be *necessary;* the world needed him. "I was elected, branded, but without talent: everything would come from my sorrows and long patience." Thus was a vocation born.

His early schooling was at the Lycée Henri IV. In 1916 his mother married a man who was, like her first husband, a graduate of the Ecole Polytechnique, and at that time in charge of the La Rochelle Naval Yards. It was during this period, writes R.-M. Albérès, "that Sartre became acquainted with that sector of the middle class—certain of its safety, its duties, and especially its rights—he would later satirize." This is perhaps true; but a reading of *Les Mots* makes it clear that Sartre had already had a foretaste of those certainties and that imposture from living with his grandfather of the godlike beard. Thus he came to adulthood already set against provincial formalities and smug middle-class morality. In 1924 he entered the Ecole Normale, in the rue d'Ulm, and was first in France in the philosophy agrégation in 1929.

It was during this period that he came to know the group of "chums" who were to become long-time friends—Raymond Aron, Paul Nizan, and especially Simone de Beauvoir —herself a philosophy agrégée—his companion in life and in thought. Instances of such lasting understanding and such continual trust between two first-class minds are rare. Thanks to Raymond Aron, who was a sergeant in the Central Meteorological Office, Sartre was able to do his military service near Paris. In February 1931, he was appointed professor of philosophy at Le Havre where he remained for six years—his tenure interrupted only by an interlude at the French Institute in Berlin, where he studied Husserl's phenomenology. An understanding education commissioner kept Sartre in Le Havre and Simone de Beauvoir in Rouen, and this made it possible for their friendship to continue to thrive. Then, after a year in Laon, he was assigned to the Lycée Pasteur in Neuilly—that is—in effect, to Paris.

The initial objective his grandfather had hoped for—a professorship—had been fully and successfully realized. His students held him in high regard. The second objective—which Sartre himself had wanted—became a reality in 1938 with the publication of his novel *La Nausée* (which was set in Le Havre), followed in 1939 by a collection of short stories, *Le Mur*. These two highly original books caught the attention of the critics and of intelligent readers. Then the war came. Sartre was called up, served as a medical orderly, was taken prisoner, but later freed. He wrote for *Lettres Françaises* and other clandestine publications. Then suddenly, in 1943, his play *Les Mouches* (*The Flies*) made him famous. He had expressed the feelings of an entire people. As Valéry said: "the rest is all sound and fury." Sartre's philosophical works will be discussed later. It should be noted here, however, that in the closing pages of *Les Mots* Sartre says he no longer recognizes himself in the author of *La Nausée*.

"I have changed. I shall speak later on about the acids that corroded the distorting transparencies which enveloped me; I shall tell when and how I served my apprenticeship to violence and discovered my ugliness—which for a long time was my negative principle, the quicklime in which the wonderful child was dissolved; I shall also explain the reason why

I came to think systematically against myself, to the extent of measuring the obvious truth of an idea by the displeasure it caused me. The retrospective illusion has been smashed to bits; martyrdom, salvation, and immortality are falling to pieces; the edifice is going to rack and ruin; I collared the Holy Ghost in the cellar and threw him out; atheism is a cruel and long-range affair: I think I've carried it through. I see clearly, I've lost my illusions, I know what my real jobs are, I surely deserve a prize for good citizenship. For the last ten years or so I've been a man who's been waking up, cured of a long, bitter-sweet madness, and who can't get over the fact, a man who can't think of his old ways without laughing and who doesn't know what to do with himself." Sartre is really being terribly coy here; for he knows very well what he is going to do with his life: he is going to give an account of it and show that his ethic, his unequivocal rejection of the imposture and bad faith of the "right-thinking" middle class all spring from his childhood. It is because he experienced bad faith in his youth, both in those around him and in himself, that he later fought against them with such anger. This ineradicable preoccupation was sometimes to cause him to be unjust, because just as "right-thinking" has its type of bad faith, so too reaction to "right-thinking" has its bad faith.

II. THE PHILOSOPHY

Sartre was a philosopher before he was a novelist. His novels, short stories, and plays are embodiments of his philosophy, and it is through his philosophy that he has "touched" his fellow men. He has always held that there is only one vital philosophy in any given period, that being the philosophy which reflects and gives expression to the main current of the society of that time. Thus, when the great lions of the French nobility found themselves tamed by the young monarchy, Descartes gave them an expression of what had been their virtues, the virtues that also animate the tragedies of Corneille. Thus too did Schlegel's romanticism make a theretofore amorphous Germany aware of itself as a nation. At any given moment some doctrine is fertilizing literature. Such was the case with French existentialism in the middle of the twentieth century.

The ideology of existentialism had two sources. The *first* is Kierkegaard, the Danish Christian who reorganized existing philosophies so as to make room for the living individual. No system of concepts can ever account for the existing man. "The philosopher erects a palace of ideas, and he lives in a cottage"—the cottage of himself. Existence, according to Kierkegaard, is the personal adventure of each individual in confrontation with others and with God. He finds this existence tragic, fraught with fear and trembling. Existentialism's *second* source is Husserl's phenomenology, which studies the manner in which phenomena manifest themselves in consciousness. What we call "the world" can consist only of these phenomena of consciousness. "In reducing the existent to the series of operations which manifest the existent, modern thought has taken a considerable step forward."

What do we know of the exterior world? Nothing except the data consciousness provides. Still, all consciousness is consciousness of something. "The true interior world is the true exterior world." There is no duality of mind and matter. Things-in-themselves exist only as objectivized by consciousness. There is however one exception. Consciousness exists "for-itself." The nature of a thing is to be exactly what it is— blind and inert. But consciousness sees itself; it is capable of cutting itself off from its past and of projecting itself on the future; *it is free.* This is the very core of existentialism. Existentialism is a philosophy of freedom which places human will at the center of everything. Man is that being for whom existence precedes essence. In the mind of the carpenter a chair is essence before it exists. But man? Who could possibly shape him after an essence? God? Sartre doesn't believe in the existence of God. If God *existed,* he would be contingent; he wouldn't be God. "God is dead," said Nietz-sche. Sartre was introduced to God by his Christian family, but: "Rather than taking root in my heart, he vegetated in me for a while, then died. Today when anyone speaks to me of *Him,* I say—with the assurance of a handsome but old man meeting a beautiful but old woman: 'Fifty years ago, if it hadn't been for that misunderstanding that made us part, something might have happened between us.'"

Have we any right to speak of man's freedom when all our knowledge is based on determinism and on a belief in the laws of nature? Yes we do, for determinism is nothing but a hypothesis necessary to scientists. It cannot impose itself on the consciousness that has itself imposed this hypothesis on things. The real is there, but its reality *for me* depends on the manner in which I actualize it. Man's freedom is absolute. One may speak of psychological determinism, one may weigh motives, one may say: "I stop fighting *because* battle is hopeless, *because* I don't have any ammunition; I stop climbing the mountain *because* night is falling, *because* my heart is beating too fast. But in the end all examination of motives boils down to this: I give up because I've decided to give up.

And of course this freedom does not imply that each individual can do whatever he wants. We exist, and we exercise our wills, within a situation that is given. I can't appoint myself King of England; I can't pass an agrégé exam if I'm illiterate; I can't run the hundred-yard dash in ten seconds if I'm a ninety-pound weakling. Man is of his own designing —that is, he is what he wants to be. He is obliged, however, in drafting his design, to take his situation into account. He can refuse to acknowledge this situation, but that would be rendering himself ineffective. Trying to stop a speeding car by throwing oneself in front of it is one example of refusing to acknowledge one's situation. Man *is,* in point of fact, *en-gaged.* Every one of us is engaged through his actions, and any one who says he refuses to be engaged is so, by that very act of refusal. All literature is engaged. If an author chooses to be frivolous, even that frivolity will be a form of engagement.

Whatever the limitations of the individual's particular situation, freedom of choice remains considerable. The proletarian is "determined" by his class, but "it is he who—freely—decides on the meaning of his condition and of that of his fellows." A cripple is "determined" by his disability; it is up to him, however, whether he makes his condition intolerable and humiliating, or contrarily a matter of pride and a source of moral strength. "I choose myself, not in my being, but in my manner of being." We cannot change the past, but we can, through our attitude toward it, modify the effect it has on the present. It's a question of inventing salvation. The die is not cast. It isn't cast until the moment of death. It is evident from this that it is wrong to consider existentialism a totally pessimistic doctrine. It allows everyone at every moment to hope, to exercise his will.

Everyone except those who are bogged down in the slime of the "in-itself." Those who avoid acknowledgment of their total freedom are "cowards." Here Sartre's vocabulary departs from common usage. The people he calls "cowards" are those who act from fear of some principle or hallowed taboo rather than from free choice. The man who gets himself killed "for duty's sake," or the woman who is faithful "out of respect for the vows of marriage" are in his terms cowards. Those who believe their existence is necessary, and those who believe there is a God directing everything are "scum." The Just, the Pharisees, most middle-class people are "scum." They cheat; they are "in bad faith." When they eat, they say they are eating to restore their strength in order to do Good. What Good? Man, cast upon the desert isle of his own consciousness, is "a useless passion." Yet he knows he is responsible, responsible for everything, even for what he has not willed—for living means choosing. But responsible to whom—since there is no God and since Sartre scorns social judgments? This responsibility is inexplicable, absurd; but every man is conscious of it. We are here in Kafka's world.

And the result of this situation is *Angst* (one of Kierke-gaard's themes). "If man *is* not, but *creates* himself; if, in so doing, he assumes responsibility for the entire species; and if there are no values and no ethic given to us a priori but we must instead in every instance make solitary choices, with no points of reference or guidelines . . . how can we help but feel anxious when it is necessary for us to act." This *Angst* is intensified, moreover, by the existence all about us of our fellows—The Others—who are equally endowed with consciousness. The gaze of these Others takes possession of me, makes me an object. In love, for example, "the lover does not want to possess the loved one as one possesses a thing; he demands a special kind of appropriation: the possession of a freedom as freedom." The whole history of woman-as-object is just one long tale of her attempt to achieve the condition of subject.

In his recent *Critique de la raison dialectique* (*A Critique of Dialectical Reason*) Sartre examines the relationship of existentialism and Marxism. Raised in an aura of bourgeois humanism, Sartre very early felt the need for a philosophy "which would liberate him from the defunct culture of a bourgeoisie eking along on its past." Marxism seemed to him to be that philosophy. "We were convinced at one and the same time that Marxism provided the only valid explanation of history and that existentialism remained the only concrete approach to reality." In his early thinking on this subject, the two doctrines seemed to him complementary. However, they contained the elements of a conflict. Marxism is a form of determinism. It teaches that the thought of any given period is determined by the methods of production and distribution of that period.

But then one must explain the Marxist in power in terms of his own philosophy. Once in power the contemporary Marxist thinks in terms of police, army, security, unity. He sees minds and even facts in terms of the "party line." If the subsoil beneath Budapest is not such as will allow the construction of a subway, that subsoil is counter-revolutionary. This is not, says Sartre, the way Marx thought. In examining the brief and tragic history of the Republic of 1848, Marx did not find it enough merely to say that the Republican petite bourgeoisie had betrayed the proletariat. He tried instead to reconstruct the whole tragedy; he tried to grasp the totality of a movement through its specific incident and small details. People today try to fit individuals and facts into prefabricated molds. They seek, through bureaucratic conservatism, to reduce all change to one and the same level.

Confronted with this lazy kind of Marxism, says Sartre, one is justified in reinvoking existentialism. "What would be ruinous to Marxism," says Alain, "would be the attempt to maintain that technological progress alone has determined all change. It isn't as simple as all that; the structure of human societies depends as well on feelings, thoughts, and even on a kind of poetry." If one reduces all forms of thought to class terms and interests, one falls back into that form of idealism which Marx condemned as "economism." The contemporary Marxist would consider it a waste of time to try to understand a bourgeois thought in its own terms. He will, in speaking of Valéry, describe his thought as "a turn-of-the-century petit bourgeois' defense reflex against the materialism of the prevailing philosophy of the day." Valéry himself does not exist in this description. It is quite true that Valéry was a petit bourgeois intellectual, but every petit bourgeois intellectual is not Valéry. Sartre himself is proof of that. This is not to deny the importance of economics and technology. It is simply to say that Valéry was as well—above all—Valéry the living individual.

What then must one conclude? Not certainly that Sartre rejects Marxism, but rather that he attempts to retrieve the living individual within Marxism. There is no history without living, individual men. Hegel had already observed that antitheses are always abstract as compared with their resolutions which are always concrete. Even so will Sartre come much closer to actual life in his plays than in his philosophy. His philosophy has made a great stir and has had a visible influence on young people. It has, however, been little understood on the whole. People have called boys and girls existentialists simply because they wear their hair long! In point of fact, existentialism is a serious and profound philosophy of freedom, which Sartre has expounded but which he can hardly be said to have invented. It has its source, as we have observed, in Kierkegaard, Heidegger, and Husserl. What one entire group of French writers (Sartre and Simone de Beauvoir especially) have succeeded in doing is to transpose existentialism into novels and plays, to which novels and plays it lends substance and resonance. Conversely, these novels and plays have enabled existentialism to wield an influence on the contemporary mind it would never have enjoyed without such embodiments.

III. THE NOVELS

Can *La Nausée* be called a novel? Yes, since it is a fiction with characters invented by the author and an imaginary town, Bouville (which is reminiscent of Le Havre, where Sartre was teaching at the time). But the novel has no action. It is the metaphysical journal of Antoine Roquentin, an uprooted intellectual living in a hotel room. Roquentin is writing, without knowing quite why, the biography of one of the Marquis of Rollebon; he is sleeping with the owner of a café although he doesn't love her; and he drags out his existence in the most dismal kind of solitude. He has no family and no friends. And he feels quite removed from the Bouville citizenry.

"It seems to me that I belong to another species. They come out of their offices at the end of the day's work, they look at the houses and squares with satisfaction, they feel it's *their* city, a good, solid middle-class city. They're not afraid, they feel at home . . . imbeciles. It revolts me to think I'm ever again going to have to look at their thick, self-satisfied faces." He hates them even more when, in the local museum, he examines the portraits of the good burghers of the past— "irritating in their frozen respectability and haughtiness." They so obviously considered themselves right with God, with the Law, and with their own consciences. "Adieu, sweet lilies, all filigree in your little painted niches, adieu, sweet lilies, all our pride and raison d'être, adieu, you Scum."

Aside from Roquentin there is only one other character of note—the Self Taught Man, who represents the illusion of culture. A bailiff's clerk with a thirst for knowledge, the Self Taught Man has set himself the task of reading, in alphabetical order, every book in the Municipal Library. The child Sartre reading the dictionary comes to mind. Doubtless he put something of himself into this character, something of what he was like at one particular stage of his education—just as Flaubert was at times Bouvard or Pécuchet. He depicts himself to an even greater degree, however, in Roquentin, the man who has found there is nothing that justifies existence and who has stopped believing in the worldly illusions of the good citizens of Bouville, in any kind of goal, or even in culture. What is left to him? Nothing. Contemplating this void, he is gripped by nausea.

Nausea is a disgust with everything, not just men but things as well. To Roquentin things seem gratuitous, contingent. Why this pebble? Why that root? Why those trees? They are there, but why are they there? "Existence is not necessity. To exist is *to be there,* and that's all; existents appear, allow encounter, but one can never account for them. . . . Everything is gratuitous, this park, this city, me. When you come to be aware of this, it turns your stomach and everything begins to float. . . . that's Nausea; that's what the Scum . . . try to hide from themselves with their idea of what's right. What a shabby lie!" No one knows what's right. "The Scum are totally gratuitous, like everybody else." They're *de trop;* we're all *de trop.*

Yet we can't help existing—and thinking. As this thought gains ascendance, and as objects (a leather bench, the root of a chestnut tree) turn increasingly grotesque and monstrous, Roquentin is overwhelmed by *Angst,* just as Kierkegaard was before him, and just as all men are once they start pondering the human condition. One is paddling along peacefully on a warm sea, and then suddenly one feels that one is hanging over an abyss. Or, like Pascal, one finds oneself with a precipice on either side. The Scum swim along confidently, refusing to think about the abyss. Roquentin (and Sartre) see the *factitiousness* of existence. It is a fact, and no more.

How can life be salvaged from this lack of meaning? Through the gratuitous act, would be Gide's suggestion. Anny, a woman with whom Roquentin was once involved, used to say: "Through perfect moments." Proust thought man could be saved through art, Pascal through faith. Roquentin rejects both the religious and the aesthetic justification. As for the Scum, they aren't even aware of the problem: they think they *are* justified. Sartre, like Pascal, sets out to undermine their false security. Originally, it was based on the moral code of their forebears. Provided one kept its commandments, one was justified. But over a period of time these moral values deteriorated into conventions. And the man who scorns these conventions finds himself alone, face to face with his responsibilities.

To the average person Roquentin's nausea seems like some morbid form of sensitivity. Why should a pebble or a root provoke such violent disgust? Sartre, it should be noted, has an unusual "capacity for nausea." He has a particular horror of anything slimy, soft, sticky—even to the point of seeing only the more repugnant aspects of the sexual act. Although Sartre may be rather ahead of most people as far as disgust is concerned, it should be noted that the feeling of isolation and *Angst* he describes is shared by many of his contemporaries. By some because "God is dead," leaving them abandoned; by others because the violence and treachery of our time have destroyed any trust they might have had in traditional values.

The role of human consciousness is to give life a value: and there is only one value, and that is freedom. *Les Chemins de la Liberté* (*The Roads to Freedom*), the major novel Sartre attempted to write after the war, depicts a character who starts off completely listless but slowly discovers what he lacks: the proper use of freedom.

L'Age de Raison (*The Age of Reason*), the first volume, takes place in July 1938, and is set in the streets and cafés of Paris, a milieu Sartre knows well. Mathieu Delarue, a teacher and intellectual, has refused up to this point to be engaged. He hasn't married his mistress, Marcelle, who is pregnant; he is thinking of making her get an abortion; and he hasn't participated, despite his convictions, in the Spanish Civil War. He is aware of his freedom, but he refuses to commit it. Like Roquentin in *La Nausée*, he is bored. He has got what he wanted—a job in Paris, a mistress—but he envies those of his buddies who aren't afraid to become involved—his friend Brunet, for example, who is a Communist. Brunet can live in calm and confidence; he has his place and his work in the Party. He has chosen.

Why doesn't Mathieu step across the rather shallow fissure separating him from action? Because he sees no reason for doing so. The war will give him a sense of what one might call "general responsibility." Those who haven't acted to prevent the war are responsible for it. Every man's weight, however slight, counts in the scales of Fate. Mathieu realizes, in 1940, that he shares responsibility for the fall of France. Refusing to be involved in politics is itself a form of politics. The second volume, *Le Sursis* (*The Reprieve*), takes place at the time of the Munich talks. Sartre uses the same characters; they continue to lead their individual lives; but the sum of their lives, and of their choices, will determine whether there will be peace or war.

Mathieu's paltry freedom is thus confronted with a world problem which involves him. In order to show better this interdependence of lives and fortunes, Sartre speaks of private and public lives—Chamberlain, Hitler, Benes, and Mathieu—in one and the same breath. The latter is not completely free with respect to a void, as Roquentin believed himself to be. Mathieu is free *within his situation*. The third volume, *La Mort dans l'Ame* (*Troubled Sleep*), brings defeat. Mathieu is ashamed of himself and feels an intense need to assert his freedom. How? By becoming engaged through an action which, though doubtless futile, will make up for all his past shirkings. Armed with only a rifle he fires from a church tower on German armored cars. A futile gesture. Yet. . .

"It was revenge on the grand scale; every shot made up for some past scruple. One for Lola whom I didn't dare rape, one for Marcelle whom I should have ditched, one for Odile whom I didn't want to screw . . . As he fired, commandments shattered—love thy neighbor as thyself—in this mothering war—thou shalt not kill—pow at that faker down there. He was firing on his fellow men, on Virtue, on the World." An absurd, useless act, but through action freedom takes on its true meaning for Mathieu. But is taking revenge on one's past freedom?

We are not told whether Mathieu is killed or not, but in any case he disappears from the scene, and Brunet takes over. He is sent in a herd of prisoners to Germany. Enter another existentialist theme. Since he is no longer free, the prisoner cannot have any over-all plan or goal; he is obliged, so as not to go to pieces, to set himself limited goals. A rigid Marxist, Brunet seeks out the Communists among his companions and prepares and disciplines them for the work they will be doing after the liberation. Sartre has released a few fragments of the fourth volume *La Dernière Chance,* but it looks as if the book may never be finished. Satre's hero—and his novel—have reached an impasse. In the end Brunet himself begins to have doubts about the Party line. This may be Sartre's tragedy as a novelist: that, having preached engagement, he is only able to create characters who lack the capacity for action.

The violence of his anti-bourgeois prejudices makes it all the more difficult for him to create convincing characters. Either his characters are bourgeois—in which case they are distorted by the author's antipathy and become caricatures —or they are pure—and his sympathy makes them glow with an inhuman aura. The English critic John Weightman points out in *La Nausée* a statement in which Roquentin says that in looking to art for solace he doesn't of course want to be compared to one of his elderly aunts who used to say: "'Chopin's preludes were such a comfort when your poor uncle died.'" One of the limitations, writes Weightman, "of Sartre's savagely anti-bourgeois mind is that it cannot grant that a petit bourgeois aunt may be listening to Chopin in the genuineness of her grief, may have some inkling of the absolute."

The short stories in *Le Mur* are illustrations of existentialist themes. In *La Chambre* (*The Room*) Eve, whose husband is mad, chooses to live alone with a man foundering in insanity rather than put him in an asylum as her common-sense bourgeois father suggests. *Erostrate* (*Erostratus*) is the monologue of a sadist who humiliates a prostitute and shoots into a crowd in order to defend himself from "The Others." *L'Enfance d'un Chef* (*Childhood of a Leader*) is a brilliant study of a young bourgeois who doesn't know "who he is," and who searches for an identity until he finally discovers that at least some people will take him seriously if he declares himself an anti-Semitic fascist. Taking this ignominious and militant stance saves him from his void.

Nothing Sartre writes is uninteresting; but just as his childhood indicated, it is in the theater especially that he gives proof of astonishing gifts.

IV. THE THEATER

It is in his plays that Sartre has most vitally and vividly embodied his ideas. It is his plays too that have won him a vast public throughout the world. His first play, *Les Mouches*, was staged during the occupation and owed its success in part to the courageous allusions audiences detected in the text. But it has permanent value as well. The subject is the return to Argos of Orestes, who is the son of Agamemnon and Clytemnestra, and whose father has been assassinated by his mother's lover, Aegisthus. Ever since the murder, millions of flies have descended upon Argos and torment the populace. They are a symbol of the remorse eating away at the entire city.

As the play opens, Orestes—young, rich, handsome, skeptical—"in short, a superior sort of a man"—declares that one must never engage oneself. He is free, but his freedom is based on his nothingness. The palace is no longer his palace, nor the city his city. How he wishes he could become a man among men!" "Ah! if there were one act, any one act that would give me freedom of the city among them . . . even killing my own mother." The erratic Orestes, however, would likely as not decide to leave Argos without acting, were it not for the sudden appearance of his sister Electra—who has lived with the guilty couple and waited fifteen years for the return of the brother who will avenge their crime and deliver Argos.

Jupiter himself urges Orestes to go away, to give up. Is it always necessary to punish? asks Jupiter. The Gods have turned this perturbation to the advantage of moral order. Orestes bristles at this. He is "a well-behaved young man of noble soul," but there are limits: " 'So . . . is that what Goodness is? Treading softly. Very softly. Always saying excuse me and thank you . . . Is that it?' " This is the turning point.

Orestes has chosen. He commits the irreparable act, kills his father's murderer and his own mother, and then, repudiated by his sister and censured by Jupiter, leaves Argos. Why does Electra repudiate him? Because he has deprived her of her reason for living—her dream of revenge which turns out after all to have been *only* a dream.

Orestes, the existential hero, assumes full responsibility for his act. "'I'm free, Electra; freedom has struck me like a lightning-bolt.'" As for Jupiter—having created free men, he is no longer in control of their freedom. Orestes will never again be subject to his law. "'For I'm a man, Jupiter, and each man must invent his own road.'" No fate can impose itself on the man who exercises his will. "'Men are powerless only when they admit they are.'" Through his act, however, Orestes has cut himself off from his youth. He has entered the adult realm, the realm of responsibility, of full manhood. The people of Argos, whom he has saved, revile him because he frightens them. When he leaves, the flies (or Erinys) pursue him. Their departure means the deliverance of Argos—a deliverance brought about by Orestes in spite of Argos.

The plays following *Les Mouches* deal with the same theme—freedom—but focus instead on the failures and limits imposed on freedom by death, social class, and the exigencies surrounding action. *Huis-clos* (*No Exit*), one of Sartre's best plays, is a richly meaningful myth. The action takes place in Hell—not the Hell of the Middle Ages, but one without devils or vats of boiling oil. The presence of other men is in itself sufficient torment. Three people are left alone together for all eternity in an ordinary hotel room. For "Hell is others"; hell is the lucidity with which others view us. In hell hearts are laid bare and delivered over to the judgment of other free persons. This hell, in fact, goes on in real life. But after death, this hell is eternal, and there is no possible recourse to an action that might reverse, suspend, or evade the judgment rendered.

Sartre doesn't believe in an afterlife or in hell, but that "being dead means being at the mercy of the living." The living judge the dead man, and who is there to defend him? From which follows Sartre's idea that when one dies "the chips are down" (*Les Jeux Sont Faits*—the title of a Sartre film scenario). The chips are down because life is over, and the dead person can do nothing either to erase or perfect it. He is obliged to draw the line and total up the sum by which he will be judged—judged by his actions, for he is only the sum of his actions. *Huis-clos* is Sartre's equivalent of Mauriac's "The blue-books are all passed in." The irrevocability of life is one of the meanings of the play, another being the torture of living beneath the gaze of others. This rich and fecund myth resembles Balzac's *La Peau de Chagrin* in containing even more than its author knows.

La Putain Respectueuse (*The Respectful Prostitute*) shows freedom destroyed by social prejudice. A Negro is accused of a crime he didn't commit; Lizzie, a white prostitute, knows the truth and could save him. But both Negro and prostitute are victims of a society run by the Scum who, in addition to imposing their justice and police on others, paralyze consciences.

Les Mains Sales (*Dirty Hands*) poses that grave problem which all men of action have had to face. Should purity be sacrificed to efficacity? Hoederer, head of a worker's party, believes in the necessity of working with other political parties against a possible invader. Hoederer's opponents want above and beyond anything to hold to the party line. Hugo, their leader, is a young middle-class intellectual who arranges to be sent to Hoederer as a secretary in order to kill him. In short, Hugo is Orestes—but Orestes in a revolutionary world in which one must take others into account and in which the grand gesture is a mistake. Hugo doesn't understand the party because he is by nature an aristocrat. " 'I respect orders, but I respect myself as well . . . I joined the Party so that all men might one day have that right.' " To which the proletarian responds: " 'We joined the Party, pal, because we were sick of starving to death.' "

Hugo has never gone hungry; he's an amateur, who has joined up by choice, perhaps through pride; in his colleague's view, "his act was only a gesture."[1] He is cut off equally from the middle class whose values he denies, and from the proletariat, which repudiates his. By volunteering to kill Hoederer he hopes to get himself accepted. Even his wife Jessica doesn't take him seriously. And is he, finally, truly serious? He plays roles—that of the lover and that of the revolutionary. Only one man sees through him—his intended victim, Hoederer. "You don't love men, Hugo, the only thing you love is principles. . . . Me, I love them for what they are. With all their nastiness and all their vices. . . . Men, you hate them because you hate yourself; your purity is like death, and the Revolution you dream of isn't our revolution; you don't want to change the world, you want to blow it up."

Hoederer wants results. And he is willing to maneuver and lie to get them. "All means are good if they're effective." Hugo is afraid—like a fakir or a monk—of getting his hands dirty. Nobody has ever done anything without getting his hands dirty. Hoederer is authentic, substantial, adult; Hugo, like Orestes, is a child. His wife Jessica throws herself into Hoederer's arms because the latter is at least genuine, a real flesh-and-blood man. Hugo shoots Hoederer three times with a pistol. Is the crime political or one of jealousy? His colleagues must know before they can decide whether to eliminate him or whether he can be regenerated. Hugo screams: " 'Unregenerable,' " which amounts to suicide, and which is, as are all his acts, a theatrical gesture. In Sartre's eyes, of course, (and in mine), Hoederer is in the right. Dirty hands do better work than bloody gloves. " 'There's work to be done, and that's that. And one must do the work for which one's fitted.' " This, for Sartre, sums up the collective ethic of the

[1] F. Jeanson

proletariat as opposed to the individualistic ethic of the young bourgeois. Yet he denies having written a didactic play. And rightly so—for a bourgeois playwright might set the business ethic up against the interests of the individual, and the same play would result.

In *Le Diable et le Bon Dieu* (*The Devil and the Good Lord*), Goetz, a mercenary soldier, is laying siege to the town of Worms on behalf of an archbishop, and he has vowed, if he takes the town, to put twenty thousand men, women, and children to the sword. He has always practiced evil with utter mercilessness—until, that is, a common priest named Heinrich convinces him that it is much harder to do Good than Evil. Goetz doesn't believe in God or the Devil; he's a ham actor who wants to play the role of absolute, to be himself either God or the Devil. He tosses a coin, but cheats in order to consign himself to doing Good, a new and tempting role. Why is Goetz bitter, at odds with himself and the world? Because he was born a bastard and during his childhood humiliated even by the affection shown him. He decides to *give*—without accepting—in order to humiliate in turn. "'Good will be done against all,'" he says— against the caste of country squires who scorn him for a bastard *and* against the peasant population whom (like Hugo) he can't manage to fit in with either. He divides his land among them in vain. He is told that this will cause a general revolt in which the peasants will be defeated. He doesn't care. He is God's emissary and refuses to turn to violence. In the City of the Sun, which he is founding, love will be the only law.

Actually, of course, it's a case of self-love; Goetz, the ham actor, is not only playing on God's side, he is playing God. He is himself so well aware of this that when Heinrich comes (after a year and a day have elapsed) to see how well Goetz has kept his side of the bargain, Goetz admits he cheated and that he fully intended his goodness to do even more harm than his previous cruelty. "'It was all sham and lie.'" How does he get out of the situation? By taking command of the peasant army and once again practicing the profession of relentless and merciless leader. " 'Never fear, I won't flinch. I'll horrify them since I've no other way to love them; I'll give them orders since I've no other way of obeying; I'll remain alone with this empty sky above my head, since I've no other way to be with other men. There's a war to wage and I'll wage it.' " Since neither God nor the Devil exists, the only solution is to do one's job as a man.

In *Sartre par Lui-même,* Francis Jeanson brings out the importance of the theme of the bastard in Sartre's work. Goetz is a bastard; so, because of his divided loyalties, is Hugo; and Sartre's pleasure in adapting Dumas' *Kean,* lies in the fact that Kean is "the Actor who is always on stage, who acts even his own life, no longer recognizes himself, no longer knows who he is. And who, in the end, is nobody." And thereby the Myth of the Actor merges with that of the Intellectual—at once bastard and player. " 'One doesn't act to earn a living,' " says Sartre's Kean. " 'One acts in order to lie, to lie to oneself, to be what one can't be—and because one is sick of being what one is. . . . One plays heroes because one's a coward, and saints because one's wicked. . . . You act because you'd go mad if you didn't.' " Kean's grievance is no different from that of Orestes, Hugo, Goetz, or Mathieu. Like each of them, Kean liberates himself through an action: that of insulting the audience and the Prince of Wales from the stage. " 'Was it an action or a gesture?' " It was an action since it ruined his life; a gesture because he did it as an actor. " 'I thought I was Kean, who thought he was Hamlet, who thought he was Fortinbras.' "

Les Séquestrés d'Altona (The Condemned of Altona) is one of Sartre's finest plays—strange, disordered, terrifying. The son of a family of industrial magnates near Hamburg is confined to his room, fed by his sister, and hidden from all eyes because he is mad. His madness is itself a refuge from his

FROM PROUST TO CAMUS

thoughts, horrible memories of the war, of murders for which he was responsible. The father of the family is suffering from cancer of the throat and knows he has no more than six months to live. All the Sartrean obsessions—incest, hatred of the father, confinement—haunt this accursed household. The room of this grandiloquent madman is still, in a sense, the world of *Huis-clos*. Frantz can't escape the past.

" 'Imagine a black pane of glass. Thinner than air. Ultra-sensitive. A breath mists it. The least breath. All History is graven on it, from the beginning of time to this snap of the fingers. . . . Everything is going to come back to life. How about that? All our actions.' " Frantz, within his room, still thinks, that Germany hasn't recovered from the war, that it is atoning, that after thirteen years grass blankets the streets. He suddenly learns the truth: Germany is more prosperous than ever, the family business is running full blast. Deprived of his madness, he can no longer go on living. He and his father kill themselves together in an automobile in a way that will be hushed up as an accident.

The power of Sartre's drama in *Les Mains Sales* and *Les Séquestrés d'Altona* lies in the fact that we are no longer dealing with didactic plays but with tragedies—one might even say—his tragedy, and ours.

V

The themes of the novels and plays reappear in the essays. Sartre has engaged in literary criticism, which could not be other than perceptive, but which deals primarily with intentions and with personalities. He is less interested in Baudelaire the poet than in the question of moral dishonesty. He comes to view Baudelaire as one of the nauseated: "Baudelaire couldn't take his efforts seriously. . . . The reason he contemplated suicide so often was that he felt unnecessary. . . . One of the most spontaneous reactions of his mind was undoubtedly the disgust and boredom that overwhelmed him when faced with the vague, mute, and disordered monotony of a landscape." I don't find this altogether accurate; Baudelaire also has moments of enthusiasm and happiness. He interests Sartre, however, only to the degree he is a Sartrean hero.

Jean Genet (*Saint Genet*) is another story. Baudelaire acknowledges guilt; Genet, who is more authentic, asserts his vices and defies The Scum. Poor as a child, he was caught by The Grownups in the act of committing a petty theft. Whereas he dreamed at the time of being a saint, he suddenly found himself an outcast. Society demanded that he repent. It will forgive anything but the sin of pride. But his answer is: "I'm a Thief," and he proudly assumes responsibility for it, just as he assumes responsibility for his sexual perversion. By declaring himself evil, he recovers his authenticity. "If he hadn't been thrown off the track at the start, Genet would have been attracted to true morality." He had the makings of a saint. Just as the Christian saint renounces Sin, and then the World, for God, so Genet renounces Good and Society in order to follow Evil. Sartre praises this literally paradoxical position.

Baudelaire's mistake (according to Sartre) is in retaining the mask, in taking his role seriously, in not being capable of doing away with the idea of God. For if God exists, man is nothingness. The history of Sartre's atheism is the history of the progressive triumph of freedom over theology. He has no doubts about the eventual victory of atheism. God is a concept which answered a need and which, as men become increasingly conscious of their freedom, will "die out." Moreover, there are no longer any authentic believers: "Today God is dead, even in the heart of the believer."

What is apparent (both in *Saint Genet* and in *Les Mots*) is the shift, which began in 1945, from a negative to a positive position. "Refusal doesn't mean saying no, but modification through work. One need not think that the revolutionary flatly rejects capitalist society: how could he possibly do so, living in it as he does? Quite to the contrary, he accepts it as a fact which justifies his revolutionary action. 'Change the world,' says Marx . . . All in good time: change it if you can. Which means accepting a good many things in order to change a few." Here again Hoederer triumphs over Hugo and the action of pure motive. "I think that on any given occasion there is something to do," Sartre tells Jeanson. I agree. One must *"act the man"*—even though that means *putting bastardy to work* and finding in the agony that lies within the heart of every man the strength to act.

In an article on *Les Mots* the critic Robert Kanters inquires: "When M. Sartre reflects on the efficacy of his political action, does he find that it has really been rather weak, rather utopian, considering the force of circumstances and of parties? When he examines his most glittering intellectual constructions, does he find them very much more than a set of mirrors wherein reason has striven to lose its reflection?" Kanters' rejoinder is that one should talk about courageous lucidity rather than hopelessness. The best of the matter is that this confession of a man waking from "a long, bitter-sweet madness" will be marked up to Sartre's credit. *Les Mots* aren't everything, but when they are well chosen, they save him who is their master.

SIMONE DE BEAUVOIR

When most readers think of Sartre they immediately think of Simone de Beauvoir, and vice-versa. One imagines that neither Sartre nor Simone de Beauvoir is displeased by this. Each has the satisfaction of living close to someone he admires. Their philosophies are similar. They have, for years, compared, reviewed, and adjusted them. Their talents have always been dissimilar. Simone de Beauvoir seems the more gifted for fictional creation. Sartre's best piece of writing is his most recent non-fiction work: *Les Mots*. It is remarkable that two writers should have been able to share their lives so intimately without either one's losing his own originality.

I. THE LIFE

Simone de Beauvoir was born into a middle-class family in Paris in 1908. If she later became extremely hostile to her own class, it wasn't because, like Gide, she had a tyrannical upbringing. On the whole, she loved her parents. Her father, a lawyer, had received the classical education of his time. He considered Anatole France the greatest French writer. His daughter admired her father. At the age of five and a half her parents enrolled her in a school bearing the rather odd and intriguing name of Desire; this was an upstanding institution where a staff of old maids and priests taught, respectively, virtue and philosophy. What she read had more

effect on her than her teachers. At nine she liked Louisa May
Alcott's *Little Women* and identified intensely with Jo, one
of the novel's heroines. Jo wrote; Simone de Beauvoir began
to write. She decided very early to devote her life to intellectual pursuits. Her best friend, Zaza, said: "Having nine
children is quite as worthwhile as books." Simone de Beauvoir, however, thought that having children who would in
turn have children was a very boring refrain; thinkers, writers
created joyous worlds, and that was a better way to spend
one's life.

Her mother was devout, her father an agnostic. Although
she liked her father more than her mother, she was, in her
early years, very much a believer. Then she discovered death
and man's innocence as regards sin. "The realization of the
silence of death horrified me. . . . God became an abstract
idea way off in the sky, and one evening I erased him."
Of inflexible temperament with a horror of compromise, she
fell abruptly from faith into atheism. It had become clear
to her that she loved earthly pleasures and wouldn't be able
to give them up. "I no longer believe in God, I told myself
with no particular surprise. This was itself a proof; if I
believed in him, I wouldn't have so lightheartedly come to
trespass against him." Indeed, her conception of God had become so abstract that his perfection excluded his reality.
She didn't miss him and was never to return to the question
of his existence. As a result of her moral training, however,
she retained a strong sense of responsibility and of guilt.

She has told in *Les Mémoires d'une Jeune Fille Rangée*
(*Memoirs of a Dutiful Daughter*) how she had no trouble
passing the exams for the *baccalauréat*, the *licence*, and
in 1929, the *agrégation* in philosophy. At that time the
number of women who elected to brave this strenuous competition could be counted on the fingers of one hand. But
she liked ideas and systems and had become intimate with a
whole group of young philosophers, all of them intelligent,
whose number included Raymond Aron, Jean-Paul Sartre,
and Nizan. She called them her "buddies"; they nicknamed

her "le Castor," French for "beaver," because Beauvoir sounded like the English word "beaver." A number of her buddies were Communists and busily engaged in tearing "middle-class ideologies" to pieces. But she found she trusted Sartre most. Always on the qui-vive, he refused to indulge in intellectual evasions, tracked down bad faith, never took anything for granted, and didn't let himself get "mired down" in any kind of conformism. She had always hoped to be guided by such a free and powerful mind. She was happy when Sartre told her: "From now on I'm taking you in hand." Which doesn't mean he forced his own beliefs on her; they were friends because their philosophies were close to begin with, and because they shared common likes and dislikes.

Thus began a team that nothing has broken up. Both feared marriage; they granted one another complete liberty. Perhaps they suffered for it sometimes. Each had his adventures; but the bond held. They thought together, fought together, and together achieved literary fame. The views they held in common kept them together in peace as in war. "One must agree politically in order to be friends," Alain said. First both were teachers, she in Marseilles, then Rouen, and finally, in 1938, in Paris. While she was in Rouen, Sartre was teaching nearby in the lycée in Le Havre, and they were able to see one another. Sartre was the first to publish, but during the war Simone de Beauvoir wrote a full-length novel, *L'Invitée* (*She Came to Stay*), which came out in 1943.

Thereafter, she participated in the meteoric rise of existentialism (which by 1945 made Sartre the favorite philosopher not only of young Frenchmen but of the whole Western world) and at the same time brilliantly furthered her own career, publishing alternately works of fiction and non-fiction. They set up headquarters in the Café de Flore on the Boulevard Saint-Germain. In the minds of the intelligentsia everywhere Saint-Germain-des-Prés became synonymous with existentialism and with the Sartre-Beauvoir duo. After the success of her book, she stopped teaching. The "buddies" were now Camus, Merleau-Ponty, Bost, and Queneau. With the Liberation and Sartre's founding of *Les Temps Modernes,* she naturally took part in the editorial direction of this political and literary review.

Then she had a series of dazzling successes. *Le Deuxième Sexe (The Second Sex),* a study of the condition of woman, found a world-wide audience. She won the Prix Goncourt in 1954 for her novel, *Les Mandarins (The Mandarins).* This prize made her rich, something she had no wish to be; but it was also a triumph which, after a life free of servitude of any kind, must have delighted her. Actually she hadn't waited for success to make her happy. Gaiety and health were characteristic of this whole group. She traveled a lot— on all continents—had affairs with an American writer and a young Frenchman, then wrote her autobiography in three volumes: *Les Mémoires d'une Jeune Fille Rangée, La Force de l'Age (The Prime of Life),* and *La Force des Choses (Force of Circumstance)*—three intelligent, candid, and forceful books. Overthrow of the ruling class seemed to her desirable. "I found myself even less than at twenty able to stand their lies, stupidity, false trappings, and fake virtue."

The fact that, anti-middle class as she was, she didn't subscribe to Communism troubled her deeply for a long time. Sartre's philosophy being different from Marxism, the Party treated him very badly. "Renown for me, meant hatred," he wrote. Then the Algerian war found Sartre and Simone de Beauvoir on the same side as the Communists. Allies, however, are not necessarily brethren. Agreement remained limited. The end of Stalinism, however, made relationships easier. The renowned couple was invited to visit Russia, where they formed friendships. Cuba appealed to, then disappointed, them.

Simone de Beauvoir's intransigence did not lessen. When Camus crashed into a plane-tree, she said: "I'm not going to cry. He no longer meant anything to me." They had had a falling-out over Camus' *L'Homme Révolté.* There has been only one fixed point in Simone de Beauvoir's life, one certain success—her relationship with Sartre. "In more than thirty years there was but one night when we fell asleep at odds with one another. . . . Our temperaments, points of view, our prior judgments remain different and our works are quite dissimilar, but they grow on the same top-soil." It is a truly remarkable example of friendship and symbiosis. The only kind of man she could possibly have become fond of was one who also hated what she hated: the political Right, orthodox thoughts, and religion. Her choosing Sartre was no accident. Contrary to reports in the press, the couple lived in relative isolation. Their material circumstances—automobile, apartment—cut them off from the proletariat; and they were emotionally and intellectually opposed to the middle class.

La Force des Choses ends on a rather sad note. She is afraid of old age and death. "My rebelliousness is dampened by the imminence of death, my joys grown pale as well." The time has come to say: nevermore! "Now the terribly brief hours speed me headlong toward my grave. I avoid thinking about in ten years, in one year. Memories waste away, myths peel and crumble, plans miscarry in the conceiving. I am here, and things are here. If this silence is to continue, how drawn-out my brief future seems." Still, all expectations have been fulfilled. She wanted her freedom; she got it. She wanted to write; her writings stand up, substantial, valued. Why is the last sentence of her *Memoirs:* "I'm stupefied to realize how much I've been swindled"? Because she's growing old? Because she's going to die? I know what Alain would have said: "Death is not a thought."

II. THE WORKS

Simone de Beauvoir's novels, like Sartre's, are kneaded out of metaphysics. She believes it is just as valid to write metaphysical novels as it is to write psychological novels,

and that the novelist's job is to depict the emotional consequences of metaphysical experience. In *her* work however,
philosophy serves only as leavening, as yeast; in Sartre's
it is the dough itself. *L'Invitée* (*She Came to Stay*) verges
here and there on being an existential novel. "I'm there,
impersonal and free, in the middle of the dance-floor. I see
all lives and all faces at once. If I turned away from them,
they would remove themselves from my ken immediately,
as a landscape one has forsaken." This passage, and others
like it, are doses of doctrine. The bulk of the novel, however,
is fleshed out; the characters step out of their frames. Simone
de Beauvoir is a born novelist who doesn't have to give much
thought to craft.

L'Invitée is built around Pierre Labrousse and Françoise
Miquel, a happy couple who love one another but also
respect each other's freedom (one cannot help but be reminded of Simone de Beauvoir's own relationship with Sartre).
Labrousse is the director of an avant-garde theater. Their
constant collaboration, more than passion, unites them.
" 'There's only one thing that interests me,' said Françoise,
'and that's our future together. Just that's enough to make
me happy!' " Pierre has affairs on the side. " 'The thing is,
I very much like beginnings,' he said. 'Don't you remember?' "—" 'I suppose,' said Françoise, 'but I just wouldn't
be interested in an affair that had no future.' " One can't talk
about their relationship in terms of faithfulness or unfaithfulness; they are one.

But then Xavière Pagès appears on the scene. She is a
young middle-class girl who is unhappy living with her
family in Rouen. Out of sheer kindness Pierre and Françoise
adopt and take her into their hotel in Paris. She is to be
their guest. Xavière is a strange, unsociable person who hates
any kind of demand. She sleeps when others are awake, sulks
when others are happy—is, in short, incapable of normal
relations with anyone. Her moods, whether of joy or rage,
are so unpredictable that Pierre and Françoise spend their

time trying to interpret what she has said. "One would have thought they were talking about the Pythian." Simone de Beauvoir succeeds in making Xavière a complete "alterity." "All one could do was circle about outside her, in eternal exclusion."

This seductive little monster succeeds, through her very mysteriousness (oh, the power of the elusive) in arousing in Françoise a feeling she has never previously experienced: jealousy. A double-edged jealousy, for she wants to have Xavière to herself, and she doesn't like Pierre's taking Xavière seriously. When he tells her that he and Xavière are in love, her first reaction is to be hurt; her second is to try what no one has ever succeeded in doing: living together à trois—"something difficult but which could be beautiful and happy." It might be possible with someone less cruel and unpredictable than Xavière, but she makes any kind of honesty impossible. Françoise gazes at "this woman with whom Pierre was in love with a lover's eyes."

What can be done? She tries being generous, thinking she may thus solve the problem of The Other. But Xavière "nullifies" her. Françoise feels that this stubborn little girl has taken away her world. After Xavière has given herself to a young man named Gerbert and made Pierre so jealous he spies on their lovemaking through the keyhole—and even after Françoise has twice triumphed over "the guest" by first regaining Pierre's love and then by winning Gerbert's as well—she still can't bear the monstrous manner in which Xavière views her. " 'You were jealous of me,' said Xavière, 'because Labrousse loved me. You've made him loathe me and for further revenge you've stolen Gerbert from me. Keep him, he's yours. Now get out of here, and get out now.' "

Françoise has won and therefore no longer has any reason to be jealous of Xavière, but she can't bear that another's consciousness should destroy her own. As Geneviève Gennari has observed, "She isn't committing a crime of passion when she turns on the gas jet in the room where Xavière is asleep —she's committing a philosophic crime." The novel's epigraph is from Hegel: "Every consciousness seeks the death of every other consciousness." Xavière has tried to "nullify" her; one must choose; and Françoise chooses *herself.* She repeats: " 'It's either me or her.' She turned on the jet." At a later date Simone de Beauvoir would no longer like the way the novel ended.

Les Bouches inutiles followed. This play is centered around the political dilemma of whether one has the right, in order to save a besieged town short on provisions, to eliminate the non-essential mouths to be fed—or whether one should sacrifice the town in order to save them. The action of the play forces decisions; even silence would be criminal. The play was not very well received. "There was one annoying thing about the idiotic fame that had fallen to Sartre [and to her]. It came high. Although he had reached a world-wide audience of unexpected proportions, he found himself cut off from the audience of future centuries."

That Simone de Beauvoir attaches enormous importance to the idea of immortality is clear from her autobiography and from the novel *Tous les Hommes Sont Mortels* (*All Men Are Mortal*). In this work, Régine, an actress, is tired of ephemeral success and aspires to immortality. She wants to win the love of a madman who thinks he is immortal, because she will thereby survive in someone's mind and heart after her own death. In the end she realizes that she must find in life itself what she had hoped to find in immortality. All men are mortal, but they must act as if they were immortal.

This same theme appears in non-fiction form in *Pyrrhus et Cinéas.* Pyrrhus outlines his plans for conquest to Cinéas, his counselor. After Pyrrhus has described each victory, Cinéas asks: "And then what?" Another plan is outlined. Cinéas continues to ask, "Then what?" Until finally Pyrrhus

answers: "Then we'll rest." "And why," asks Cinéas, "don't
you begin resting right now?" At first glance this seems a
perfectly astute observation. But Cinéas is wrong. Despite
everything, new goals spring up and urge us on. Pyrrhus is
right to conclude: "It's today that I exist; today propels me
into a future which is defined by my present goal."

In *Pour une Morale de l'Ambigüité* (*For an Ethic of
Ambiguity*) Simone de Beauvoir maintains that existence is
more ambiguous than absurd. It isn't meaningless; however,
each of us can give it whatever meaning he chooses. Moral
values exist only to the extent that man creates them. She
believes neither in the Ten Commandments nor in the
"moral law in our hearts" Kant posits; each mind must
invent its own meaning for life and live according to the
exigencies of *its own* truth. Maurice Cranston, an English
critic, has remarked on the degree to which such a position—which breaks equally with God and with reason—
is difficult, even painful, for the French, Descartes-oriented
mind. The existentialists, he says, are very like Hume, who
found no evidence for the existence of God and no trace of
a moral law. The difference, however, is that Hume doesn't
suffer from this state of affairs. An Englishman who doubts
has no trouble carrying on with life. He has only to follow
British tradition, conventions, and laws. But for a Frenchman
who has lived more by reason than by tradition, and especially a Frenchman during the time of the Occupation,
the choices are harder.

In her non-fiction Simone de Beauvoir intends to cut
deep, and does. "I'm not interested in resorting to emotional
appeals when I have truth on my side." In her novels, on
the other hand, she concentrates on nuance. "My non-
fiction reflects my personal choices; my novels the state of
wonderment the human condition—both as a whole and in
its particulars—throws me into." Only a novel could allow
her to sort out the multiple swirling significations of the

changed world she awoke to in 1944. "The ground was strewn with broken illusions." She had witnessed "the triumphant return to power of the middle class" as well as the clashes that had put an end to some of the precious friendships of the days of the Resistance. This gave her *distance,* so necessary a quality for the novelist. She wrote *Les Mandarins.* She wanted to depict intellectuals, a special breed "whom people advise novelists not to rub elbows with." But people are wrong; an intelligent man's experiences can be equally as interesting as those of an illiterate; and intellectuals are, after all, human beings with human feelings.

Many have talked about *Les Mandarins* as a roman à clef, pointing out that Dubreuil and Henri are Sartre and Camus, and that Dubreuil's wife, Anne, is Simone de Beauvoir herself. But this is totally to misunderstand the nature of fiction. A novelist gives his characters certain traits of actual people, but he doesn't paint portraits. He transforms, he mixes, he shifts, he constructs. Dubreuil is an elderly man and very different from Sartre. Henri is like Camus in being young, dark-complected, and the editor of a newspaper, but "the similarity ends there." Dubreuil and Henri have a falling-out, just as did Sartre and Camus, but in the novel they become reconciled, which is not what occurred in real life. Camus left his paper for reasons that had nothing to do with Sartre.

The same is true of the minor characters, who are so lifelike. Paule, Nadine, and Scriassine are wonderfully real. They are not, however, copies of real people. "All of the materials that I drew from memory, I broke up, twisted around, hammered out, exaggerated, combined, transposed, distorted, even sometimes made their opposite, and in each and every instance recreated. I hoped that people would take the book for what it is—not autobiography or reportage, but an evocation." That, indeed, is just what it is—the compelling evocation of a group, of a period, of a state of mind—and a great novel, one of the best of our time.

III. *THE SECOND SEX*

Le Deuxième Sexe (*The Second Sex*) is a remarkably intelligent, instructive, and impassioned book. It shows Simone de Beauvoir the philosopher as "an angry young girl." This anger gives her style vigor. The book is very well written, with precision and clarity, and employs the very broadest scientific and philosophical frame of reference. It has two parts: "Les Faits et les Mythes" ("Facts and Myths") and "l'Expérience Vécue" ("Woman's Life Today").

The facts part describes woman's position as it may in actuality be observed. This position is analogous to that of the proletariat: woman is inferior, an object. Man considers himself Subject, Absolute; woman is The Other. It never occurs to a man that his thoughts might be determined by his sex; but he says to a woman: "You think like a woman." In order to justify this superiority, man has appealed to philosophy, theology, and science. It's true that ideas on the matter have changed to a great degree during the last fifty years. Indeed, Christianity had long since asserted that "Woman too has a soul." One is reminded too of Saint Paul's celebrated pronouncement: "There is no longer Jew and Greek; no longer slave and free man; no longer man and woman, for you are all one in Jesus Christ."

In fact, however, the humiliation of woman has remained on a par with that of the victims of racial prejudice. There is a myth of the Eternal Female, just as there is a myth of the soul of the Negro or the nature of the Jew. Except that women aren't, as are American Negroes, and as are Jews, a minority; there are as many women as men on earth. They have, nevertheless, accepted being treated as beasts of luxury (Balzac's coquettes and courtisans) or as beasts of burden (our harried suburban housewives) or as the devil's hand-maiden. Man's function is living life, woman's reproducing it. Man's place is in the world, woman's in the home. Such was man's view for ages. Why did the women of so many different societies allow it? Is this state of being Other, object, inferior, part of the nature of things?

Simone de Beauvoir asks biologists, Marxists, and psychoanalysts for their answer to this question. The biologist replies: "Woman is weaker than man. The killer and hunter rules over the begetter of children. . . . It is the vigorous son who inherits the father's prerogatives, not the daughter, who is too weak to exercise them." To which Simone de Beauvoir in turn responds that the notion of physical weakness is meaningful only in terms of the laws, attitudes, and level of a civilization. A woman protected by laws is no longer weak. True, the biologist agrees, but adds, what are the laws if not reflections of the nature of things? It may not seem fair that the adulterous woman should be more severely punished than the erring male, but it is "natural" because woman's unfaithfulness brings an intrusion, the illegitimate child, into the home. To which again the woman might raise the objection that physical force is no longer all that important in an era when you can kill merely by pulling a trigger or pushing a button, and that, moreover, in an age of contraceptive devices one need no longer fear the intrusion of the illegitimate child. But this sort of argument can go on forever, and the biologist will further point out that male brutality continues to terrorize (or reassure) a great number of women. Consider prostitutes, for instance, who are slaves of their pimp.

As for the Marxists, they view the history of manners and morals in terms of the history of technological means. When civilization was agricultural, women shared equally in the work; early industrialization reduced her to a state of slavery; mechanization will free her by doing away with forced labor. Beauvoir is not won over by these simplistic ideas, which take no account of individual relationships. Nothing would keep a man, even a stronger man, from treating a woman as an equal if it weren't for his desire to dominate her. The psychoanalysts, on the other hand, blame woman's inferiority complex, which, they say, is the result of feelings of failure and incompleteness and of her envy of men. But is this true?

Why does man persist in reducing woman to a state of slavery? Because she is of all objects that one through whose possession he believes he subdues nature. Adam hopes to find in Eve a transcendence, a means of going beyond himself; Flaubert viewed the female sex organ as an arch through which man hopes to arrive at the infinite. Doomed to infirmity, old age, and death, man naïvely hopes to find in woman a remedy for all these evils. He wants his woman young, sound, in good health, *especially* if he is himself frail and at death's door. The older he is, the more he hungers after young flesh. "Breasts and buttocks are prime objects for him because of the gratuitous and contingent nature of their blooming." But far from being his salvation, Eve plunges Adam into the immanent world. Far from finding infinity in her, he is again made conscious of all the servitudes of being human—secretions, odors, fatigue, words, boredom. She doesn't deliver him from his guilt; she buries him beneath it. Then, with persistent bad faith, he projects this guilt on her. She becomes Fate, Death, Circe, Diana, the vamp, the sorceress—none of which prevents her in moments of desire from being the ideal, poetry, the goddess. *C'est trop,* says Simone de Beauvoir. Don't put woman too high or too low, but at your own level. Deliver her from the myth of the Eternal Female and let her create *herself.*

In short, put woman in an existential perspective. A person who exists creates himself at every moment through his goals. Little by little man has triumphed over the base servitudes of the animal state by acting, by actualizing his goals. Woman, on the other hand, has at no time had anything to do with personal goals. Mother and housekeeper, she has had little leisure to devote to a personal life. She can transcend herself only by having some activity of her own, as is proved, indeed, by Simone de Beauvoir's own life. She has *lived* her experience.

"L'Expérience Vécue," the second part of *Le Deuxième Sexe,* deals first with the matter of women's education. Woman, like the Negro, does not exist; she is the product of her environment. She is trained to think of herself as inferior. She observes that priests, who are God's educational agents, are always men (which is a step backward from Antiquity even, when there were priestesses). In the home she notices that her father has more power and prestige than her mother. The books she reads as a child depict men either as heroes or powerful monsters (Prince Charming, Bluebeard), and women as victims (Cinderella, Snow White). As she grows up, classical plays and novels continue to inculcate in her the myth of the Eternal Female and to teach her how to be seductive and to compensate for her weakness with coquetry. Thus does every mother forge a new link in "the chain of inferiority."

Objection. Is it really true that woman is an artificial construction made in accordance with man's wishes? Isn't it, in fact, physiologically fated that women should have children? And doesn't marriage best insure that fulfillment to a woman—and that being the case, shouldn't she "win" a husband, that is, seduce him? Simone de Beauvoir doesn't consider marriage the best solution to the male-female relationship. She contrasts love, which is a gift freely given, and marriage, an economic and social function. "Marriage is obscene in principle in so far as it transforms into rights and duties those mutual relations which should be founded on a spontaneous urge." Bernard Shaw said: "Marriage is popular because it combines the maximum of temptation with the maximum of opportunity." And that, cyncially and bluntly put, is man's assessment of the matter. Marriage for bed and board remains an alternative, and many women choose it; but it is a form of prostitution.

Of course "it is still true that most women are married, or have been, or plan to be, or suffer from not being." In marrying, however, woman becomes an appendage of her husband's world. Her parents say they are *giving* her in marriage, her husband says he is *taking* her to wife. "It is still agreed that the act of love is, as we have seen, a *service* rendered to the man; he *takes* his pleasure and owes her some payment." Which means that woman is not a free agent in choosing the man of her erotic destiny. She belongs to one man. Her desire and pleasure are at the mercy of an institution, and for a long time man denied even that she had any right to pleasure. Montaigne considered it dangerous to get one's own wife "over-excited." He said: "We want them healthy, vigorous, in fine fettle, plump, *and* chaste— that is, both hot and cold."

And therein lies the inconsistency of the male: he wants women to be passionate when they're in bed with him but cold and indifferent to men as a whole. He asks that a wife always be present but never obtrusive; he wants her to be entirely his but not himself to belong to her, to live together and remain single. "Thus she is betrayed from the day he marries her." The terrible thing about marriage is that the man promises happiness and doesn't give it—that he cripples the young woman by consigning her to a life of repetition and routine. Bound to one man, with children to tend, her life is over. Until she was twenty she lived a free life filled with studies, friendships, sexual awakenings, and the anticipation of love. Then she found herself with no future outside of her husband's, and—often—sexually ungratified. For traditional marriage is far from creating the most favorable kinds of conditions for the awakening and growth of female sexuality. Since the preliminaries of love before marriage have not prepared her, the wedding night seems to the virgin the absurd fit of some crazed epileptic.

Thereafter her lot consists of discharging her duties in bed and in the home, in which she maintains a position only by virtue of acceptance of her bondage to a master who is both mentor and satyr. At first, then, she starts out by living her early married life in dishonesty; she convinces herself that she is deeply in love with her husband. Then, like Sophie Tolstoi, she comes to her senses. She discovers that "she is not faced with the imposing figure of a Sovereign, Lord, and Master," and she sees no reason why she should be his slave. So she either assumes the role of victim or she is unfaithful to him—both sad solutions.

But "the middle class . . ." (Beauvoir hasn't forgotten her arch-enemy) "the middle class has in recent years invented an epic style of expression in which routine takes on the cast of adventure, fidelity, that of a sublime passion; ennui becomes wisdom. . . ." The truth is, however, that the lot of two individuals who loathe one another yet can't get along without one another is not the truest nor the most touching, but rather the most pitiable of the possible kinds of human relationships. Ideally, human beings should be entirely sufficient one to the other, and whatever bond may exist between them should be based on common love and consent.

It is true that traditional marriage seems to be changing, that girls now work and meet men, that the working woman has made "arranged" marriages unnecessary, and that divorce, which is now part of our culture, enables a woman to have a succession of experiences. Yet it is still true that man fulfills himself concretely in work or action, whereas woman's freedom is always freedom from—never freedom for—work and action—as one so clearly sees in America where the emancipated woman chooses either to remain in the home and conform to traditional type or fritters away her energies and time in useless activities.

Another form of fraud is "to maintain that through maternity woman becomes concretely man's equal." Simone de Beauvoir deals at great length with unwanted motherhood, the unmarried mother, and with abortion. "The unwed mother is still in disrepute." (In 1966 this is no longer entirely true; I know some contented "bachelor mothers." Still, Simone de Beauvoir was probably right in 1949.) "It is only in marriage that the mother is glorified"—that is, to the extent that she remains subordinate to the husband. Even though she spends more time and effort tending the children, so long as the husband remains the economic head of the family, they depend much more on him than on her.

Simone de Beauvoir concludes that woman, like the working classes and the downtrodden races of the world, should be freed. Despite the myths, neither physiological inferiority nor eternal hostility between the sexes really exists. Woman, finding herself confined to the immanent, has attempted to hold man down to the same level; she has done her best to cripple him, to destroy his values. That, however, has been the reaction of the slave; woman freed will no longer maintain a state of war. Her salvation will be in sharing, at a professional level, the responsibilities hitherto assumed by man alone. Simone de Beauvoir uses her own experience as a universal yardstick. She doesn't, however, have any children. The minute a woman becomes a mother, she is faced with a choice, even in socialist countries. Simone de Beauvoir thinks that motherhood and freedom can be combined, and it's a fact that a number of women have succeeded in making this combination work. "The words mystery and fate are convenient alibis; woman is shaped by civilization; humanity is responsible for her limitations, failings, and her misfortunes as well as for the hostility between the sexes. The future is open, and it is this book's intent to seem out-of-date in the very near future."

Fifteen years have passed, and it is *not* out-of-date. It retains its cogency and urgency. A few things have been done on an institutional level to improve woman's lot. Much remains to be done on the emotional level. Equality, of course, will not mean identity. "To emancipate woman is to refuse to confine her to the relations she bears to man, not to deny them to her . . . mutually recognizing each other as subject, each will yet remain for the other an *other* . . . the words that move us—giving, conquering, uniting—will not lose their meaning. On the contrary, when we abolish the slavery of half of humanity, together with the whole system of hypocrisy that it implies, then the 'division' of humanity will reveal its genuine significance and the human couple will find its true form."

IV

The three volumes of Beauvoir's autobiography have been very well received. "But," she says, "it makes me uneasy if the middle classes take to my work. . . . Too many women readers enjoyed in *Mémoires d'une Jeune Fille Rangée* the depiction of a milieu they found familiar without being interested in the effort I have made to escape it." I don't consider this statement well-founded, for *La Force de l'Age* and *La Force des Choses,* which describe milieus with which middle class readers have little familiarity, have been equally well received. No, these books attract readers because they are authentic.

Simone de Beauvoir has herself voiced a number of criticisms of these volumes. They cover much the same ground, she says, as some of her other books. One does, indeed, come across certain episodes which appear in her novels; but they are presented in an entirely different light and are, moreover, transposed. On the contrary, I find it fascinating to measure the distance between the raw material of life and its fictional expression. Anyone interested in the art of fiction enjoys seeing how the real Olga is turned into the character Xavière. "However much I may have drawn on Olga in creating Xavière, it was done through a systematic process of distortion." In similar fashion Charles Haas, in becoming

Swann, acquired charm, taste, and an aptitude for suffering infinitely superior to his gifts in real life.

Simone de Beauvoir doesn't claim that this autobiography is a work of art. "That word," she says, "makes me think of some bored statue in a public park. . . . Not a work of art, but my life with all its enthusiasms, its anguish, and its tremors." That is just what it is; she has done what she intended to do, and it is not a work of art.

"I tried hard to be impartial. . . . Of course I am objective only to the degree my objectivity includes *me*." Which amounts to saying that this objectivity in tinged with the subjectivity of the opinions, dislikes, and fears of the author. "We must learn," said Alain, "to like differences." Nothing can keep men from being subjectively involved. Each individual judges a given matter according to his personal experience of it. Ideas and temperaments are shaped by experience. Every writer thinks in terms of his own context. We have to accept the fact that those who have lived lives and fought battles different from ours also have different thoughts. Simone de Beauvoir is not Virginia Woolf; the former escaped her environment; the latter loved hers; both accounts ring true.

ALBERT CAMUS

HIS LANGUAGE was strong and straightforward; his style studded with striking turns of phrase; his thought was courageous, vigorous, exact. Yet his tremendous literary success comes as something of a surprise. A young man, he was not an "intellectual giant" (this tag made him laugh) but the living reflection of a whole generation of French youth. Foreign readers took to him with such enthusiasm that he was awarded the Nobel Prize at an age when many still dream wistfully of the Prix Goncourt. Was he then a Balzac or a Tolstoy, a great creator of characters, the animator of a world? However high one's opinion of him, one could never claim that. His novels are essays in fictional form; his characters do not haunt the reader. And yet his fame seems to us, in the end, deserved. This disparity and this accord need explaining.

I. SKETCH OF A LIFE

Albert Camus was born in 1913 of an Algerian father and a Spanish mother. He spent his entire childhood living with his mother (his father having been killed in 1914) in a destitute quarter of the city of Algiers. He himself has told us what the sun of Algiers and the extreme poverty of the Belcourt quarter meant to him. "Poverty prevented me from believing that all is well with everything under the sun and in history; the sun taught me that history is not everything." Poverty taught him respect for suffering, led him to identify with the poor; but his was not that grudging kind of identification of the bourgeois who has risen above his class and feels obliged to "make amends" in order to be forgiven. Camus had a natural taste for frugality and doing without. He felt at home "on the island of poverty."

Considerable importance should be attached to the fact that Camus' mother was Spanish. The Spanish have a special kind of dignity, a nobility in poverty, and defiance in the face of death. There was a good bit of the Castilian in Camus. "A Castilian turn that served me ill," he said. Perhaps, but it also helped him command respect. Honor made him write *The Rebel* (*L'Homme Révolté*), a book which was to get him in trouble with some of his friends and upset some of his readers. A man of passion, a very Spanish trait, he was throughout his life unmarked by one passion: envy. His sense of honor kept him from envy, which makes men malicious, and from complacency, which makes them stupid. Roger Martin du Gard speaks of "his insurgent bitterness." I find only scattered evidence of such. Camus refused absolutely to allow it. If at times he felt bitterness, he felt it as bitterness mastered.

The sun had provided for that. It is difficult—accustomed as we are to rain, fog, and chill mornings—for us to imagine the physical joy of a child living naked on the shores of a temperate sea. Frenchmen are sometimes amazed by the stubbornness with which Algerians in exile elect to remain in the Midi. But it is altogether natural. People who have lived in a mild climate can no longer forget or do without it. "I lived in destitution but also in a kind of sensual delight." He was molded by "that winter, unlike any elsewhere, glittering with cold and sun, that blue cold." Each moment of life "had its own miraculous quality, its own semblance of eternal youth."

One should read his *Noces à Tipasa* in this regard: "Under

the morning sun a great happiness hangs in space . . . Here I understand what is meant by glory: the right to love bound-lessly. There is but one love in the world. Clasping a woman's body is also to embrace this strange joy that extends down from the sky toward the sea . . . The wind is brisk and the sky blue. I love this life without restraint and wish to speak of it with none; it makes me proud of being a man. And yet, people have often told me there is nothing to be proud of. But there *is* something: this sun, this sea, my heart pulsing with youth, my body tasting of salt, and the vast arena in which tenderness and glory meet in yellow and in blue." This paean, composed as it is of very simple words, has its own special beauty. It is like the Gidean fervor of *Nourritures Terrestres* but cooler and more salutary.

One would think this contact with light and water would have moulded a robust man. It seemed so at first. In grade school and high school, then as a member of the University of Algiers Racing Club, Camus was an athlete—a fine soccer player. He was a mental athlete too. His philosophy professor, Jean Grenier, who remained his mentor in later life, thought highly of him and urged him to pursue graduate work. How-ever, he contracted tuberculosis, which necessitated health cures and visits to the sanitorium. To get these treatments he went to Europe, which transformed him. "Pleasure takes us away from ourselves; travel is a form of ascesis that brings us back to ourselves." It appears that Camus was cured, for the face familiar to us in photographs is that of a hale and hearty-looking man whose ravined face questions and dis-turbs us deeply. "A burdensome, blind obstinacy," he said.

He started writing at a very early age. He wanted to ex-press his joy at being alive, rather like Goethe, but with "the unromanticized nostalgia for the poverty of my youth." The wellspring of his spirit lay in that poverty-stricken and light-filled world. He was only twenty-two years old when he wrote a group of essays—*L'Envers et l'Endroit* (*Betwixt and Between*) on this dual aspect of things. The style had to an astonishing degree the mature qualities of a master. He was drawn to the theater, both as actor and as author, and tried his hand at it—writing at this same period his graduate thesis on Plotinus and Saint Augustine (the relationships of Hellenism and Christianity). It is clear that he read widely and deeply, readings which Jean Grenier must have supervised. Meanwhile he married, a first marriage that didn't last, and he joined the Communist Party, with which he broke the following year.

Indeed, he wasn't at all cut out to be a Party man. "Principles are needed in large matters," he said; "compassion suffices for the small"—and in his *Notebooks:* "It is generalizations which have done me the most harm,"—which brings to mind Alain's: "All generalizations are false, and that is a generalization." The world seemed to him neither explained nor explicable. He wasn't a Christian, Marxist, or anything else; he was Albert Camus, offspring of the sun, poverty, and death. Was he an intellectual? Yes, if an intellectual is someone who splits himself in two, who enjoys life even as he watches himself live it. Was he an artist? Assuredly, although he himself doubts it. At twenty-three he has "the distinct feeling that there is nothing left to be done in art. Only action, adventure, remain." He records a line from *Faust* in his *Notebooks:* "Action is everything; fame nothing." In any case, if he is to become a writer it will be only in order to express his thought *plus* his life. "A great artist is above all a man who lives to the full." He turns down a teaching position in Sidi-Bel-Abbès "so as not to be swallowed up."

In 1938 he joins the staff of *Alger Républicain,* then run by Pascal Pia. That same year he writes *Caligula* and begins to outline *L'Etranger* (*The Stranger*) and *Le Mythe de Sisyphe* (*The Myth of Sisyphus*). During this period he formulates, with an astonishing precociousness, all of the essential themes of his work. *La Peste* (*The Plague*) figures, in projected form, in the notebooks of this period. It is a mistake, therefore, to consider this particular book a product of the war and occupation. It would be more correct to say that, having already a great subject in hand, he brought the war into it. We shall see later what ideas were occupying his mind at this early period, but we must now round out this brief *curriculum vitae*. Remarried in 1940, he went to France, worked for *Paris-Soir*, and then in the resistance movement *Combat*. With the liberation in 1944 he became editor-in-chief of the newspaper *Combat*, which grew out of that movement. Then with a suddenness right out of *The Arabian Nights* the success of one of his books and of one of his plays made him one of the most famous writers in the world. Within five years he had won a world-wide audience. Around 1946, when I was traveling in South and North America, I was everywhere questioned about "Sartre and Camus," whom young people appeared to link together and with whom they identified. Actually Camus consistently refused to acknowledge any similarity between his and Sartre's thought. Indeed, *The Rebel* was later to cause a break between the two men.

Around 1956–57, Camus, an Algerian and Frenchman both—and deeply distressed by the civil war—called for a truce between the two communities. In 1957 he received the Nobel Prize, as much for the exemplary character as for the quality of his work, and as well by reason of a desire on the part of the Swedish Academy, in view of the tragic upheavals in Algeria, to express its sympathy to an Algerian who neither hated nor censured. This signal honor subjected him, as was to be expected, to a good deal of insult and attack. When questioned by Jean-Claude Brisville in this regard, he replied that it was perfectly natural. "They don't like me. Should they for that not be blessed?" There was a touch of the Christian in this agnostic.

In 1959 a blowout on a French highway killed him. His was a brief but full life. No lapses. No lies. It is perhaps appropriate to recall here that "Those whom the gods love die young." The gods had little left to give Camus. His marriage with death was quick and painless. "How describe eternity except as that which will endure when I am dead?" Let us now pass from the temporal, the Camus of the flesh, to the Camus that endures.

II. *THE MYTH OF SISYPHUS*

We must begin with the myth of Sisyphus. This is not the chronological order, but for Camus' early works there is no true chronology. Everything from *Caligula* to *The Plague* was equally present in the thoughts of the young man. *The Rebel* alone marks the beginning of a new stage. *The Myth of Sisyphus* contains the essence of the ideas that also inspired *The Stranger*. It is a book of ideas, an essay of remarkable density of language, which had a deep and lasting influence on a whole generation.

"The gods had condemned Sisyphus to ceaselessly rolling a rock to the top of a mountain, whence the stone would fall back of its own weight. They had thought with some reason that there is no more dreadful punishment than futile and hopeless labor." This myth is a metaphor for human life. What is our life on earth but "futile and hopeless labor"? How do men spend their brief and singular lives? "Rising, streetcar, four hours in the office or the factory, meal, streetcar, four hours of work, meal, sleep, and Monday Tuesday Wednesday Thursday Friday and Saturday according to the same rhythm." If we manage, by dint of hard work, to hoist the rock to the summit, then some illness, or a war, makes it fall again, and in any case the whole thing ends in death, which is the final fall.

To become aware of the senseless character of this activity, of the futility of all this suffering, is to become aware of the absurdity of the human condition. Why are we condemned? By whom? For what crime? In a world thus stripped of illusion, man feels himself alien, *a stranger*. A stranger, yes, because he is not at home. The universe he inhabits is so constructed that it can neither satisfy his desires nor reward his efforts. He has been thrust into it with a need to understand which nothing can satisfy. "This divorce between man and his life," between actor and setting, is actually consciousness of the absurd. "The absurd is born of this confrontation between the human need and the unreasonable silence of the world." Logically this consciousness should lead the absurd man to suicide. That is the subject of this essay. Can an honest man, one who doesn't cheat, continue living after he has become aware that life is not worth living?

Yet suicides are rare. Is there then no connection between the opinion a man has of life and the steps he takes to forsake it? The first answer to this question is that there is something a great deal more powerful than any philosophic conviction in a man's attachment to life. "The body's judgment is as good as the mind's, and the body shrinks from annihilation." The habit of living precedes that of thinking. In most instances the mind must *deceive* the body in order to bring it to the fatal act. Squeezing a trigger is in itself easy, seemingly innocuous. But as soon as the body comprehends, it resists.

There is also evasion: the hope of another life, a happy one, to be earned (Christian salvation); or there is the cheating of those who live not for life itself but for some great idea larger than life, an idea that elevates it, seems to give it meaning—and betrays it. Those, for instance, who say: "Yes, my life is ineffectual, absurd, but I have fought for justice and someday justice will triumph, which will give my action a posthumous meaning." This is cheating, for death is an absolute. Posthumous justice is only for the people who haven't died. Nevertheless everyone lives as if no one knew he must die. "Under the fatal lighting of that destiny, its uselessness becomes evident. No code of ethics and no effort are justifiable a priori in the face of the cruel mathematics that command our condition." It is cheating also because mankind as a whole, just like the individual, is Sisyphus. If it raises the rock of freedom, the rock falls back as soon as it has been pushed to the top.

A sense of the absurd is born when those stage sets that screen the real for us crumble. Most men live for years without giving it a thought. "But one day the 'why' arises and everything begins in that weariness tinged with amazement." As I write this sentence the shade of Camus impels me to touch the absurd walls that surround us. Yes, why write? Why work so hard? When in a few years, perhaps tomorrow, we must die. For fame? But fame is uncertain and if it should chance to survive me I should not know of it. Moreover the kind of society that takes an interest in such writings as mine will very quickly disappear, as will one day the earth itself. Then why? We learn in childhood to live for the future: "Tomorrow—Later—You'll understand when you're older." Tomorrow, always tomorrow, but tomorrow means death. There comes a day when the grown man sees through this deception and perceives that time is his worst enemy. "That revolt of the flesh," which then grips him, "is the absurd."

The absurd is not in man alone nor in the world alone. It is in their co-existence. What is absurd is the confrontation of that irrational universe where atoms and electrons, just and unjust, innocent and culpable, spin at random and hold on as best they can, and of "the wild longing for clarity whose call echoes in the human heart." To understand, for the human mind, would mean reducing the world to the human level, putting the human brand on it, making men's thoughts effective therein. But what do we understand? Nothing. Why these stars, these trees, these sorrows? Why me? Am I not alien to myself? Has Socrate's "Know thyself" greater value than the "Be virtuous" of our confessionals?

Both phrases and others like them are just so many futile exercises in the face of such afflictions.

What possible answer is there? Neither suicide nor hope. We must somehow get beyond absurd consciousness. It does not in itself prescribe any rule of action. It does, however, instigate revolt. This pitiful reason, which sets man up against all creation, must be held to—with acceptance at the same time of the irrationality of the outside world. "Living is keeping the absurd alive. Keeping it alive is, above all, contemplating it." There is no tomorrow: literally. Therefore there is no point in living for the future. We should, rather, savor the moment, sensation, the richness and variety of the world. We should return to our nuptials in Tipasa. Become an athlete, or a poet, it doesn't matter which. "The present and the succession of presents before a constantly conscious soul is the ideal of the absurd man." To a man without blinders there is no sight more beautiful than that of the intelligence at grips with a reality greater than itself.

For Sisyphus is aware of his wretched condition. "The lucidity that was to constitute his torture at the same time crowns his victory. There is no fate that cannot be surmounted by scorn." Camus is here at one with Pascal. The greatness of man "is that he knows he dies." The greatness of Sisyphus is that he knows the rock will fall. "But crushing truths perish from being acknowledged." Camus admires Sophocles' Oedipus when he says: "Despite so many ordeals, my advanced age and the nobility of my soul make me conclude that all is well." This is a holy remark. "It makes of fate a human matter, which must be settled among men."

"I leave Sisyphus at the foot of the mountain! One always finds one's burden again. But Sisyphus teaches the higher fidelity that negates the gods and raises rocks. He too concludes that all is well. This universe henceforth without a master seems to him neither sterile nor futile. Each atom of that stone, each mineral flake of that night-filled mountain, in itself forms a world. The struggle itself toward the heights is enough to fill a man's heart. One must imagine Sisyphus happy."

One must imagine too the effect of this book, appearing as it did in 1942, on the young people of France. Never had the world seemed more absurd. The war, the Occupation, the apparent triumph of violence and injustice all harshly contradicted any notion of a rational universe. Sisyphus—man—had at the beginning of the century raised the rock fairly high on the fated slope. Before 1914, all was not well—far from it—but much, at least in France, seemed better. Hope, progress, were words still frought with meaning. Within four years the First World War had brought the rock tumbling back to its lowest level, but Sisyphus had bravely applied himself once again to his eternal task. The Second World War destroyed hope. The rock had crushed everything. Sisyphus lay still, strength and courage spent, beneath the debris. Then this young voice was raised and said: "Yes, that's how it it: yes, the world is absurd; no, nothing is to be expected from the gods. And yet, faced with this implacable fate, it is of consequence to acknowledge this fate, scorn it, and, insofar as it is humanly possible, change it." One sees why people listened. It was that or nothing.

III. THE NOVELS

Rather than "the novels" I should have called this part "the embodied ideas." Camus' narratives are moral tales—dramatizations of his essays. *The Stranger* is the myth of Sisyphus lived. First we see the everyday and commonplace existence of a young Algerian, Meursault, an office clerk. His mother dies and he buries her. He becomes involved with a young typist, Marie. He experiences neither painful grief nor rapturous love. He wakes up, lies abed on Sundays, is too lazy to go out and buy bread, eats his eggs straight out of the pan, smokes cigarettes. One can't even say he is bored; he lets time pass; he fritters away his unique existence; he isn't even conscious of it.

His mother's burial is composed of tiny touches, untinged by emotion. It's a hot day. The undertaker's assistant mops his brow with a handkerchief and says, pointing to the sky, "Terrific, isn't it?" Meursault replies: "Yes . . ." "A bit later, he asked: 'Is it your mother we're burying?' I again said: 'Yes.' 'Was she old?' I answered: 'So-so' because I didn't know her exact age." There is an odor of dung about the horse-drawn hearse, and the smell of shellac and incense. His only thought is that when this is over he will be able to go back to Algiers and go to bed and sleep for twelve hours. "It's over; mother's buried." In short, he is the absurd man before rebellion, that is, like all men, caught up in the everyday, which he barely notices.

Then drama enters this drab life. As a result of an untoward reflex reaction Meursault kills an Arab with the revolver a friend has entrusted to him. Suddenly he finds himself arrested, thrown into jail, and put on trial. Everyone—lawyer, prosecutor, and judge alike—sees him as a "stranger" because he doesn't lie properly. Society expects conventional reactions from him. "Did you love your mother?" asks Meursault's lawyer, who wishes to "naturalize" him, make society accept him as normal. His client's response is: "Certainly I was very fond of mother, but that really didn't mean much. All normal people had to one degree or another desired the death of those they loved." The lawyer entreats him not to repeat this answer before the examining magistrate. Meursault, however, does so, and everyone—magistrate, prosecutor, the citizens of Algiers—feels threatened.

Why threatened? Because this man who has spoken the hidden truth is a menace. He threatens to waken humanity to awareness of its own insensibility. Meursault is an intruder; he doesn't play the game everyone else plays, and he is all the more irritating because he keeps repeating: "I'm just like everybody else"—which is true as regards his feelings but not his words. And men are judged according to their words. "The prosecutor said that if the truth were to be told I had no soul, that nothing human, not one of the moral principles that dwell in men's hearts was available to me." A society based on respectable lies rejects this "stranger" who isn't one of them and who doesn't want to be. Meursault is sentenced to death.

Then a reversal occurs. Backed up against the walls of the absurd, the condemned man in most cases clutches at one hope: that of eluding the wheels of justice either through escape or through pardon. Meursault, however, is the incarnation of the absurd man for whom there is neither flight nor recourse. The prison chaplain offers him the promise of an afterlife. Meursault replies that he doesn't believe in God. "Your heart is blind," the chaplain tells him. "I will pray for you." Suddenly something in Meursault snaps. "I had seized him by the collar of his cassock; I poured out on him all my innermost thoughts and feelings in spasms of half-joy, half-rage . . . Once he had gone I became calm again . . . As if that great burst of anger had cleansed me, emptied me of hope—and, looking up into the sign- and star-strewn night, I lay myself open for the first time to the benign indifference of the world."

Thus Meursault, a demonstration dummy rather than a true fictional character, closes the circle begun in *The Myth of Sisyphus*. He had been a slave to the hell of the everyday, pushing his rock without giving it a second thought; then, by refusing hope, any kind of hope, he gains his freedom, and can now enjoy life, yes, in his cell, enjoy the sounds of the countryside that reach his ears, the odors of the night, of earth and salt; in short, he has returned to his "nuptials in Tipasa" and to the sheer intoxication of being alive, because he has accepted death, and the rock, and the total indifference of the immense universe about him. He is saved by that which destroys him.

The Plague (*La Peste*) is to collective life what *The Stran-*

ger was to the individual life. Even as Meursault discovered
the beauty of life through a severe shock that resulted in revolt, so here an entire city is wakened to consciousness when
it finds itself cut off, faced with a deadly scourge. The city
is Oran, the scourge an entirely fictional epidemic of plague.
This fine book owes nothing to direct observation; here again
the characters are fleshed-out ideas. However, like all great
comic writers—from Swift to George Orwell—Camus endeavors to lend his fiction credibility through the use of concrete
detail. His description of Oran, which opens the book, com-
pares with Balzac's best; it depicts not only the physical character but also the moral climate of the city, which slumbers,
before the scourge, in its business affairs and routine.

The gradual introduction of the fictional into the real
is truly a masterpiece of technique. A rat dies, vomiting
blood; then ten, then a hundred, then armies of rats; finally,
the first human victim. The description of symptoms; the
opposition of the civil authorities, who shrink from the
scourge even as a tribunal shrinks from a murderer; all these
seem to me consummately rendered. In *The Plague* Camus
is mainly interested in the reactions of men faced with the
collapse of everything they had believed secure: communica-
tions systems, trade, health. It is no longer a single Sisyphus
but a city of Sisyphuses who find themselves crushed by disaster.

How will the infected behave? Better than one might have
thought. First of all, almost all of them, the moment the
quarantined city is cut off, become conscious of the ties that
bind them to those from whom they are separated—husbands, wives, absent lovers. Pain lends validity and strength
to feeling. Most particularly, however, there are those who
act. Among the latter is Dr. Rieux (the narrator) who,
without a thought for his own safety, fearlessly cares for the
sick. Rieux is an atheist. To Father Paneloux, who believes
that the plague has been sent by God to punish a city of
sinners, and who thinks only of saving these latter through

repentance, Rieux replies: "Man's salvation is too big a chunk for me. I don't go that far. It's his health, his physical health that concerns me." To him it is a simple matter of practicing his profession properly. "There's nothing heroic about it. It's a matter of integrity." Which would be Antoine Thibault's moral view in Martin du Gard, and which, I believe, would be mine too. To do as well as one can what must be done wherever you happen to be. Why? For no reason. To be in tune with yourself.

Then there is Jean Tarrou. He is not a native of Oran: an artist, he keeps a kind of diary which complements, through vivid tiny details, Rieux's technical account. Tarrou offers to help Rieux in the epidemic by organizing sanitation squads. The doctor draws his attention to the risk he will be running and asks him why he has accepted it. One detects in this dialogue between the doctor and Tarrou Camus' own dialogue with himself. Tarrou, an intellectual, feels a confused desire to act the role of saint—without faith; Rieux, a man of the people by birth, is a member of that obscure brotherhood of poor people, who help one another by acts rather than words. Both Tarrou and Rieux exist in Camus, child of the Belcourt quarter—the desire to be a saint without God and the imperative to do one's daily duty.

The Plague is the book of a humanist who will not allow himself to accept the unjustness of the universe. In the eternal silence of these infinite spaces, a silence broken only by the shrieks of the suffering, man should stand by man, perhaps through heroism, perhaps through saintliness, but above all through taking into account certain basic feelings: love, friendship, brotherhood. This, moreover, is fairly easy in times of danger. But everything deteriorates again once the scourge goes away. The epidemic subsides; the quarantine is lifted; the city reopens; people forget. Consider, for instance, how many genuine heroes—after the plague of World War II—returned to their weaknesses. The plague of souls survives that of bodies. "I know with a certain knowledge," says Tarrou, "that each man carries the plague within." But those who know this can keep a watch on themselves and try to do their fellows "as little harm as possible, and even a little good."

Thus, after *The Plague,* "the feeling of human brother-hood rose," for Camus, "like a dawn upon a world of dying men"; but contrarily, in *The Fall (La Chute),* a subsequent novel, all remaining hope seems to vanish. "We cannot affirm the innocence of any one person whereas we can with certainty affirm the guilt of all." In other words we find in our consciences as civilized men sufficient reason to believe any crime possible. Here again we are dealing with a philosophical novel. In a sailor's dive in Amsterdam we meet Clamence, a lawyer from Paris and once a highly respected member of his profession, who has slowly convinced himself of the hypocrisy of a profession in which he judges those he defends as if he himself were not guilty. Disgusted with himself, he has left Paris and confesses his transgressions to strangers, adding: "I have never had other than good intentions," which immediately enmeshes him once again in the universal hypoc-risy.

The book is one long monologue by Clamence, who tries to discover the exact moment his fall began. He finds that it partook of all moments; the further he delves into the past the further that moment recedes in time. "I had principles, of course, one of which, for instance, was that the wives of friends were not to be touched. I simply ceased, in all sincerity, a few days before anything occurred, to feel any friendship for the husbands." "In the end nothing meant anything to me. War, suicide, love, poverty—I gave them my attention, of course, when circumstances obliged me to, but only in a polite and superficial way . . . How should I put it? It slid. Yes, everything slid off me . . ." "In short, I never bothered with larger concerns except in the intervals between my little flings." This frankness prompts his inter-locutors to confess that they are no better than he is. This is what he has been waiting for. Having thus acquired, through their admissions, the right to judge others, he considers himself authorized to practice any kind of vice.

It's an odd fable. Who ever doubted that men are imperfect or that a number of them live hypocritical lives? A few Jansenists have insisted upon purity in the name of religion, a few ascetics in the name of philosophy. But on what is Clamence's rigor based? On nothing, for it ends up in madness à la Caligula, who was cruel in order to have revenge for being guilty. "How many crimes are committed simply because their author could not bear to be at fault." The book abounds in such paradoxical and brilliant apothegms, but to what end? It is difficult to say. "In this play of mirrors in which author's disclosure and character's confession, exorcism and comedy, truth and lie are interreflected,"[1] one admires the style and the humor; but one is shocked by the bitter quality of an irony that dissolves absolutely everything. "It isn't a fall," Marcel Thiébaut has said, "but an impasse."

It is true that man's follies justify the blackest sort of pessimism. But to what end? One must attempt to go on living, and, as we shall see, *The Fall* is not Camus' final word.

IV. *THE REBEL*

I shall discuss this fine and important work before going on to the plays because Camus' plays fall between the two poles of thought represented by *The Myth of Sisyphus* and *The Rebel*.

"Man is the only creature who refuses to be what he is," in short, who rebels against his condition. This rebellion is what is essential about his being. "I believe that I believe in nothing," says the rebel; however, I am unable to doubt my protest—that is, put in Cartesian fashion: "I protest,

[1] J. C. Brisville.

therefore I am." The rebel is a man who says no, but he cannot say no to what is without saying yes to something else. Some scale of values is implied in every act of rebellion. Seemingly negative, rebellion becomes positive when it discloses what there is in man to be defended. The act of revolt offers a basis for human solidarity and in turn finds its sole justification in that solidarity. In the realm of the absurd (*The Stranger, The Myth of Sisyphus*) experience was individual; in the realm of rebellion it is communal (*The Plague, The Rebel*), for everyone is a victim of the disjunction of man and the world. This fact saves the individual from his aloneness. "I rebel, therefore we exist."

Metaphysical rebellion sets man's own inner notion of justice against the injustice he finds in the world. It is an act in defiance of the gods: the myth of Prometheus. However, the Greek gods were one with nature, and we are part of nature. How then is it possible to rebel against oneself? Resignation was the answer given by Epicurus and Marcus Aurelius—two noble but cheerless thinkers in whom only the disillusioned find solace. A personal God better lends itself to balancing up accounts. Ivan Karamazov takes man's side against God, placing emphasis on man's innocence. Christianity replies by making Christ undergo the most agonizing tortures and even death. It promises that in the Kingdom of Heaven redress will be made for injustices.

Contemporary nihilism is no longer content with this promise. "God is dead"; Nietzsche based his entire thought on this postulate. There is no Kingdom of Heaven. However, if God is dead, why accuse him? If windmills do not exist, Don Quixote is mad. Which Nietzsche was. There is neither good nor evil; everything is allowed. Since the world has no direction, man should give it one that will result in a superior form of humanity. A superman must be developed; but that, unfortunately, leads to the Storm Trooper and the Commissar. Hegel and Marx do not promise "the beyond" but the "later," which amounts to the same thing. Camus violently attacks Hegel because the latter prophesies that even if no one is virtuous today, everyone will be one day—through the simple action of dialectic and history. When historical contradictions are resolved "the true god, the human god will be the State." Meanwhile one may do anything one likes. Whence terrorism. A "proletariat of university students" takes up the torch of the revolt and gives that revolt its most violent aspect.

Then, too, the stage of individual terrorism is succeeded by State terrorism. The entire Germany of 1933 submitted to the degraded values of a few men. The morality of the national-socialist gang (as of all Fascist gangs) consists of rancor, revenge, and conquest without end. For Marx man is only a dialectic of means of production. A classless society is his Kingdom of Heaven. A golden age, relegated to the culmination point of history, and coinciding—in double polarity—with a second coming, justifies all. Marx's prophecy has, in fact, proved false. Capitalism and the proletariat have evolved in a fashion he could not have foreseen. Whether bourgeois or socialist, collectivist systems put justice off to some future date to the profit of brute power. "How could a socialism that called itself scientific come to be so at odds with the facts?" asks Camus, and adds: "The answer is simple; it wasn't scientific."

"Here ends Prometheus' surprising itinerary. Proclaiming his hatred of the gods and his love of mankind, he turns away from Zeus with scorn and approaches mortal men in order to lead them in an assault against the heavens . . .

"They must be saved from themselves. The hero then tells them that he, and he alone, knows the city. Those who doubt his word will be thrown into the desert, chained to a rock, offered to the vultures. The others will march henceforth in darkness, behind the pensive and solitary master. Prometheus alone has become god and reigns over the solitude of men. But from Zeus he has gained only solitude and cruelty; he is no longer Prometheus, he is Caesar. The real, the eternal Prometheus has now assumed the aspect of one of his victims.

The same cry, springing from the depths of the past, rings
forever through the Scythian desert."

This is neither Christian nor Marxist; neither the Kingdom
of Heaven nor the Radiant City. Then what is left? The
book's conclusion is a courageous one. Camus does not repudiate rebellion; he does not scorn action. But he extols and
requires moderation. It is necessary to act according to the
level and scale of mankind. He quotes René Char: "Obsession with the harvest and indifference to history are the two
extremities of my bow." Europe in its present torn state needs
work and mutual understanding rather than intransigence.
"Real generosity toward the future lies in giving all to the
present."

Here, right now, is where we should labor. It will be hard.
There will always be injustice and rebellion. It is the devil
who whispers in our ears: *"Eritis sicut dei*—You will be as
gods." To be man one must refuse to be god. Camus does
not exactly say with Voltaire: "We should cultivate our gardens." Rather, as I see it, he says: "We must help the
humiliated cultivate their gardens . . ." "The only truly
engaged artist is the one who, without refusing the fight, refuses to join the regular army; by which I mean: the sniper."
There we have Camus' last embodiment, and we should not
forget that of all fighting men the sniper is the most exposed
to danger.

V. THEATER

Camus said in an interview that *The Rebel* was much less
a statement of belief than a confession, a disclosure of his
readings and his thoughts, and moreover that he didn't want
to be judged on the basis of a single book but on works that
form a whole wherein each throws light on the others. We
are here, indeed, in the presence of an author who never
ceases to question himself about the human condition and

whose different responses are colored by experiences which are themselves diverse. We find this same indefiniteness in his works for the theater, for existence never affords an exact and final answer.

Robert de Luppé divides Camus' dramatic works into two groups of plays: plays of the absurd and plays of revolt. This corresponds to my own division of Camus' thought between two poles. *Caligula* is the absurd man in a pure state. Aldous Huxley once wrote that to judge a man one must imagine what he might have been like if Fate had made him a Roman emperor. Great power allows the fulfillment of what is in most men but dream or inclination. Camus, as an emperor, would have been Marcus Aurelius; Caligula was Caligula.

In Camus' play Caligula discovers the absurdity of the world through the death of Drusilla, his sister, for whom he had a carnal passion. All of a sudden he has grasped a truth that is "altogether simple, and altogether clear, rather banal, but hard to bear."

And what is that truth?

Men die, and they are not happy.

His friends' protestations that everyone lives with this truth are in vain. Caligula denies it. Men live in falsehood. He will open their eyes. "Today and from this day forth, my freedom knows no bounds." When an emperor's freedom no longer knows any bounds, cruelty and injustice no longer know any limits. Is Caligula mad? No, he is the victim of a mania for logic; he wants to act, by pushing the bases of the intellect to their limits; he is the absurd man who wants to destroy all traditional values. This state of mind in an intellectual would give birth to a hoax; in an emperor to a slaughter. If he could, Caligula would destroy this world, the absurdity of which offends him. Not being God, he will at least destroy mankind, all they have respected, all they have loved.

The worst of it is that they will submit, that the patricians will hand their wives over to him, that they will write poems in his honor. There is an element of farce in every catastrophe. Didn't Mussolini make his ministers run and jump through flaming hoops? Didn't Hitler, after violating every divine and human law, try to bury himself beneath the ruins of the world? *Caligula* was not the story of a madman; it was, alas, a chronicle of our times. Less hideous even than our times. Hitler never got beyond his hatreds; Caligula continues the search, beyond his murders, for a more authentic life. He knows that he too is guilty. "But who would dare condemn me in this world where none is innocent?" He stretched out his arms to love—to Drusilla—and then to the impossible. "I didn't take the right road, I came out nowhere. My freedom is not the right kind." We are already approaching *The Rebel* here. Immoderation has failed.

Written as early as 1938, and performed in 1944, *Caligula* had the success it well deserved. Actor, director, author, Camus was in the line of great men of the theater. He had the essential gift, that of dramatic flow. The rhythm was set in the first scene, then the play leapt forward without a hitch. *The Misunderstanding (Le Malentendu)*, written in 1942–43, is another cut from the same cloth. A mother and her daughter living in an isolated house in Moravia murder the travelers they take in. The mother is weary of all these murders, the daughter rebellious against her fate, which is to live in this solitary, loveless fashion. A traveler comes by. It is the son of the family, Jan, who had gone away years ago and who does not make himself known. The two women murder him, then from his passport discover that he was their son and brother.

This is a misunderstanding that goes well beyond the immediate crime. "The characters," Brisville writes, "are ever on the verge of recognition." But aren't we all, with our friends, our relatives, all men, ever on the verge of recognition? This is a threshold we will never cross, any more than the two women in the play. We will die, as we have lived, in one great universal misunderstanding. "Neither in life, nor in death, is there homeland or peace." A play of despair, written at a time when everything contributed to despair, *The Misunderstanding* lacks flesh and blood. The development has been masterfully handled; but the ideas remain at the level of abstract models.

So much for the plays of the absurd; the plays of revolt present a similar picture: one stirring flesh-and-blood play—*The Just Assassins (Les Justes)*; and one demonstration-play —*State of Siege (L'Etat de Siège)*. Indeed *State of Siege* is *The Plague* adapted to the stage. The novel took place in present-day Oran; the play is set in Cadiz at no specific time. It is deliberately symbolic, in the manner of the morality and mystery plays of the Middle Ages; the Plague appears here as a character and the nihilist's name is Nada (Nothing). I am sorry to read that Camus had for this play the fond predilection a father often has for a malformed child. He had hoped to create a kind of total theater in which the role of spectacle would outweigh that of dialogue. This in itself was not an impossible aim; indeed, the embodiment of abstract ideas has on occasion been done successfully—by Lope de Vega among others. However, I attended the dress rehearsal of *State of Siege* and had occasion to observe the public's stolid lack of interest. The text did not catch the audience's attention. The ideas did not get beyond the footlights.

On the other hand, *The Just Assassins,* which I have just reread, moved me. It is based on an actual instance of Russian terrorism that occurred in 1905. It is possible that this historical foundation (which *Caligula* had in Suetonius) contributed to the credibility of the play. The subject is the conflict between the absolute revolutionary—the Caligula of the opposition—who shrinks from no injustice in order to bring victory to the cause—and the revolutionist who retains respect for moral limits. Kaliayev, assigned by the party to kill the Grand-Duke Sergei, doesn't throw the bomb because at the crucial moment he finds that two of the Grand-Duke's nephews are in the carriage. "Killing children is not honorable." The more callous Stepan disapproves of his scruples: "Such nonsense makes me sick. The day we make up our minds to forget about children will be the day we'll be masters of the world and the revolution triumph." This is the counterpart of the State's logic. Non-State logic has identical requirements. The terrorist is just as callous as Richelieu. The man of moderation—Camus—Kaliayev—does not want victory at such a price. Not through weakness. Kaliayev will end up killing the Grand-Duke and be hung. It is rather from the belief that victory gained by immoderation will itself collapse in immoderation. One does not found justice on injustice.

VI. THE FINAL STATEMENT

Jean-Claude Brisville once asked Camus: "What compliment annoys you most?" Camus replied: "Honesty, conscientiousness, humanity, you know, the whole modern hogwash." I shall be careful therefore, in describing him, not to use these words. Rather I shall ask him to speak for himself. He did so in Stockholm after receiving the Nobel Prize.

He first said that there are periods when the artist may abstain and remain in the stands while the martyrs and lions have it out in the arena, but there are others so desperate that abstention itself is deemed a choice. In the latter instance the artist is caught up in the tide of the times. This is the case with our own period. In the face of so many horrors the artist can no longer content himself with inconsequential amusement, with formal excellence. Frivolous art is fine for happy elites who have the leisure to unravel subtleties or scan meters. The modern artist denies himself this deceitful luxury; he feels he speaks for naught if he doesn't take the woes of history into account.

(There is room here for argument. The artist of past centuries did not always remain in the stands. Voltaire went down into the arena; Victor Hugo went down into the arena; so did George Sand, and Zola, and Anatole France. Moreover, is it certain that formal perfection is necessarily "inconsequential amusement"? Pure beauty imbues the mind with a certain idea of order and the soul with a disinterested rapture that prepares men for real battles. Flaubert and Mallarmé were not unuseful hornets in the human hive. That, however, is "another story.")

To return to Camus' argument: his *first point* was that the modern artist is a rebel who depicts realities he has lived and suffered. His *second point,* however, is that the artist thereby risks falling into another trap that is equally sterile. If his rebellion is entirely destructive, he allows the desire to be a *poète maudit* to take over. A barstool Caligula, he becomes intransigent in order to become great. He tears the traditions of his art to bits and does not affect mankind. To speak to all one must speak of what is common to all: pleasure, sun, need, desire, the fight against death; and one must speak of these honestly. "Social realism" is not realistic. The academicism of the far left, like the academicism of the right, is deaf to mankind's afflictions.

Whence his *third point:* art is nothing without reality, and without art reality wouldn't be much. Art is a rebellion against the world and aims to give it a different form. To change the world, however, one must start with the world as it is. Neither total rejection nor total consent. To make a still life two elements are necessary: a painter and an apple. "If the world were lucid, art would not be." In this scheme classic art occurs halfway between the artist and his object. "Thus emerges from time to time a new world, different from the everyday world and yet the same, particular but universal."

Here Camus is at one with Chekov and all great writers. "I plead for a true realism against a mythology that is both illogical and deadly, and against romantic nihilism whether bourgeois or allegedly revolutionary . . . I believe in the necessity of some kind of rule and of some kind of order. I only say that it cannot be a matter of just any rule." Some-one asks: "Isn't that what separates you from the intellectuals of the left?" To which he replies: "You mean that that is what separates these intellectuals from the left. It has been traditional with the left always to be battling against obscu-rantism, injustice, and oppression."

He had a horror of being considered a teacher of ethics, either private or social. "I am not virtuous," he said. And I think indeed he must have had "his moments of excess." Happily. A great artist is above all a man who lives to the full. He copied in his notebooks the four conditions Poe described as necessary to happiness: 1) outdoor life; 2) being loved by someone; 3) indifference to all ambition; 4) cre-ation. It is a fine list, and I believe Camus followed it. He was greatly honored and bitterly criticized. I believe he came to accept honor and censure with equal courage. "I am be-ginning," say the *Notebooks*, "to stop being affected by the opinion of others." I think that Sisyphus died happy, leaving the rock at the summit.